TIM LaHAYE & CRAIG PARSHALL

MARK OF EVIL

THE END SERIES
BOOK 4

ZONDERVAN

Mark of Evil
Copyright © 2014 by Tim LaHaye

This title is also available as a Zondervan ebook.
Visit www.zondervan.com/ebooks.

Requests for information should be addressed to:
Zondervan, *Grand Rapids, Michigan 49530*

978-0-3103-3464-4 (HC, Library Edition)

Library of Congress Cataloging-in-Publication Data

LaHaye, Tim F.
 Mark of evil / Tim Lahaye & Craig Parshall.
   pages cm. -- (The End Series ; Book 4)
 ISBN 978-0-310-33454-5 (trade paper)
1. End of the world--Fiction. 2. Good and evil--Fiction. I. Parshall, Craig, 1950- II. Title.
 PS3562.A315M35 2014
 813'.54--dc23
                         2013037376

Interior design: James A. Phinney

Printed in the United States of America

---

14 15 16 17 18 19 20 RRD 28 27 26 25 24 23 22 21 20 19 18 17 16 15 14 13 12 11 10 9 8 7 6 5 4 3 2 1

Dedicated to all the faithful pastors and teachers of the Bible who take God's Word to mean what it says—particularly regarding end times prophecies—and to the unique wisdom and understanding that such students of Scripture possess about the current chaos in the Middle East.

ONE

IN THE FUTURE

Athens, Greece

Ethan March had just confronted the horror once again. He now struggled to steady himself and to clear his mind after seeing the hideous face. He murmured to himself, lips barely moving, as he spoke the two words that seemed to explain everything.

"The beast."

A lightning-fast shiver shot down his spine, like an aftershock following an earthquake. One thing he knew for certain: he had not dreamed it and it wasn't just some nightmare; he was sure of that. Just more evidence, he thought to himself, that the final reckoning approached.

Ethan had spent the previous night sleeping up on the flat, tiled roof of his apartment building. The air-conditioning inside the building didn't work and it was cooler up there. It was likely the rioting across the city and all the fires had caused the electrical failures everywhere. Economic desperation had wrestled Greece into an economic choke hold, just like the rest of the world. And the masses were getting restless.

At the first glimmer of dawn that morning he had wakened on the rooftop, stretched, rubbed the sleep away from his face, and said his morning prayers. The sun was just breaking over the mountains, spreading its burning light across the miles of whitewashed office buildings and apartments crammed into the Greek capital. It was then—with his eyes wide open—the same vision had appeared to him, just as it had so many times before. Ethan was convinced it was a message from God. He didn't care what other people thought. Although the truth was he had told very few others about what he saw in those moments. He couldn't afford to. He also understood that in some strange way the visions were for his benefit, even though they unsettled him deeply, down to his gut.

Each time the sequence was the same: the image of a handsome man would appear to Ethan out of nowhere. But those features would linger only momentarily and would quickly disappear like a morning fog evaporating in the sun. And then, suddenly, in one great, sickening jolt, there would come another face—a repulsive, red-eyed creature. A moment later and it would all be over. The vision would leave Ethan drenched with a sense of dread and wondering why, out of everyone in the human race, he'd been chosen to encounter the image of that grotesque creature, over and over again.

Ethan was still up on the flat rooftop, and now his eyes searched the four corners around him. He had to be ready for nasty, unannounced visitors, like the violent men who were probably at that very minute scouring the city for him. Tracking him down.

But today he was expecting his buddy Jimmy Louder, who was supposed to arrive any moment now. Louder was one of the most trusted men in Ethan's Remnant group—the underground network struggling to survive in this new order of things. Like Ethan, Louder had once been an air force pilot, but he was several years older. He had a laid-back manner, but underneath there was a reserve of toughness, something that had come in handy during his confinement in a North Korean prison camp. Although Louder and Ethan didn't focus on physical survival—their mission was bigger than that—it was still a necessity, especially for Ethan, who was at the top of the Most Wanted list of the Global Alliance.

From his position up on the roof, Ethan could now hear the sirens wailing across the city and see smoke spiraling up from half-a-dozen fires set by vandals, rioters, or looters. This was life as usual. He knew similar scenes were happening in every other major city on the planet.

With no sign of Louder, Ethan decided to make use of the time. He yanked up the bottom edge of his sleeveless T-shirt to wipe the sweat off his face, cracked the stiffness out of his nineteen-inch neck, and rose to his feet, shaking his muscular arms to loosen them up. Then he dropped down for fifty rapid-fire push-ups. Then fifty sit-ups. Then leg raises, followed by an explosive volley of running in place. He must have been shaking the roof, because someone in the apartment below began screaming out the window. Ethan understood a little Greek and knew the man downstairs was yelling for him to stop. He was shouting a few other choice things too.

Ethan smiled and called back an apology. *"Sygnomi!"* He grabbed his canvas rucksack, which was filled with fifty pounds of bricks, and prepared for his daily routine. For the last two years he had been forced to live his life like an endless series of stunts on a movie lot—scampering down the sides of apartment buildings, leaping from rooftops, and jumping out of moving cars—just to stay one step ahead of the Global Alliance agents who pursued him. That meant every day was a training day.

Strapping the heavy rucksack to his back, he sauntered over to the edge of the three-story building where a four-foot black, wrought-iron fence surrounded the rooftop. A rope had already been cinched to it and hung over the side until it nearly reached the street level. He climbed over the fence and quickly rappelled down the rope. Then came the hard part—with a heave, he scampered back up the rope to the rooftop with the pack full of bricks still strapped onto his back.

While he caught his breath on the roof, a voice brought him out of his thoughts. "I figured I'd find you up here."

Ethan snapped around. He relaxed when he recognized the thin frame of Jimmy Louder with his reddish hair receding in a widow's peak at the temples.

"Always pushing yourself physically," Louder said.

Ethan shrugged and smiled. "Force of habit, I guess."

"Going all the way back to your Triple-A baseball training, I suppose? Nearly making the pros—yeah, that always impressed me, by the way."

"Well, it didn't impress the pitching coach much," Ethan shot back with a smirk. "I had a pretty good fastball. But about as much control over the ball as my mom had over her tomcat. And then there were those other problems I had with the game . . . So, next stop, the United States Air Force."

Louder had a glint of admiration in his face. "And all of that special-ops training they put you through. Now, me? I was just one of those ol' run-of-the-mill fighter pilots who only got the basic survival camp."

"Which came in handy, I bet, when you got shot down on the wrong side of the DMZ."

"Sure. For the four days I was on the run. Until I ran smack into a North Korean patrol. Oh well. Water under the bridge. And God was good. Two years later He sent Joshua Jordan and the rest of you guys to get me out."

Ethan still struggled over that. He always felt a sting of regret that he didn't really do a lick of work on that rescue mission. It had all been God and Josh Jordan as far as he was concerned. Oh yes, and the pretty, dark-eyed Rivka. She had been in on it too, big-time. How could he forget her?

"The minute I noticed your new location on the encrypted Remnant GPS," Louder continued, "I wondered what happened to that cheap hotel room where you were living before—the one on the western end of the city."

"High-crime area," Ethan said with a wink. "Bad neighborhood."

Louder chuckled. "Since when are you afraid of a little violence and mayhem?"

"Actually," Ethan explained, "some agents from the Global Alliance's security police showed up one day and started asking the landlord about me. I had to split in a hurry. So I found a room here in the Plaka district. It turns out this landlady's one of us. So what's new with you?"

Louder quickly surveyed the rooftop. They were still alone. "Two things. First, on a personal note"—he broke into a grin—"I ran into Rivka a few days ago at a safe house in Jerusalem. She was traveling through on her way back to Hong Kong. She said to say hi."

Ethan's face brightened slightly. "Oh? Did she say anything else?"

"Only that she would really like to see you soon."

Ethan shrugged. "Well, she knows the encrypted underground number. She can locate me that way anytime she likes. In fact, she could have done that a year ago."

Louder snickered. "Do I sense that you've got some feelings on that subject?"

Ethan waved the comment off. "What's the second thing?"

Louder sobered. "Speaking of the Global Alliance, I think I was tailed today. Two rough-looking guys."

That was something Ethan didn't want to hear. He could feel his jaw tensing. "Did you lose them?"

"Yeah, about a block from here. They didn't look like Global Alliance police. More like bounty hunters. Probably sniffing after the reward money the Alliance is offering."

"I wondered when the Alliance was going to raise the bounty."

"Well, on you they have. Big money. But for the capture of little ol' me," Louder said, "they're just offering dresser change." He gave out a fake whimper. "My male ego is still aching about that."

Ethan managed a grin. But silently he mulled over the bounty hunter issue. He hoped Louder had lost the guys tailing him.

He shook it off and changed the subject. "All right, on the subject of an underground barter payment system, where are we on that?"

"I've been in contact with the black market guy. His name is Gikas. A local Greek. He's the Athens point person for Mr. Big."

"Jo Li?"

"Right. I've already set up the introductory meeting with Gikas."

"Where is Jo Li now?"

"Don't know. But we may find out shortly. You and I have a meeting with Gikas up at the Acropolis, like, right now. That's why I came by to pick you up. Sorry about the short notice. If he clears us for the next step, then we get a meeting directly with Jo Li."

"Good," Ethan said, snatching his short-sleeved shirt off the roof and slipping it on.

"Just one thing," Louder said. There was caution in his voice. "We just don't know a lot about Jo Li's operation. I've only heard rumors. We have to be careful."

"Sure. But those of us in the Remnant who refused to get laser imprinted with the BIDTag identification don't have any choice," Ethan shot back. "Ever since the Alliance linked the universal monetary system to everybody's BIDTag via the web, we've been stuck. I'm hoping Jo Li's system will be our ticket to an alternate method to buy and sell."

Louder smiled as he watched Ethan launch into one of his favorite subjects.

"If we fail in this," Ethan continued, "our people won't eat. Won't be able to pay for housing. And we'll be strapped for communications money to deliver the truth to a world on the verge of imploding. And then there's our field operations budget. Without that, how are we going to protect God's people from the evil empire? This is a 'Moses at the Red Sea' moment."

"I thought you said you weren't called to be a preacher," Jimmy cracked with a sly smile.

Ethan shrugged it off. "Okay, so I guess I'm cranked up this morning." He looked out beyond the rooftops and up to the ancient ruins on the top of the hill in the distance. He studied the columns of the ancient Acropolis from his position on the rooftop, and then he asked a question that came out more like an answer. "Most people just don't think their own civilization will crumble, do they? Josh kept telling me how one day the whole planet would start collapsing into chaos, right before God wraps up history once and for all. Brings Christ back to establish His kingdom. Like an idiot, I didn't take it seriously back then. But Josh was right. He was right about a lot of things."

Louder studied him. "You miss him, don't you?"

"I miss all of them," Ethan shot back. "The whole Jordan family. Josh. And Abby too. Boy, she really sized me up when she first noticed I was interested in her daughter!" He laughed. "And I miss her too. Deb Jordan, I mean. I know now why it never would have worked between the two of us, though I didn't have a clue at the time. And I miss Cal, of course. We ended up like brothers. But right now I know that none of them are looking back. No regrets. And meanwhile you and I, because we dragged our feet in making a decision about Jesus, ended up being left behind."

Louder bobbed his head. "At least we're on track now."

Just then Ethan heard a sound, as if someone approached. He was instantly on the alert, like a hunting dog. The noise came from the far end of the rooftop where it was accessed by a single door set into a copula. Ethan narrowed his eyes and pointed to the door. "When you came up to the roof, was anyone hanging around in the stairwell?"

Louder shook his head.

Before Ethan could reply, the door burst open and two men rushed out onto the rooftop. In the lead came a bounty hunter sporting a Mohawk and a sleeveless shirt that revealed tattoos running down both arms. He was followed by a tall, lanky man with his hair tied back in a ponytail who hung back.

"Hold it right there!" the tattooed guy screamed as he stood his ground at the other end of the roof. He pointed a strange-looking gun in their direction. "We've got a piece of paper from the Global Alliance. And you know what?" He broke into a big grin. "It's got both your names on it."

"They had those kinds of papers in Nazi Germany too," Ethan called back.

"Nice history lesson, Jesus freak," the man yelled, following up with a string of profanities. "But I didn't come this far to chat. Wait till the Alliance starts putting the screws to your head," he said with a laugh. "I wish I could see that."

Ethan whispered to Louder, "I'm not carrying at the moment. Are you?"

"Nope," Louder replied in a hushed voice.

Ethan sucked in a deep breath and stared at the two tough guys edging cautiously toward them. "Looks like we'll have to do this the hard way."

TWO

Ethan and Louder raised their hands. As they stepped slowly toward them, the bounty hunters eyed them like jungle animals stalking a prey that could fight back.

Ethan kept his eye on the little black weapon with four barrels that was gripped in Tattoo Guy's hand. "Looks like one of those Russian pistols. The PB-4M," he whispered.

"Rubber bullets?"

"Maybe." Rubber bullets or not, Ethan knew that a shot to his skull from one of those would knock him out, and could even be fatal. And a hit anywhere else would certainly disable him. "They must want us alive."

"What's the plan?"

Ethan surreptitiously glanced around. They were standing about five feet from the wrought-iron fence at the edge of the building's flat rooftop. "You slide down the rope. I'll handle the *illustrated man* with the gun."

"I thought you were the master rope climber."

"But you're the old guy. Age before . . . whatever."

"Shut up!" the tattoo guy yelled. Without warning he fired his pistol, winging Ethan in the thigh. Ethan howled, grabbing his leg. He grunted to Louder, "Yeah, rubber bullets. Get down the rope. Meet me at the Acropolis."

The two bounty hunters were now about five feet away. Louder turned and launched himself over the fence, sliding down the rope. The tattooed shooter aimed for him, but Ethan leapt forward and buried his head in the man's midriff, taking him to the ground as the pistol clattered out of his hand. The tattoo guy gasped for air, the wind knocked out of him.

The tall man with the ponytail jumped into the fray and locked his arm around Ethan's throat from behind. Ethan grabbed the ponytail and tossed the man over his shoulder, sending him onto his back with a smack.

Struggling to his feet, Ethan began to limp toward the edge of the building. But the tattoo guy had recovered enough to catch him by the ankle and trip him. As Ethan jumped to his feet again he saw Mr. Ponytail scrambling over to the pistol. Ethan hobbled toward the fence, coming within a couple of inches of the rope before the tattooed bounty hunter caught up to him and wrestled him to the ground. As the two men struggled, Ethan caught a glimpse of Ponytail picking up the pistol. An instant later the man had the multibarrelled gun in his hand and with three shots left was running full speed toward Ethan.

It was now or never. Ethan punched his assailant solidly in the face, knocking him out. As the ponytailed gunman ran toward him, Ethan lifted up the listless bounty hunter and held him like a shield. Mr. Ponytail fired and hit the bleary-eyed tattoo guy squarely in the back. With a low groan he registered the strike, now only semiconscious.

Ethan dropped him and vaulted over the fence to rappel down the rope. By the time he reached the porch of the second floor below, Mr.

Ponytail was aiming his gun down at him. Ethan swung himself out of sight onto the patio.

An elderly couple sat there on the deck in folding chairs. They watched him, wide-eyed with mouths agape.

"Folks," Ethan announced hurriedly, "you'd better go inside." He pointed to the sliding door that led to their little porch. "Stay there for your safety. I'm borrowing one of your chairs."

The elderly man nodded hesitantly, like he was trying to understand. He and his wife rose unsteadily to their feet, Ethan helping the wife until she had both feet planted beneath her, and made their way into their apartment.

Ethan snatched up a folding chair and collapsed it. He stepped up to the edge of the patio and waited. Two seconds later Ponytail came sliding down the rope with his gun now jammed in his pocket. When he saw Ethan staring back at him, he grabbed frantically at the weapon, trying to yank it out of his pocket as he swung back and forth on the rope.

Ethan raised the folding chair. "Stop persecuting God's people." He swung the metal chair and smacked it into the man's midsection. Mr. Ponytail dropped off of the rope and fell straight down, clipping through an awning and finally landing on his back on the roof of a car.

Ethan grabbed the rope and finished rappelling down to the sidewalk below. The ponytailed thug was rolling around in pain on the car's roof like a turtle on its back. Reaching into his pocket, Ethan pulled out a gospel tract and tossed it onto the man's chest. "Read that," he said to him. "Seriously. You're on the wrong side. There's still time to turn your life around."

Then he placed under the windshield wiper of the car a few old-fashioned international CReDO currency bills. He'd heard a few merchants were still accepting those remnants of the last one-world currency that had been in circulation before the world's money system went totally digital. Those bills would cover the damage to the car roof. He felt bad about the torn awning, but there was nothing he could do about that now.

He limped across the street to another apartment complex and made his way through the lobby to a back entrance that led to an alley. He'd have to use a staggered route for the first part of his walk up to the Acropolis to avoid detection. He was feeling the heat from the Global Alliance in Athens.

Only one thing to do: *After the meeting, time to leave the area and relocate.*

Ethan made his way to Therios Street, where it took a steep turn up to the Acropolis and its overshadowing marble structures, the Parthenon and the Temple of Athena—monuments to the long-dead prestige of pagan Athens. Therios Street would put him in the wide open, but there wasn't any other way to get there. Once up among the ancient ruins, things might be safer, at least on the ground. With the devastating effect of worldwide depression, tourism was a bust. The grounds surrounding the ancient sites were usually vacant, except for hordes of homeless people sleeping under trees.

As Ethan glanced up at the familiar remnants of ancient Greece where he would meet Louder and Gikas, he began to silently pray. For a successful meeting. For some way to provide a financial system for millions of new Jesus Remnant members around the world. And for some way to protect them as long as he could while the rest of the world continued to collapse.

THREE

When Ethan arrived at the large rock outcropping near the ancient ruins of the Acropolis, Louder and Gikas were there, along with a big, ominous-looking "assistant" who Ethan took to be the bodyguard. Gikas, a short, stocky man with bushy eyebrows, announced that he was the local agent for Jo Li, the reputed mastermind behind an underground network for buying and selling. But Gikas looked distracted. He kept nervously scanning the sky. When Ethan started to dialogue, Gikas put up his hand to silence him. Gikas craned his head quickly back and forth, surveying the Acropolis. After a moment he said, "I thought I heard one of them."

"One what?" Ethan asked.

"One of those Global Alliance drone-bots they use for flyovers. Very little armed security on the ground here in the ruins."

"We've noticed that," Louder said.

"Yeah, now they are doing it from the air," Gikas continued. "They use the drones for nontaggers like you guys."

Gikas launched into a diatribe on the problems that global surveillance had created. Everyone—and especially Ethan—knew what Gikas was talking about. Ethan didn't need a lecture on the dilemma of nontaggers who, like his own group, had refused to receive a BIDTag—the invisible, biological identification tattoo with a hidden QR code, required by force of law to be lasered onto the backs of hands or on the foreheads of every citizen on the planet, including those in America. People had been told it was for homeland security purposes. But with the onslaught of global depression, the BIDTag had been converted for another use as a human debit card—a cashless, worldwide electronic system for payment and banking.

When they'd worked shoulder to shoulder in Israel, Josh Jordan had continually drilled Ethan on the significance of those events. Josh kept reminding his younger apprentice how it fit into the tapestry of Bible prophecy. So when Josh and his family were raptured, Ethan was already trained to understand "the signs of the times," as Josh would put it: the geopolitical events happening around the world and in the United States. Like the fact that the United States Congress had voted to join the world's universal payment scheme, but President Hank Hewbright had promptly vetoed it. Then Congress overrode his veto in a squeaker of a vote. That's where matters still stood in America. Appeals to the Supreme Court had been fruitless; the vanishing of several Supreme Court justices at the Great Disappearance meant a weakened high court, with several members missing and President Hewbright unable to get any of his judicial nominees confirmed.

Standing there in the shadow of the huge rock outcropping, Gikas was going on and on about the robotically operated drone planes that had been employed by the Global Alliance for surveillance and police work. "If they scan you from the air and don't see your BIDTag, you get one warning over the loudspeaker from the drone, telling you to stop and to wait for someone to arrive on the ground to arrest you. A second warning if you don't stop. Then they start shooting from the air."

Ethan nodded. This was old news for him. Except that he knew something Gikas didn't: for Ethan there would be no second warning, or even a first.

"Yeah," Louder replied. "We're pretty up on all of that." He gave a knowing glance at Ethan. Both of them knew that because Ethan was a leader of the resistance, his image had been cataloged into the facial-recognition program of the Global Alliance ID data centers—the main one in New Babylon, Iraq, and the others in Rome, London, Frankfurt, and Singapore—and they were all digitally linked and uploaded to the drone-bots around the world.

Gikas concluded his point. "Just have to be careful. Need to keep an eye on the sky."

"The drone-bots have a recognizable pitch to the engines," Ethan said. "I can usually hear them coming."

"Anyway," Gikas went on, "let's get back to why you're here."

Ethan jumped to his main point. He explained how he needed assurance that if his Remnant followers joined Jo Li's underground economy they would not be linked to anything criminal. No dirty money. No tie-in to drugs, prostitution, human trafficking.

Gikas stretched out his arms in wonder. "What kind of people do you take us for?" He laughed loudly and so did his bodyguard.

"Ethan March is a guy with principles," Louder said. "I thought you knew that."

"Okay, okay," Gikas replied. "I know about you people. Goody-good. Nicey-nice. All squeaky clean and talking all about God and Jesus. Which is why I'm happy to tell you that our trading system is completely legit. The people who trade back and forth in our system are just people who didn't get BIDTagged, and so they need to be able to buy and sell some other way. Jo Li's system is legal because he found a loophole in the law."

"I need to see how his financial system actually operates," Ethan said. "I need more information."

"For that, you will have to talk to Mr. Jo Li himself," Gikas said.

"Where is he?"

"Not here," Gikas replied.

"Close?"

"Not very. Hong Kong."

Ethan took a moment to consider that. Then he asked something very different. "Tell me, Gikas, do you believe in God?"

Louder smiled as if he wasn't surprised.

Gikas answered, "Sure. Yeah. Why not."

"You don't sound very convinced," Ethan said.

Gikas winked at his bodyguard as he answered. "It's just that, you know, there's a lot of unknowns."

Ethan asked, "Do you know anything about this huge rock we're standing next to?"

Gikas took a step toward the historical marker attached to the outcropping and eyed it. "Yeah, something about Paul the apostle doing something here. Some religious thing."

Ethan began to explain how two thousand years ago, at that exact spot, Paul had told the great philosophers of ancient Athens about the God who had been unknown to them but could be known through His Son, Jesus.

The big bodyguard shuffled his feet and nudged Gikas, motioning with his head, like it was time to leave. But Gikas took a second to study Ethan. "You people are a strange bunch," he said and thrust an index finger toward Ethan. "I'm going to have to figure you out."

"Will you arrange the meeting with Jo Li?" Louder asked.

"Maybe," Gikas said with a shrug. "It's up to him, not me. He's the big guy. I'm a nobody."

"Wrong," Ethan said with a smile. "God thinks you're somebody."

Gikas was about to reply, but now Ethan hushed him as he held a finger to his lips. He gazed straight up. "There's a drone-bot approaching. I can hear it."

A second later they were all eyeing the sky.

Ethan searched for somewhere to hide. The high mount Acropolis was too far away. He would never make it. Down towar city? That was a mile at least to the nearest building. Probably mo.

Now they could see the clean white underbelly of the dro. approaching their position.

"We're exposed!" Ethan yelled. He pointed to the grove of trees off to the side of Mars Hill. "Head to the trees."

Gikas yelled back, "They've got body sensors. They can still scan us in the woods."

As he started racing toward the trees, still limping slightly, Ethan explained, "But the bullets may get blocked by the trees!"

He watched the drone dropping in altitude over their position. Then the laser orb on the belly of the unmanned attack plane flashed. On the ground Ethan was bathed with red light. "I've been painted!" he cried. "Everyone scatter. Get away from me!"

"Ethan!" was all Louder had time to scream.

A mere three seconds later—just enough time for the onboard computer in the drone to recognize Ethan from the sky—bullets from the fifty-caliber gun in the drone's belly turret started blasting down at him. He yelled to Louder as he kept running clumsily toward the grove of trees. "Jimmy, get out of here! Meet me back at the apartment. Gikas, make the arrangements for the meeting with Jo Li." Pistoning toward a full run as bullets exploded around him, he ducked inside the small wooded area. The bullets ripped through the treetops.

He found a large tree and wrapped his arms around the trunk, pressing against it as hard as he could, and waited. He could still hear the drone up in the sky, cruising back and forth over the trees. He glanced at his Allfone watch. The usual protocol was a seventeen-minute gunnery pursuit, and then the drones usually departed if they hadn't confirmed a hit on their target. The only thing he could do now was wait it out and not move a muscle.

He stood absolutely still, pressed against the rough bark of the olive tree, until he heard the sound of the plane's engine fading. Finally the drone was no longer visible in the sky. He let go of the tree and breathed. And breathed again.

Thank You, God.

But he couldn't relax. Not yet. He had to get out of Athens. He knew that in a matter of minutes the plaza around Mars Hill would be crawling with Global Alliance police forces.

As he made his way down the hill, he had another thought. *So much for taking me alive.*

FOUR

AMMAN, JORDAN

Bart Kingston sipped a cup of Turkish coffee at a sidewalk café. The Jordanian man on the other side of the little glass table held a small, handheld AllView image display unit. He looked uncomfortable and was passing it back and forth from one hand to the other. The Jordanian was obviously a man under pressure.

Kingston wondered about the overly public place his contact had picked for their rendezvous. "Can I ask you something?" he said. "Why here? Why not a quiet hotel room?"

The Jordanian laughed, but not as if something was funny. More like a cynical snort. "Hotel rooms have only two exits. The Global Alliance breaks down the door and now you have only one way out—through the window." He put the AllView unit down and finished his coffee. Then he glanced around and picked the unit up again. "At least here I keep my options open. You know, for running."

Kingston, a former journalist for GNN, knew the stakes. The news footage chip in the image unit was the kind of stuff that could make the Jordanian—or a newsman like Kingston, for that matter—disappear forever if he was caught with it.

"You say, Mr. Kingston, that you are now with this AmeriNews group?"

Kingston nodded.

"I hear the Alliance hates you people," the man added with a scowl.

"Sure," Kingston answered. "Because we are American based. Because we're the only web-based news service left in the world that's still independent. Not controlled by the Global Alliance, or by any of its ten world government regions. Or by the Alliance's web-news network, for that matter."

The Jordanian man set the compact device on the table, exactly in the middle between the two men. "Two thousand units. Agreed price. The digital video chip is already in the recorder."

"Agreed," Kingston said.

Before Kingston began to electronically transmit the money, both men glanced around the café again, just one more time. Looking for snoops. Spies. Agents of the Alliance. Close by, a couple sat arguing about something. Two tables away, a young man was smoking a cigarette and eyeing a trio of attractive women passing by. It all looked normal enough.

"Okay," Kingston said. "I need your BIDTag."

Kingston held out the screen of his Allfone, and the Jordanian man placed the back of his hand to the screen of the digital communications device until it could read his BIDTag. The screen flashed. Next Kingston passed his finger over a tab with a dollar sign on it. His Allfone was an older model, and the symbol was a relic of the past now that the dollar had been abandoned as the monetary unit in America and anywhere else.

The screen on Kingston's handheld read *Transaction Ready*. Kingston placed the back of his own hand to the little screen. Another flash. The screen read *Amount to Transfer?*

After the monetary units were typed in, the screen lit up again. *Monetary transfer complete. Thank you, Mr. Kingston.* The corner of the screen flashed with a summary of the payment and the identities of the parties involved.

"Done," Kingston announced and displayed the screen of his Allfone to the Jordanian, who nodded and looked satisfied but still very nervous. The Jordanian slid the video recorder over to Kingston. Then he added, "Please do not tell who I am or where you got this."

Kingston nodded.

"I think I know why you want this," the Jordanian said, pointing to the image recorder. "The raw footage from the Alliance Network. Used for those news stories about the disappearance of the Christians."

"We call it something else."

"Yes, yes. I know."

"Followers of Jesus call it the Rapture."

The Jordanian searched Kingston's face. "Then why, if you are one of those Jesus persons, aren't you disappeared too?" The man gave a little laugh and raised an eyebrow.

"Because," Kingston said, "I was a foolish man back then. I didn't make my decision about Jesus until after the Rapture had happened. So here I am."

The Jordanian pointed at the recorder. "Me? I think that the Alliance Network is right when they say this Rapture didn't happen. I think what happened was like they say: millions of Christians went out into desert places and all killed themselves, because they thought it would bring Jesus back to earth."

"And if that's true, where are the bodies?" Kingston said with a grin. Then he added, "As for that mass suicide business, it's a lie from hell." He leaned across the table, closer to the other man, and tapped the video recorder. "And I intend to prove it."

The Jordanian stood up and looked around, ready to leave, but stopped and pointed at Kingston's right hand with a surprised look on his face. "You have a BIDTag. And yet you are a Jesus person?"

"Yes, before I ever became a Christian," Kingston said, "I got tagged. Another foolish thing."

The Jordanian shrugged, shook his head, and in a moment was gone.

Kingston flipped open the screen of the recorder and swept his finger over the *Play* tab. He needed to verify what he had just bought.

The screen displayed a Global Alliance logo and a warning in several different languages, including English. The good news was that Bart Kingston was now in possession of the raw footage he had been tracking for more than a year. The bad news became clear the instant he read the warning notice.

Global Alliance Information Network
Property of the News Division
WARNING!

Unauthorized viewing or possession of this material is a violation of the international code and will be punished to the fullest extent of the law. Any usage of this material by a member of a subversive organization that causes harm to international peace is punishable by imprisonment of a minimum term of twenty years and a maximum punishment of execution through humane, lethal injection.

After reading that, Bart Kingston thought about his long career in the investigative news business. And how that business had taken a deadly turn.

FIVE

NEW BABYLON, IRAQ

Alexander Colliquin, chancellor of the two-year-old Global Alliance of Nations, left his office on the top floor of his twenty-thousand-square-foot "Hanging Gardens" suite. At his side walked stone-faced Ho Zhu, his deputy chancellor. The men were flanked by a squad of security guards. In his breathless, long-legged pace, Colliquin strode ahead of them on the moving walkway, making his way over to the adjoining white stone headquarters of Global Internet Connectivity.

A private, heavily guarded corridor led directly from Colliquin's office to the IC building, part of the new massive complex of buildings that took up one hundred square miles—land that had been deeded to Colliquin years ago by the United States when his friend

Jessica Tulrude, the former U.S. vice president, was finishing out the term of critically ill President Virgil Corland.

Now Colliquin stopped at the bulletproof, triple-layered glass door leading into the IC center. He placed his right eye in the pupil recognition socket and placed his index finger and thumb on the fingerprint ID pad. A laser beam scanned his Romanesque facial features—the kind of face you might expect to see on the cover of *GQ* magazine—and then electronically outlined his tall, athletic profile from head to foot.

A digital voice spoke from the security console. "Thank you for your cooperation, Chancellor. Have a nice day."

The airlock hissed as the thick glass door opened, followed by another, and another, until Colliquin reached the lobby of the IC facility where the chief of digital imagery, dressed in a light-blue lab coat, waited for him.

The guards held back at the entrance of the glass doors. Ho Zhu went through the same security clearance process, and when the airlocks opened for him too, he joined his boss in the lobby. The lab chief led them to an open testing space the size of two football fields. A hundred cubicles were filled with a hundred data engineers, digital architects, network specialists, and electronic image designers.

As the chief strolled with the two men through the maze of cubicles, he described the progress to date. "We're approaching completion of the first phase. At this stage all we have is just a great deal of computer code and schematics and the single prototype system here in this facility. But we are quickly nearing completion."

Colliquin smiled. "The world is about to become a better place. And you, Chief, can be part of this historic evolution."

The chief smiled. "Yet," he replied, "the problem still remains. We need a central data hub with enough computing power, speed, memory, storage capacity, and network reach to serve as the nerve center for the kind of global transmissions you are proposing. And no such data center—at least none within the jurisdiction of the ten-nation global alliance—currently exists."

Colliquin nodded toward Ho Zhu. "Mr. Ho here has located such a data center, have you not, Mr. Ho?"

Ho nodded with a grin. "I have. To be sure."

"And where would this great data center be located?" the chief wondered.

Ho replied. "In Utah."

The chief blinked. "But . . . ," he stammered. "You are referring to the highly secure government surveillance complex at the United States Data Center in Bluffdale, Utah?"

"We are," Colliquin said.

"But that is under the control of the United States government."

"Presently, yes," Colliquin agreed with the nonchalance of someone who had a plan.

A stunned look settled on the chief's face. "But as we all know"—he stammered a bit as he said it—"the American president has refused to become part of your Global Alliance, Chancellor."

If the chief expected a response to that, Colliquin wasn't giving one. Instead, he simply stared at the chief and with a calm voice, like an elementary school teacher, explained the next step. "Mr. Ho here has discovered something important. Isn't that right, Mr. Ho?"

Ho nodded.

Colliquin continued, "And Mr. Ho will be transmitting, directly to you, the information he is gathering on the U.S. Data Center at Bluffdale. Correct, Mr. Ho?"

"Certainly," Ho agreed without emotion.

Colliquin abruptly dismissed his deputy chancellor, who turned on his heel and left. Colliquin continued his conversation with the head of his radical Internet project. "Now, about the imagery details . . ."

The lab chief nodded energetically and talked as he led Colliquin to a separate, locked laboratory. "The cloud-networked, holograph-to-human interactive digital program. Yes, of course. We're all very excited about that. The concept is at the very frontier of technology— the idea of physically linking humans to the Internet and then using a web-based holographic image to influence neural responses in the brain."

After inputting code into the trio of computers connected to the digital image laser tubes, the chief waved his hand over a few tabs on the master screen. Then he turned to Colliquin. "Where in the room would you like it?"

Colliquin smiled and pointed to the space above a storage cabinet at the far end of the laboratory. "Let's start there."

"Easy enough," the chief said. He activated the 3-D GPS locator function on the screen and touched the spot that showed an outline of the room and the cabinet. Then he pressed an icon on the screen. That was when the 3-D image of the face appeared, hovering over the cabinet.

Colliquin smiled. "Make it bigger. Much bigger."

The chief tapped a tab on his screen and the hologram suddenly filled the entire room, eclipsing Colliquin and the technology chief with the giant human likeness that seemed to have a life of its own.

Colliquin grinned broadly and raised his hands in a kind of strange blessing at what he saw. He could have cried for joy, but he didn't have the ability. Not because of some physiological defect of the tear ducts, but rather because of something else altogether— something deep inside of him that was invisible to the eye, but very dark. And it was growing unchecked with the passage of time, like a malignancy.

51X

JERUSALEM, ISRAEL

A young bearded man named Micah walked at a hasty clip, his eyes darting around him. He was on his way to a clandestine meeting just off Bab as-Silsila Street, formally the dividing point between what used to be called the Jewish Quarter and the Arab Quarter. But then, those kinds of geographical labels didn't make much sense anymore since the migration of most Arabs and Palestinians out of Israel following the spectacularly failed Arab-Russian invasion several years back.

Micah didn't dare break into a run. That would catch too much attention from the Global Alliance police force. And there were a dozen of them in their blue helmets, some shouldering automatic weapons, stationed here and there on the plaza adjoining the old Western Wall where Micah now crossed quickly, head down. Micah also knew that it wasn't just the Alliance police on the ground that posed a threat, or even the drone-bots that patrolled the airspace. There were also the heavily armed droid-bots patrolling Jerusalem on foot. He had walked past a few of the big droids from time to time, though he hadn't been stopped by one.

Not yet.

The Alliance authorities still permitted pedestrians to cross the plaza under the shadow of the huge temple in order to enter the crowded, winding alleys of the commercial *souk*. Because of the negotiations between Prime Minister Sol Bensky and the Global Alliance's Alexander Colliquin, the Jews had finally been given complete control of their most sacred piece of geography: the Temple Mount. Up there on the Mount they had completed construction of their replica of the ancient Herodian temple. But in exchange, Israel had paid dearly.

Micah paused for a moment on the edge of the open plaza to gaze up at the monumental Jewish temple. He saw the smoke spiraling up from the altar of burnt sacrifices that lay between the entrance to the massive porch of the temple and the Court of the Priests near the second eastern gate—that place where animal sacrifices were now being offered for the first time in more than two thousand years. A few animal rights activist groups had tried to protest at first, but they didn't have a clue about the significance of it all. Micah shook his head at the sight of the temple. He was someone who knew what it meant and the thought of it made him mutter to himself.

"The coming cataclysm."

But Micah's delay was a mistake. An Alliance officer with a machine gun slung over his shoulder called out to him.

Micah froze. The officer, joined by another blue-helmeted policeman with a sidearm, jogged over to him.

The officer with the automatic weapon spoke with the hint of a French accent. "Speak English? Hebrew?"

"Both," Micah answered.

"Papers, please."

Micah pulled out his IIA certificate with his International Identification Agency number on it. He had received his BIDTag and IIA number back before the Great Disappearance of the Christians.

While the cop looked over his papers, Micah kept cool, managing to look nonchalant until the officer passed his IIA number over to his partner and said to him, "*Vous verifiez ceci avec la liste.*"

That's when Micah swallowed hard. Because he understood the command for the other officer to check his number against the list. Micah knew French, but they hadn't asked him that.

Micah also knew exactly what the two Alliance cops would find on the list. And then it would be all over. They would learn how he was an Orthodox Jew and that he had recently become a follower of Jesus and a member of the Remnant—which had now been labeled internationally as a subversive terror group. After all, hadn't the Alliance concluded, based on media reports, that the Christians had committed the world's most bizarre and horrendous act of mass suicide, even dragging children into it? And doing it in desolate areas to avoid detection? According to the Alliance, those like Micah and others becoming Jesus followers after the "disappearance" posed a similar threat to the "peace and order of the global community."

Micah had just a few seconds to make a decision. He knew what arrest would mean. He glanced over at the entrance to the covered souk to his left where he could disappear in the complex of marketplace alleys. It was only about thirty feet away. He was a fast runner. He could make it.

Micah kept up his calm smile and tightened his calf muscles as he silently gave himself the order.

Now!

He barreled off toward the entranceway, his arms pumping like a machine. Behind him the officer with the automatic weapon yelled for him to stop. Then yelled again. As Micah reached the entrance to the souk, he dodged to the left and heard the sickening sound of several *pops*. A paving stone ahead of him and to the right exploded from the bullets.

The other Alliance cop fired a second round from his handgun, but by then Micah was already inside the twisting, covered alleyways of the souk, running through a crowd of people. A shop owner and a few pedestrians screamed at him as he plowed his way through them, bumping into shoppers and almost tipping over a fruit stand in the narrow, shadowy passageway. He passed by the entrance to Men's Delight, one of several brothels that had recently been permitted along the souk, much to the outrage of the Orthodox and Christians alike. He raced past the Amsterdam Café, where marijuana and hashish were now sold, and almost tripped over a dazed man lying next to the café entrance.

Fifty yards into the heart of the souk he took a hard right, up a worn set of stone steps to an aged metal door with a modern keypad attached to it. It led to the upper terrace of the Old City. He frantically typed four numbers and two letters into the pad. The door clicked open, and he swung through and closed it tight behind him. Then he raced up the tall flight of stone steps, taking them two at a time. He was almost to the top, where there was daylight and possible safety on the upper street level.

Micah burst out from underneath the covered stairs and paused, taking a second to catch his breath in the warm sunlight. But as he bent over, panting heavily, he became aware of a presence standing very close to him. Startled, he looked up and stumbled backward. A six-foot, seven-inch semihuman-looking droid was standing within arm's reach of him. It was plated on the outside with glistening blue bulletproof Kevlar with a blue-and-white Global Alliance logo on its chest where the ends of short-barreled automatic weapons spouted out. Behind its black-screened face, two red digital eyes flashed out at him. Then it spoke.

"Halt, suspect Micah Schotze. You have been visually identified and matched with a terrorist religious group. You are under arrest. I am authorized to use deadly force if you resist."

Micah settled himself. He knew what to do. He had heard rumors about it and its success. But now it would mean the difference between life and death. The droids had the strength of six men, speed and agility that would put Olympic athletes to shame, and were armed with forty-five-caliber weaponry. There was only one way out.

Micah spoke the words out loud, bending a little closer to the cop-bot, as his friends would call these global police robots. He said it as clearly as he could, this short phrase he had been told would override the security code in the electronic brain of the droid. And then he stood perfectly still, staring at the black plastic shield that covered the face of the droid. Waiting for the verdict.

A few seconds later the droid spoke again in a perfect human voice tinged with only a slight digital echo. "You are free to go. Have a good day."

"Thank You, God," Micah said out loud and sprinted off.

Ten minutes later he quietly slipped into an apartment safe house belonging to Rabbi Zechariah Gamaliel. Rabbi ZG, as the Remnant followers called him, was pointing to an electronic screen behind him as he lectured the group of thirty or so who had crammed into the room. There was a picture of the Temple Mount on the screen. He was recapping how Israel's prime minister, Sol Bensky, had arm-twisted the Knesset into supporting his decision to give international supervision of Jerusalem over to the Global Alliance of nations and granted generous oil leases to that body so it could distribute the oil from Israel's newly discovered shale oil deposits. In return, the Alliance negotiated for the Temple Mount to be handed over to Israel and the historic Muslim edifices—the Al Aqsa Mosque and the Dome of the Rock—to be dismantled and moved to Saudi Arabia. In addition, the Alliance pledged to help Israel fend off all terrorist incursions. In the end an empty gesture, since the massive defeat of the Arab-Russian invasion had already taken care of much of that problem.

The rabbi touched a tab on his handheld control and the screen lit up with footage of the newly completed construction project on the Temple Mount. He raised a finger in the air as his voice grew intense. "The rebuilding of the Jewish temple on the Temple Mount. Can't you see the fulfillment of the prophetic words of *Yeshua*, Jesus the Messiah? In Matthew chapter 24, the Lord Jesus predicted the desecration that will take place in the Holy of Holies, clearly referring to the temple, which presupposes that the temple had to be rebuilt. In the same way, beloved friends, 2 Thessalonians 2:3–4 predicts the same thing, the ultimate fulfillment foreshadowed by the prophet Daniel. This temple construction, taken in conjunction with the Lord's Rapture of His Church from the earth a little more than two years ago, signals the approach of something dark and terrible. The rise of the Antichrist. The lawless one. And the beginning of the first half of the seven-year Tribulation period on the earth—God's judgment on the unrighteousness that is rampant."

Then the rabbi said, "Mark him well, this man of sin, when he appears. For he seeks to rule the world and all that is in it. He is a liar and the father of liars. And he will tell us anything, and he will say it with brilliant, soothing words that tickle the ears. But no matter what he says, or how enticing his appearance, he seeks to destroy the followers of Jesus and to make the human race his slaves."

Another person, a young man, shouted out, "How can we—any of us—withstand such a force?"

Rabbi ZG smiled. "Be of good courage. Remember the promises of God. The Lord of hosts is faithful." The rabbi paused, touching his index finger to his beard. "And there is also good news. All of these events shall serve as God's great trumpet, giving mankind yet another chance to embrace Jesus the Messiah. The perfect Lamb of God."

He looked over to the young man who had asked the question. "So, how can we withstand so great an assault of evil?" He smiled. "Come, come! Remember the Scriptures! What does it say? God shall send us His wonder-working witnesses, who will soon be among us." A few in the audience nodded, but the rest had a questioning look in their eyes. Rabbi ZG continued, "And those witnesses shall be two."

SEVEN

WHITE HORSE, YUKON TERRITORY, CANADA

Beyond the edge of town, in a heavily forested area a half mile off the road, John Galligher stood poised at the top of a makeshift ladder that leaned against a pine tree. He had a canvas bag slung over his shoulder, and he had just finished readjusting the wireless surveillance camera positioned high up on the trunk of the tree. If his calculations were correct, with the adjustment he had just made, the cameras should be able to capture a sweeping view of Klondike Highway a mile outside of White Horse. That would help him monitor the influx of Global Alliance troops in the city.

Now that Canada had joined the Global Alliance, Alliance military hardware and manpower were flooding into the Yukon. The smart money was on the idea that the Alliance would eventually surround the United States from Canada in the north and Mexico in the south. What they had planned after that, though, was anyone's guess. But as Galligher saw things, his assignment wouldn't focus on the U.S. Instead, he was to protect at all costs the Remnant's unique high-tech installation in White Horse from any interference by evil-doers, including the Alliance. At least that's what he'd been told. So that's what he would do. But it didn't mean he had to like it.

Okay, I'm a good soldier. I can take orders. Even if it means that a former federal agent from New York City who used to chase terrorist cells ends up moving to the land of Paul Bunyan and has to climb pine trees.

Galligher, still on the ladder, put his Allfone against his ear and listened to the voice mail left by his ex-wife, Helen. It had come in while he was fiddling with the surveillance camera. The message started bad and went south from there. Helen ended it on a note so low and nasty it could have qualified for the *Guinness Book of World Records*.

You know, John, I've really liked not hearing your voice these many months. But you spoiled that by calling. I've enjoyed not having your overweight presence lumbering around my home. Leaving the refrigerator open. Leaving the toilet seat up. Never listening to me when I tried to talk to you. Then slipping out of bed in the middle of the night so you can whisper on the phone to your FBI buddies about some terror group you're going after. And then packing your bags and disappearing on your next mission for the Bureau without so much as a "Good-bye, Helen. I'm going to miss you." So listen to me, John, when I say you can take this garbage about "my life has radically changed now" and you can stuff it. It makes me want to vomit. Divorce from you was the beginning of my new life. Got it? So don't screw it up by bothering me.

Galligher stared at his Allfone as he clicked it off.
Best regards to you too, Helen, dear.

He sighed. He had called her with good intentions. Oh well, maybe some other time. Maybe Helen was just having a bad day. But the "overweight" business was a low blow. Galligher had worked hard to maintain his fighting weight. Two hundred and thirty-five pounds dripping wet.

He heard something. A snorting, huffing sound down on the ground. Then he felt something bump his ladder. He looked down. His day had suddenly gotten worse.

A mammoth brown bear stood at the foot of the ladder, staring up at him. Part of Galligher knew he had planned for this eventuality; preparation for chaos was a specialty of his. The other part of him broke out in a cold sweat. The grizzly looked to be fully grown. When he first arrived in the Yukon two weeks before, he'd read up on the species, just in case. The females would often reach four or five hundred pounds. The males could be even bigger, sometimes up to eight hundred pounds. But he had no interest in resolving the gender question on this one. All he knew was that it was grotesquely huge.

The humpbacked grizzly now opened its massive jaws and roared, so loudly Galligher thought he could feel his hair blowing. Then it raised itself on its hind legs like it was going to climb up the ladder after him. He was tempted to kick the ladder down to the ground, but quickly thought better of it.

Stick to the plan.

Galligher carefully lifted the canvas bag off of his shoulder, making sure he didn't drop it. That would be a disaster. As the brown bear reached up to the fifth rung of the ladder, he pulled out a plastic freezer bag. In it were two big salmon he had thawed out that morning, heads, fins, and tails still intact. He waved the bag in the air. The bear halted, sniffed loudly, and stared at the bag with a deadly kind of resolve.

Now for the hard part. Galligher lifted the plastic freezer bag high and cocked his arm, then let go with a solid throw. The bag with the smelly fish sailed through the air and landed on the ground about fifty feet away.

The bear had been reaching up the ladder with its massive front paws, hind feet on the ground. When Galligher tossed the bag, the monster barely flicked its shaggy head in the direction of the throw before returning its eyes to the man at the top of the ladder. Galligher was now sweating bullets. He'd had only the one trick up his sleeve, and he had just used it. He had nothing left.

Lucky for him, the bear leaned to one side and then, with the grace of a giant ballerina, pushed off from the ladder, almost sending Galligher tumbling down. The animal loped over to the bag of fish.

Galligher clutched his Allfone, one arm wrapped around a tree limb and his foot hooked between the slats of the ladder to keep it from falling. He repositioned the ladder beneath him until it was safe to climb down. Then he descended while keeping a close eye on the big brown bear sitting on its haunches and calmly ripping the plastic bag apart. He fought the temptation to run. It would have been fruitless; he'd read grizzlies could hit thirty miles per hour. But he walked quickly, keeping his arms to his side to avoid catching the bear's attention, as he made his way to his jeep parked about a hundred yards away. When he got there he locked the doors and turned on the ignition. It wasn't until he heard the jubilant sound of the engine revving that he finally relaxed.

Thanks, Lord, for having my back. Galligher shook his head and added, *Again.*

Putting the jeep into gear, he bumped along a fire trail, ending up at the highway, which he then drove into White Horse, crossing through to the other side of town. He pulled up in front of a three-story, 126-year-old hotel and shut off the ignition. He was feeling pretty good about besting a big brute of a brown bear.

He strode into the nineteenth-century hotel. The first-floor lobby was dolled up in gold rush décor, with lots of gold brocade and velvet curtains. It looked like the kind of place that would have been amenable to tourists once upon a time, before the global depression slowed the tourist trade. Manning the front desk was Bobby Robert, a young Native American from the Tlingit tribe who wore his black hair in two long braids. Like several others who worked the fake hotel, he was a local member of the Remnant. He was posing as the desk clerk and was reading a magazine.

As Galligher shared with Bobby the story of his close encounter with the hungry grizzly kind, he expected a minor show of admiration. Instead, the Indian man began to laugh.

"What's so funny?"

Bobby shook his head. "So you think you saved yourself with that trick, using that bag of fish?"

"I know I did. Why? What's wrong with that?"

"Oh, just this," Bobby replied, suppressing more chuckles. "Bears can smell food for miles. That bag of fish is probably what drew that bear to you in the first place."

Galligher rolled his eyes, gave a hapless shrug, and went into the back office, where he clicked on the monitor that included the surveillance sector by the Klondike Highway. He needed to make sure that after all the excitement the camera had been aimed correctly and the video feed gave him a good view of the highway. He checked it out. Mission accomplished.

So he trotted out of the office and climbed the red-carpeted spiral staircase up to the second floor. Making his way down the narrow hallway with fake gaslight sconces on the walls, he slipped a key into his door and opened it up. It wasn't just one room inside; it opened up to all the other rooms lining that side of the hallway. The whole place was crammed with computers and paper-thin monitor screens linked together. Rows and rows of floor-to-ceiling racks held electronics equipment and big cases that looked like digital suitcases wired together. Black fiber-optic cables connected everything.

In the middle of all of that sat Chiro Hashimoto, a Japanese man in his forties with a wild lock of untamed hair, in a little secretarial-type chair on wheels in front of a computer screen. The only other computer geek in the place besides Chiro was a fellow named Manfred who sported a little goatee on his chin. Manfred, like Chiro, had at one time been an employee of IntraTonics, the world-class technology company with headquarters in Washington State. Manfred was at the far end of the computer network room, peering into one of the racks.

Galligher was still getting to know Chiro, and there was a lot about this high-tech outpost of the Remnant that he didn't understand. All he knew was that it was a secret computer facility posing as a gold rush tourist hotel. So he decided to do a little probing.

"When Ethan March sent a message to me, asking me to provide security up here," he said, "I was game. But the thing is, Chiro, I've got a lot of unanswered questions."

Chiro smiled. "Go ahead. Ask me."

"Well, I realize I'm not supposed to be privy to the endgame about this computer network. And what it has to do with the Remnant, exactly. And I'm good with that. In my career, I'm used to the 'need to know' approach. But I'm worried about the Alliance being able to pick up what you're doing from the outside. You know, some kind of external scanning."

Chiro nodded. "I had new siding put on the building. Reflective material, impervious to audio surveillance. Blocks incoming radio waves. Our wireless field inside is all segregated within the rooms. Can't be seen or tapped from the outside. Even if a computer expert came into this building carrying a wireless Internet receiver or an advanced packet sniffer—the kind that not only invades Wi-Fi hot spots but also bypasses even secured systems—he still couldn't find us."

"I'm pretty old school," Galligher remarked with a tired grin. "I still don't trust any hardware that doesn't use AA batteries, so you've left me in a cloud of dust. But what I think I'm hearing you say is that your computer work here can't be intercepted from the outside."

"Exactly. No way. I'm totally sure of that."

Galligher eyed the Internet genius. He had read up on Chiro before heading north to meet him—this guy who had been hired by China to leave Tokyo and move to Beijing, where he invented the most sophisticated international computer hacking scheme the world had ever known. He'd later had to flee the Walled City when his life was threatened by the Communist bigwigs, arriving in the United States to become the head of Internet research for the megapowerful electronics company IntraTonics in Seattle. But then he left that company and went rogue for reasons that defined the word *ironic* for Galligher, even though Galligher wasn't the kind of guy who would ever use that word.

"So," Galligher asked his host, "I hear you're the one who created this whole mess. You know, the BIDTag laser process."

Chiro stopped in his tracks and turned to face Galligher, but he looked down as he spoke. "I did. I am guilty of that. Created it for IntraTonics. Didn't know back then that the U.S. government and President Tulrude and all other nations would buy it—and use it against citizens. When I realized the monster I had created, I quit. Hid out in Olympic National Forest in Washington with my buddies in an abandoned camp lodge. Built a lab and figured out a way to design a fake BIDTag for people who didn't want the government controlling all their private, personal information. Controlling their every move. I used to call my camp in the wilderness Ice Station Zebra, after the movie. Then one day I finally watched the movie. And I said to myself, *That is a stupid name for my lab in the wilderness; it is nothing like the movie!*" Chiro laughed with machine-gun staccato. *Ha-ha-ha-ha-ha.*

Galligher studied him. *I think I'm going to like this Chiro guy. He's a little weird, but in a good way.*

Chiro said something that broke him out of his thoughts. "I have asked God to forgive me many times for this terrible thing I created—the BIDTag system."

"Go easy on yourself, Chiro," Galligher said. "My list of screwups is the size of the New York City phone directory."

"Okay," Chiro replied, looking intense, "but how would you like to be known as the guy who made the human-marking process that the Prince of Darkness is going to use to rule the world?"

"Whoa, whoa, cowboy," Galligher shot back. "You don't know that."

"Not yet, but in a few hours," Chiro said, glancing at his wrist Allfone, "we have an encrypted video call from Ethan March. Maybe that is when he will finally tell us that my suspicions are true."

Galligher stepped over to Chiro and slapped him on the back. "One step at a time. Be anxious for nothing, right? That's what it says in the Bible."

"Book of Philippians," Chiro added with a nod. He slid into another solemn expression. "Just so you know, when I was at IntraTonics I also helped with the robotics program. Worked on the decision-making code for the military robots—the droid-bots. I guess that was bad too."

"You can put down your cat-o'-nine-tails and stop whipping yourself," Galligher said. "Military hardware is value neutral. It's who uses it, and how, that matters. But there's something I'd like to know: How did you finally settle up with Jesus?"

"I was in the Olympic forest in my hideout. Abigail Jordan and her son, Cal, tracked me down there. I was big-time impressed, because I thought I was deep under cover, but they found me anyway. I already knew about her husband, Colonel Joshua Jordan. Who hadn't? Well, Abby Jordan needed a fake BIDTag for a specific mission. When we talked, she told me about Jesus. And told me the signs of the end times out of the Bible. I kind of thought she was crazy at first. But she and Cal seemed like good people. Brave. Straight-up people like Josh. So I said to myself, *Okay, you need to check this Bible stuff out.*"

Chiro paused. "You know how I said that I finally saw the movie *Ice Station Zebra* and it exploded my preconceptions?"

Galligher nodded.

"Same thing with the New Testament. After Abby and Cal left, and after all those millions of other Christians disappeared—*whoosh*—just like Abby said would happen, I said to myself, *You need to actually read what the Bible says about Jesus. Don't assume.* So I read. And I told God I believed that Jesus was the Son of God, that He died on the cross to be, like, God's perfect recoding system through His blood, to solve the bad programming in our hearts and in our spirits because of sin. The ultimate infection, you know, that has been like a computer virus in the whole human race. And then I read how Jesus defied death and climbed out of the tomb. So I took Jesus into my heart. I became a new spiritual man."

"Yeah. Something like that happened for me too," Galligher said. "Minus the computer jive talk." They both chuckled.

"Oh," Chiro said, "and about those droid-bots I worked on with IntraTonics?"

"Yeah?"

"After I became a Christian, I asked a friend of mine—a guy who still worked in the company—to do a favor for me."

Galligher smiled. "This sounds like it's going to be good."

"Oh yes. I asked him to add another override security code with a phrase that I gave to him."

"Did he do it?"

"He said he did. But I never tested it. I haven't ever run into one of those droid-bots on the street yet."

"And you're not likely to up here in Bigfoot country," Galligher said. "Unless they're undercover, dressing like gold miners or lumber-jacks."

"Anyway, we will be talking with Ethan March soon," Chiro said.

"We've got the next regular video conference coming up. Then we'll find out more. Ethan's a real-life hero, I think."

Galligher considered that for a moment before he spoke. "I know that Josh figured Ethan for his successor. And as far as I'm concerned, what Josh said goes. But I knew Josh pretty well. Worked shoulder to shoulder with him in some life-and-death deals. Real cliffhangers. Now, I don't know Ethan well. But from what I do know, with all due respect, I don't think Ethan is any Joshua Jordan."

Chiro tossed him an odd look. Galligher added, "But then, what do I know, right?"

E1GHT

HONG KONG

Rivka Reuban was a slender, athletic woman in her midthirties with a pretty face and dark eyes. Anyone looking closer might notice the muscular arms and legs and a special sense of alertness and a kind of heightened quickness. It was something that came from the harsh, tensile strength she had developed in her prior profession with the Israeli Mossad.

She was in the Wan Chai district. But she had made her way off the Hennessy Road area with the nice shops and gleaming skyscrapers, where the men dressed in silk business suits and rich ladies with designer purses strolled down the avenue. Rivka was now in a grimy alley in the red-light section, outside a bar with a flickering orange-and-yellow neon sign that buzzed loudly overhead, and where the

trash barrels filled the back street with a steady stench. She was waiting for a man she had never met before, named Chow.

After Rivka had waited nearly a half an hour, a young girl in a
green satin dress slit way too high up her thighs walked out from the
bar and into the alley. "You waiting for Chow?" she asked with a voice
devoid of emotion, matching eyes that were listless and unfocused.

Rivka nodded.

"Wait here. He coming out."

The young girl turned to leave, but Rivka reached out and touched
her skinny arm. "You don't have to do this."

"Do what?" the girl asked, half turning.

"I know you are owned by the Triad. Working in the brothel. You
don't have to, you know."

"Who says?"

"God says."

"Hmmm." The girl shrugged. Rivka figured she was on drugs,
though she didn't see any needle marks. Probably one of the designer
meth cocktails.

Rivka stepped closer. "You can be free. Jesus came so that you can
be free from sin, from drugs, from selling your body. All of it."

"Free?" the young girl said. And then she turned and disappeared
through the back door. The sounds of the noisy bar inside could be
heard for a second or two until the door closed.

A few minutes later an extremely wide man who looked like he
could have been a sumo wrestler sauntered out into the alley. He took
a last drag from his cigarette, looked down both ends of the alley, then
tossed it down on the ground.

"What you want? You want work? I can give you work. Plenty.
You've got a pretty face. Men would like you."

"No. I don't want work. I need to talk to Jo Li."

"Who?"

"I've been told that you know him."

"I don't know nothing."

"I think you do."

"You're making me angry. You don't want to make me mad, little lady." Chow strode up to Rivka until he was just inches away from her face. "I don't like the way you disrespect me."

"I don't want trouble, Chow. I just want to know what you know about Jo Li. About his underground financial system. Are you connected with him? Do you run your business through his barter exchange?"

Chow leaned a little closer. "And if I did, why would I tell you?" Without warning, he brought his massive right hand up and wrapped his fingers around Rivka's neck, squeezing.

"Let go of me," she said through gritted teeth. "Don't want . . . trouble."

He squeezed tighter. "Too late. You've just found it. I am going to take you for myself right now," he grunted. "After that, I'm putting you to work for me."

Rivka stared him in the eye. She'd had enough. She let loose with a furious right kick that dislocated his left leg at the hip. Then she brought her left knee up like a hammer into his groin. He let go and started falling backward, but before he hit the ground she let loose with another roundhouse kick to the side of the head. His immense bulk collapsed onto the concrete of the alley with a *thud*.

Dropping down with the heel of her boot jammed onto Chow's neck, Rivka tried again. "How do I get a hold of Jo Li?"

He was seriously dazed. She slapped his face and he started to sharpen. "Englishman . . . ," he grunted slowly, choking under her boot.

"What Englishman?"

"Lawyer . . . or something."

"What's his name?"

"Hadley Brooking."

"Where is he?"

"Here in Hong Kong . . . Office on Hennessy." Chow's face was turning purple "I'm choking . . ."

Rivka lifted her boot off his neck. "I have just one more question. The young girl in the green dress—what is her name?"

"Suzi."

"No," Rivka said. "Her *real* name."

"Meifeng."

Rivka stepped back and watched as Chow rolled over onto his uninjured side like a beached walrus and slowly tried to get back up on one leg. He grabbed a drainpipe that ran down the building and groaned as he pulled himself to a semistanding position. By the time he looked around for Rivka, she had vanished.

An hour later, in the lobby of a small office furnished with cheap knockoffs of English and Oriental artifacts, Rivka sat looking at Meifeng, who had sunk back into the two-seater sofa with her eyes almost closed. "It will take a day or two for your body to get rid of the drugs," Rivka said, trying to be reassuring.

Meifeng blinked slowly. Rivka asked, "Do you understand?"

"Sure, sure," Meifeng replied drearily. "Know English a lot. Lot of my man customers speak English. America. Canada. England. Australia . . ."

Rivka shook her head and wondered at this sad, lost girl. *Good heavens.* "Are you afraid of running away from Chow?"

"Maybe."

Rivka grabbed her hand and squeezed it. "With God's help, I'll protect you."

A tall, thin man with fair skin walked into the lobby. He had a mop of silver hair that looked like it needed a good trim and was wearing a rumpled linen suit and an ascot. "May I help you?" he asked.

Rivka stood. "Mr. Hadley Brooking?"

"At your service," he said and reached out to shake her hand. She noticed his initials—HJB—monogrammed on his French cuffs, but the ends of the cuffs were a bit frayed. This English lawyer had seen better days.

Brooking glanced over at Meifeng. "Would she like an Orangey water?"

Meifeng shook her head no.

"Very well, then . . ." His voice trailed off.

Rivka asked to see him privately in his office, and the two of them stepped into an adjacent room filled with Oriental vases and framed reproductions of English landscapes. Brooking sat down behind his mahogany desk and smiled. Rivka noticed that the varnish on the aged desk was peeling.

Rivka started. "Are you a lawyer?"

"Of sorts. Used to be a solicitor in the U.K. But nowadays I engage in other pursuits."

"Your sign on the door says Consultations—Imports/Exports. Perhaps you can explain that."

"Perhaps you can explain what it is that you need help with, Miss . . ."

"Call me Rivka. I need advice about markets, buying and selling."

"Not currency, of course," he said. "Now that the whole world ditched the paper CReDO and went electronic—*skin transactions*, I call them—currency exchanges don't exist. But you know that, I'm sure."

"Yes. But what if someone doesn't want to engage in those kinds of electronic transactions?"

"Well then," he said, "you're not going to get very far. Bit of a jam, that." After taking the time to size her up, he continued, "You don't have a laser tag ID, do you? No BIDTag?"

She smiled.

"Are you one of those . . . Jesus followers? The Remnant?"

"Why do you ask?"

"Oh, I hear things."

"I want to find out about Jo Li's underground barter system," she said.

"He's a popular fellow."

"Oh?"

"Another Jesus person apparently wants to meet him too. Some kind of rebel leader of the Remnant group has made inquiries. You know, those chaps seem to be popping up everywhere lately. Can't remember his name, though."

"No matter," Rivka said. She kept her face placid, but she knew he was talking about Ethan March, and she had an idea why he would want to come to Hong Kong. She struggled not to smile. There was a history between them in Israel. For a while, when Ethan became a Jesus follower after the Rapture and then she did a little later, their paths had seemed to follow an identical trajectory. Getting closer and closer. She'd been falling for him hard and fast. But then, somehow, things started getting in the way and it all disintegrated between them. She wasn't sure why. Maybe it was the stress of survival in a world that had gone from dangerous to insanely brutal. Maybe it was because they were both type A personalities, mission driven. Both of them demanding and perhaps a bit controlling? Yes, that too. They found themselves rushing into the fray, helping fellow Remnant members, fighting the good fight, but growing further apart as they did.

When Rivka looked over at Hadley Brooking, he seemed to be drifting in his own thoughts. He stared into space and muttered, "Strange times, these." Then he paused, patting the desk lightly with both hands, and went on. "Back in the U.K., I was raised in the Church of England. Pretty 'stiff upper lip' and formal, and all that. Oh yes, it had some meaning for me, but . . . well, I had my own questions. I rather sensed that something was out there. But nothing like what's going on now. Those mass disappearances. And what has followed. By the way, I was here in Hong Kong as a young solicitor way back in 1997 when Britain gave the island back to China. I was so impressed with it all, thought the whole thing was a thoroughly revolutionary state of affairs. But since then, well, the world seems to have become even more confusing. And more dangerous. And yet the same questions are still there. It can cause a man to think."

Across the desk, Rivka saw a man who was searching. But she was there with her own questions and she needed answers, and she needed them quick. So she pressed. "Is Jo Li's barter system mixed in with the Triad here in Hong Kong? The brothels and drug trade? That's what I'm worried about. Or is there a legitimate way to buy and sell, underground, without worrying about being part of all that dirty money?"

Brooking studied her closely. "In the old days, when someone gave you a dollar or a pound note or some other currency, did you ever have any assurance that the last person who used that currency before him wasn't a criminal? I don't know you very well, Rivka. For a stranger, you're asking some very intriguing questions." Then he added, "From everything that I've heard, Jo Li is an economic genius. And a pure capitalist. I know plenty of people, good solid people, who say his system works—and it avoids the unpleasantness of knowing that all your transactions are being watched by Big Brother."

Rivka thought Brooking was playing it coy, giving her the "from what I've heard" line. He could be an insider in Jo Li's underground economy; when she'd had her boot at Chow's throat, he'd confirmed Brooking might know something.

"Is there any downside to Jo Li's system?" Rivka said. "For us 'Jesus people,' as you refer to us?"

Brooking looked as if he was still sizing her up. Rivka could see that something was at play, something about Hadley Brooking that remained hidden under the surface. "Let's talk more about this soon," Brooking said as he slid his card across the desk. "Call me. We'll talk. I would like to help you. If I'm able, that is."

NINE

MAVERICK COUNTY, TEXAS

The two border patrol agents lay flat on their stomachs, hidden in a grove of sand sage and yucca, each of them peering through binoculars.

The junior agent said, "I hate doing this on my belly. I've heard about the coral snakes."

"Maybe," the senior agent replied, "but at least those are easy to spot, the colors being what they are. Rattlers are more likely around here." He tensed as he saw something off in the distance through his binoculars. "Speaking of snakes. Down there, coming up over the ridge. See them?"

The other border patrol agent shifted his focus and saw what his senior partner was looking at: three blue Humvees mounted with machine guns coming over a slight ridge. They were flying blue-and-white Global Alliance flags. He cussed loudly. "Okay, now what?"

"We report back, then get out of here."

"That means they're now fifteen miles inside the borders of the United States. We need to do something—"

"Just report back," the other agent spit out. "Nothing more."

"I say we request authority to use force."

"Right. We're going to fire our Smith & Wessons at that armored convoy? Think again."

"Man, oh man. First the Mexican kidnappers and the drug cartels. Now this."

"Let's go," the senior agent said. They both raised themselves slightly off the ground and half duckwalked, hunched over, through the brush until they neared their white vehicle with the diagonal green stripe. The patrol vehicle was on top of the ridge about fifty feet away, but in an area clear of underbrush or cover.

The senior agent said, "We'd better make this fast. Once we climb into our ride, I'll call it in to HQ and then we can bug out of here."

They were still hunched over as they scuffled through the dirt toward the patrol Hummer. Then the junior agent stopped and half turned around. "Did you see that? A puff of smoke! Couple of feet behind me, coming off the ground. They just took a sniper shot at me!"

"Keep heading to the Hummer," the senior agent growled.

As he continued toward the patrol vehicle, the other agent raised his profile a bit, unholstered his Smith & Wesson, and aimed it at one of the Global Alliance vehicles.

"Drop your weapon!" the senior agent yelled. "Don't give them—"

But it was too late. Smoke rose from the machine guns on top of two of the Alliance vehicles in the distance, and then a millisecond later the sound of *ratta-tat*. The junior agent's chest exploded as several rounds ripped through him and he dropped to the ground screaming in pain. The senior agent dropped to his side and cradled him, covering his bloody body, but no more shots came. The agent dragged his partner over the sandy ground to the Hummer, lifted him into the back, and then leaped into the driver's seat and jabbed his finger onto the fingerprint tab of the emergency satphone.

"Man down, man down!" he yelled. "Verify that you have our coordinates. We've taken shots from an Alliance convoy. We need a medivac chopper stat! Do you read? Over."

☐☐☐

OVAL OFFICE OF THE WHITE HOUSE

Washington, D.C.

There was a moment, just then, when President Hank Hewbright wondered whether he had made a mistake. Whether he should have convened this meeting in the soundproof, surveillance-immune confines of the Situation Room. *Too late now*, he thought as he eyed the four cabinet-level appointees and two White House advisors seated around him. But then there would also have been a risk with a meeting even in that hyper-secured location. The word would have leaked out to the rest of the staff that a Situation Room meeting was in progress and they would wonder why. Rumors would fly. At this point Hewbright didn't really know whom he could trust. And he couldn't afford to risk a leak to the international community that America was at a Level Red over this newest outrage. He had to keep them guessing.

The president finished reading the two-page briefing memo on the incident and felt a combination of rage and nausea at the report. He leaned back in the embroidered white couch that sat just a few feet from the outer rim of the seal of the United States of America embossed in the carpet. "Two border agents were shot at. One killed?" he asked with a shake of the head.

Elizabeth Tanner, Homeland Security director, nodded from

her position directly across the large coffee table from the president. "Regrettably, the junior agent suffered massive chest wounds and expired before the medivac helicopter arrived on the scene."

George Caulfield, the White House Chief of Staff sitting next to her, interjected, "The Command Center of the Global Alliance has already released a public statement. Their story is that one of the U.S. border agents had 'threatened deadly force against the Alliance convoy with his weapon,' and they fired on him in self-defense."

President Hewbright turned to William Tatter, his director of the CIA. "And your assessment of these movements along the Mexican border?"

"They are definitely coordinated," Tatter said. "The Alliance has been making the encroachments along our entire southern border almost daily—ever since the vote in the Senate to ratify the Charter of Global Alliance. It seems clear they believe that the action of Congress makes the United States part of Global Region One, eradicating our borders with Mexico in the south and with Canada to the north."

The president turned to Terrance Tyler, his secretary of state. "What's your take on the most recent incursion, Terry?"

Tyler was leaning back in the upholstered swivel chair, moving it slightly back and forth. "I would say, Mr. President, that this is a deliberate course of provocation. Alexander Colliquin and his compatriots at the Alliance's Iraq headquarters know we are very vulnerable right now. We are facing a constitutional crisis—"

Curt Levin, the clearly frustrated White House counsel, broke in. "Your use of the word *crisis* implies there is a reasonable legal debate over the effect of the Senate vote. But there simply isn't! The Senate is empowered to ratify treaties. But the Global Alliance isn't a treaty. It is a wholesale usurpation of the U.S. Constitution, making our nation and its laws and our three branches of government all ultimately subservient to a unified world governmental body with ten international regions and with veto power over every significant decision by the United States government."

"Curt, I know your legal position on this." President Hewbright responded. "And you know that I share your viewpoint. This Global Alliance initiative is tantamount to an amendment to the U.S. Constitution."

"Exactly, Mr. President," Levin shot back. "Which can only be accomplished under Article V of our Constitution in two ways. Either two-thirds of the states call for a constitutional convention—and that's never happened in American history since the adoption of our federal constitution. Or two-thirds of the Senate and two-thirds of the House approve the proposed amendment and send it to the states for ratification by three-fourths of the states. Sure, the Senate achieved one minor part of that process, but barely, by just one vote, to reach the two-thirds threshold. But the House has been stalled on a procedural vote for approval of the Global Alliance idea as a constitutional amendment. So this so-called 'treaty' has only passed first base so far. No further."

"Mr. President, we're ignoring the political reality here," George Caulfield added. His voice was strained, and it carried a tone of urgency. "For good or for bad, the Senate did what they did because our nation is on the brink of financial implosion. And maybe even over the brink. Americans are panicked. We could be entering the most explosive, uncharted epoch in world history. The Senate is betting on the fact that we can gain some security in being part of a single, global governance system—to stabilize the world's chaotic economies, to create a band of mutual protection, and for some kind of international harmony—"

"And destroying our borders in the process!" Secretary of Defense Roland Allenworth's voice erupted at a full shout. "And eradicating nearly two hundred and forty years of constitutional sovereignty of this nation."

"Rollie," President Hewbright intoned calmly. "You know I share every one of your sentiments. The point here is to figure out if—and, more important, when and how—I order our military to start pushing back against these incursions."

"The Global Alliance is taking the following position," Secretary Tyler explained. "First, that America, through the Senate vote of ratification, has effectively joined the Alliance. Second, that the United States has therefore become part of Region One, along with Canada and Mexico, both of which have already agreed to become part of the new global governance scheme. Third, as a result of that we no longer have any national borders. That means that we have no legal standing to oppose the incursion of Alliance troops crossing our borders. So, Mr. President . . ." Tyler exhibited a momentary embarrassment. "That makes you, if you pardon my saying so, a rebel against your own country, according to the Alliance, and an enemy of the world order."

Hewbright turned to Curt Levin. "Still no hope from the Supreme Court?"

"The justices won't take up our legal challenge to the Senate vote. The rumor is they're afraid a vote by such a small portion of the full court now will just create more lack of confidence among the American people. We all know that the membership of the Supreme Court is still a few justices short ever since, well, you know . . ." And he paused to grapple for the right words. "You know what I mean."

"The Disappearance?" Hewbright interjected. "That's what everyone is calling it. I call it something else, of course."

There was an uncomfortable silence in the Oval Office. George Caulfield, Hewbright's former national campaign manager and now one of the president's closest advisors, spoke up. Caulfield pursed his lips, visibly struggling for a way to say what had to be said next. "Mr. President. We all know how this mass disappearance—or, to use your word, the Rapture—affected you. Stimulated you into a religious experience."

"Spiritual birth," Hewbright added. "Let's call it what it was. Being born again through a faith in Jesus Christ. Believing that His death on the cross accomplished forgiveness of my sins. And that His rising from the grave three days later proved He was truly the Son of God, who came to bring eternal life to everyone who calls on His name."

"I understand all of that, Mr. President," Caulfield interjected quietly. "But unfortunately, so do your political enemies. They think you are now setting national policy by your own religious beliefs. Endangering the Union. Splitting us in half. Practically bringing us to the brink of a civil war."

Hewbright remained unperturbed. He had heard all of this before. Read it on the Internet news and web television shows. "Has anyone in this room," he asked, "ever bothered to read the seventh chapter of the Old Testament book of Daniel? The prophecy in verses twenty-three through twenty-five?"

Silence in the room.

"I would suggest you do so. America is one of the few nations that still has old-fashioned printed Bibles even after the worldwide digital transformation of everything to the Internet. I would suggest that you folks see whether your grandmother's Bible is still up in your attic. Pull it out. Dust it off. And read what God said through His prophet Daniel several thousand years ago about ten kings—or world leaders, you might call them—of ten kingdoms, and see if it doesn't look like the Global Alliance of ten international regions."

"Actually," Secretary of State Tyler said, "I had occasion to read that part of the Bible, Mr. President, and I believe it was at your insistence, not too long ago. What I find interesting is that it also predicts that three of those ten kings—or leaders—will resist this supposed global kingdom, but as a result they will be struck down." Tyler raised his hand and pointed his index finger straight up. "There's America. That's one. And you've managed to talk Great Britain into seriously considering a retreat from the Alliance. That would be two. And then there's Australia, which also seems receptive to your arguments about withdrawing from the Global Alliance. And that would be three. Of course if Australia doesn't bolt from the Alliance at your urging, there's always Canada."

Tyler leaned back in his chair and swiveled it a bit. "In other words, some of your opponents would say you're deliberately fashioning a foreign policy designed to bring to pass biblical prophecy. A self-fulfilled prophecy, they would argue."

Elizabeth Tanner cleared her throat and squirmed in her chair. Secretary Allenworth looked like he was about to detonate, and President Hewbright could see that. He'd known Rollie for a long time. Even before he'd been Jessica Tulrude's former secretary of defense—the first time he had served a president in that position. That had ended when Tulrude forced him out after she fully understood his hawkish, pro-America views. Hewbright knew Rollie, and unlike Tulrude, he loved the man's approach and knew that Rollie Allenworth would defend his presidency to the death. But right now he didn't want or need that.

Hewbright raised a hand in Allenworth's direction and smiled to keep him from taking the bait from Secretary Tyler. Then he turned to Tyler. "Actually, Terry," he said, addressing his secretary of state, "bringing to pass biblical prophecy would be way above my pay grade." A few of the group chuckled. "God is the only One who brings to pass what He has declared in His Word. The rest of us are just instruments—either willing or unwilling—in His grand plan."

He folded his hands across his chest and tapped his thumbs together. "Gentleman and Madam Director," he said, "I am asking that George Caulfield and Curt Levin work together to create a draft statement. The statement will explain why I believe the United States has in fact *not* joined the Global Alliance but remains a sovereign nation, a constitutional republic with sovereign borders and legitimate federal, state, and local laws that are not subservient to the Global Alliance of nations. Nor will they ever be as long as I am chief executive of this country. Prepare that document. I will review it. I will make my own changes. And then I will decide when I will release it to the media and to the American public."

Secretary Tyler leaned forward. "And the question that everyone in the international community is going to ask—"

"Yes," Hewbright interrupted. "The question about whether President Hewbright will take up arms against these Global Alliance incursions in the south? And thus risk war with the rest of the civilized world?"

Tyler waited.

"I'm still working on that one," Hewbright said. "But the rest of the world won't have to wait very long to get my answer."

□□□

When the Oval Office had cleared out and the president sat alone, he had another thought. It was about the persons he had not invited to the meeting. He had deliberately avoided including anyone from the Department of Justice or the FBI. There were too many persons of questionable loyalty and tainted credibility in those offices—holdovers from the Jessica Tulrude administration.

And then there was his vice president, Darrel Zandibar, whom he had also left out. That was a different story altogether.

He wondered just how long it was going to take before his enemies learned the details of the discussion that had just transpired inside the Oval Office. He was convinced it was not a matter of *if*, but *when*. And he also wondered about something else: whether he could discover the identity of the traitors in his midst in time to avert a cataclysm for America.

TEN

GOMA CITY, DEMOCRATIC REPUBLIC OF THE CONGO

In the twenty-five-thousand-seat indoor coliseum, the fight fans dripped with sweat in the sweltering Congo weather, even with the air-conditioning working. But no one seemed to mind. They were there to see a death match.

This was the biggest, most outrageous championship in the UEFM—Ultra-Extreme Fight Match—in the history of the sport. The center ring was walled in by bulletproof glass with two doors, one on each side for each competitor. A monstrous, cubical Jumbotron hovered high over the ring so the audience could see the close-ups of every blood splatter and hear the sound of every punch and whimper in the man-to-man combat. The high-sensitivity microphones imbedded in the glass cage would pick up and then broadcast to the audience the actual sound of bones breaking. And in the typical fight, there would be plenty.

The gambling booths on the first floor were taking final bets. Billionaires, playboys, movie stars, and sports celebrities were in their box seats. And so was Alexander Colliquin, in his own private box, along with Mr. Martisse, his chief of security. In addition to the legalized brothels and marijuana emporiums Colliquin had helped establish in this country, as he had already done throughout Europe and Asia, he also supported these deadly UEFM fight matches. It was an effective way to get the war-torn Congo back on its feet economically after years of rebel strife and corrupt leadership.

The first contestant, Diego "The Monster" Sabiella, entered the coliseum to background music of one of Eddie Van Halen's screaming guitar solos from the late seventies. He was given a polite ripple of cheers from the crowd. Despite his size, the six-foot-eight, 260-pound weightlifter and wrestler from Argentina was reported to move in the ring like a halfback. Sabiella went to his corner and started loosening up.

It would be difficult to understand why the oddsmakers rated him the underdog—unless, of course, one knew something about his opponent, Vlad "The Impaler" Malatov. A few sportswriters occasionally joked about Malatov's custom of always wearing a mask in the ring. But of course no one would dare to laugh about that if Malatov was in the same room, or even in the same building.

A dull roar filled the auditorium as refreshment hawkers strolled up and down the aisles yelling out to the chattering fans. But the noise evaporated the very instant the house lights dimmed. The ring was illuminated with spots, and a light shone at the far end of the auditorium where Vlad Malatov would appear. There came the sound of kettledrums beating, first softly, then louder, until the percussive pounding of drums filled the entire coliseum.

Malatov, the six-foot-five, 235-pound Russian, now stood in the spotlight in the doorway, dressed in black trunks. He had a black ski mask covering his face except for two eyeholes and one for his mouth. His body was a chiseled slab of marble. The crowd exploded as Malatov slowly strutted down the raised walkway almost rhythmically, leading with one shoulder and then the other as he loosened his massive biceps while he walked slowly to the glass-enclosed ring.

Alexander Colliquin turned to his security chief and explained his other reasons for being there. "I wanted to see this," he said, nodding his head toward Malatov. "I can tell a lot about a man by seeing how he functions under stress. When life and limb are at risk. You've compiled the dossier?"

"We have. But it took quite a bit of digging, Your Excellency. As a boy, Malatov was raised in America. Then migrated to the Russian Republic with his father when he was twelve. Studied international affairs before being recruited as a clandestine operator. First with the KGB just before the end of that agency, and then with its successor, the FSB—the Federal Security Bureau. He was assigned to counterterrorism and covert operations."

"Why did he leave?"

"He was actually relieved of his position by Moscow."

"Why was that?" Colliquin asked.

"I believe," Mr. Martisse replied, "it was for excessive violence."

Down below, the ringmaster entered. He grabbed the microphone that had been lowered into the ring and introduced the two fighters, then announced that the time for placing bets on the match had closed. He then scurried out of the ring and was replaced by the referee, who carried a taser gun strapped to his side.

Each fighter stood ready in his corner. Then came the bone-jarring sound of a horn blowing like a warning siren before a *blitzkrieg*, signaling the start of the match.

Sabiella charged aggressively into the center of the ring and started dancing, but Malatov came out of his corner slowly, confidently, almost nonchalantly.

Mr. Martisse whispered to Colliquin, "In past matches, this Sabiella fellow has shown a ruthless ability to overpower his opponents with his size and his judo blows. Renders them helpless with his famous guillotine choke hold until they are lifeless. He has sent four of his opponents to the hospital."

Malatov now circled around Sabiella, eyeing him, but his hands remained at his side. Mr. Martisse continued to narrate. "Malatov has only participated in nonsanctioned, unofficial UEFM matches at underground sites. So the rumors about him are formally unsubstantiated, except for some black-market sportswriters who claim to have witnessed his famous attack strike."

"What kind of attack strike?"

Martisse, a veteran of special operations in the French military, hesitated. "Your Excellency, it is rather gruesome . . ."

On the mat, Sabiella moved to within striking distance of Malatov, reaching out and grabbing at the back of his neck. But Malatov was ready for him and with lightning speed struck Sabiella in the face, and then again and again. The huge Argentinean was stunned for a moment and stumbled slightly, but that was all that it took.

As Sabiella staggered back, Malatov grabbed him by the throat with his left hand and then positioned his other arm straight up in the air with his fingers aligned together like a human knife. His powerful arm hung poised like an industrial forge, ready to drop with deadly force and terrifying swiftness. As Malatov held his hand aloft, a hush fell over the thousands in the audience, as if they knew what was going to happen next, though still not quite believing it.

Then, in a blur of motion, Malatov swung his right hand into Sabiella's chest with blinding speed, penetrating it and holding his hand there for an instant until the giant of a man collapsed backward, hit the ground, and did not move. While the referee rushed to Sabiella and checked for a pulse—but shook his head, *no*—Malatov held his right hand up and brandished it to the crowd as if it were a deadly weapon. The crowd could see that Malatov's striking hand was now red with his opponent's blood. He had pierced the other man's chest cavity with a single ferocious blow.

A physician entered the ring with a stethoscope and a towel and checked Sabiella himself, examining the gaping chest wound and attempting unsuccessfully to stop the flow of blood. Unable to render any aid to the man, the doctor covered Sabiella's face with the towel.

The microphone was lowered and the ringmaster quickly hustled to the center of the ring, but Malatov held out a hand to stop him and instead took the microphone himself. He began to speak in perfect English without a trace of a Russian accent.

"Ladies and gentlemen, regarding the death of this man, I extend my condolences to his family. It is a pity he was not a worthy opponent."

Malatov dropped the microphone and left it swinging back and forth as he strode out of the auditorium.

Colliquin turned to Mr. Martisse. "He sounds like a very well-spoken American rather than a Russian."

Martisse nodded in agreement.

"Is his intention to become a full-time professional in this sport?" Colliquin asked.

"Oh no, not at all. The rumors that I have heard are that he participates in these matches . . ."

"Yes?"

Martisse finished his reply. "He participates in these fights merely for, well, personal entertainment."

Colliquin smiled broadly. "And his other talents?"

"Several languages. Espionage, infiltration, advanced cyber-warfare and computer hacking, intelligence gathering . . ."

Colliquin rose. He had heard and seen enough. "Arrange a meeting with Mr. Malatov," he said. "I want to meet him."

ELEVEN

CRETE, GREECE

Ethan March had just finished an encrypted Allfone call from Quiet Partner, code name for Dr. Iban Adis, his secret contact inside a lab in New Babylon. During the call he had received more intel on Alexander Colliquin's secret technology venture. The pieces were starting to take shape. According to Adis, New Babylon was in need of a massive amount of data computing power. There were several possible sites to set that up. One was in the United States. The more Ethan heard about it, the more nausea rushed over him. It was the sinking feeling that an inevitable terror was approaching, and quickly.

Now he was trying to clear his mind. Shake it off. He had fled Athens with the Alliance hot on his trail. But God had been good to him. Ethan had reached the island of Crete and was temporarily living in the lap of luxury in the villa of a Remnant supporter. He wanted to catch his breath before the next call.

He glanced at his Allfone watch and knew that in a matter of minutes he would be getting an update from Pack McHenry, a former chief of clandestine operations with the CIA from years back. After Pack and his wife, Victoria, had left the Agency, they continued as independent contractors. Then America started skidding off the rails, and Josh Jordan started his Roundtable group in an effort to stop the train wreck. So Pack and Victoria started doing intelligence work for them. And now for Ethan and the Remnant.

Ethan still had a few minutes to relax before the call. From his position on a stone wall on the veranda, he had a great vista of the sparkling azure waters of the Mediterranean. He could also see the harbor of Agios Nikolaos down there too, full of fishing boats and old stone buildings and ringed with palm trees. The breeze blew through his hair, and for a few moments he was at rest, tranquil. He closed his eyes.

His Allfone watch buzzed on his wrist. He looked down at the little screen and saw the encryption code for Pack. He tapped in the confirmation and the *okay* for the video feed. Pack's square face and salt-and-pepper hair appeared.

Ethan gave him a warm hello and they exchanged pleasantries. Pack explained that he'd been roaming the planet.

"Sightseeing?" Ethan said with a smile.

"No. Dreary places, mostly," Pack said. "And some depressing news."

"Shoot."

"Over the last few weeks I've discovered a series of murders and disappearances," McHenry explained. "All of them computer-tech gurus from ICANN—the Internet Corporation for Assigned Names and Numbers. Back around 2010, ICANN, which is a private agency that governs the tech side of the Internet, decided it needed a plan in the event there was some kind of worldwide cyberattack that brought everything down. So they created a start-up code for the entire Internet and then divided up parts of that code among seven very high-tech players—insiders with ICANN—giving each of the seven a keycard with parts of the code. If everything crashed, they were to meet at some global network site and put their code cards together, input the code, and restart the Internet."

Ethan was looking over the blue waters below his veranda. But he was thinking farther east, to New Babylon. "And how many of these high-tech cardholders are involved?"

"Five so far. Either dead or gone missing. All very recently. I've located a sixth cardholder, Professor Fin Luxendorf, who teaches in the Netherlands. I'm on my way right now to reach him. Try and keep him safe. And try to figure out whether all of this is connected with the Global Alliance. And some kind of Internet power grab."

Ethan urged Pack to keep him closely advised and said his good-byes. Then he put in a call to Chiro up in White Horse, in the Yukon. Ethan was glad to hear his friend's familiar voice on the other end of the call.

"Hi, Ethan! So great to talk," Chiro said. "I have been working hard with my new friend Mr. John Galligher up here at our communications center."

"Chiro," Ethan replied, "you've got a good man in Galligher. Josh Jordan thought very highly of him."

"Okay," Chiro said, going right to the heart of the matter. "So you've been telling me about the intel we keep getting from our inside source in New Babylon. About some kind of digital doomsday plan. Do we have any more data on that?"

But Ethan didn't respond. Not at first. His eyes searched the blue horizon from his view on the porch. "Did you know," he said with a half smile, wonder in his voice, "that the Bible says when God creates His new heaven and new earth, there won't be any oceans?"

Chiro was silent at the other end. Then, "No, Ethan. I didn't know that."

"And no more tears. Or pain. Or death."

More silence on the other end.

Ethan answered Chiro's question. "The doomsday plan. Yes, I'm getting more data from some reliable sources. I can't say anything more at this point. When I get specifics, I will tell you. But the hub of this global connection sounds like it's going to be located at some high-level computer facility. Apparently Alexander Colliquin needs that computer capacity if he's going to implement his plan." Then Ethan added, "Do me a favor, will you?"

"Anything."

"Have Galligher get in touch with another FBI buddy of his— Ben Bolling. Another retired special agent. He should still be back in America. Find out if John thinks he's a good candidate for our crew."

"I will be glad to."

"And one other thing: ask John whether he or Ben Bolling still have any contacts within the Secret Service. The White House detail."

"This is sounding *very* interesting," Chiro said with a laugh.

Ethan took a deep breath as he calculated the furious battle ahead. "I could describe it another way."

"I will pray for you, Ethan March," Chiro said.

"I wish I could tell you where I am right now," Ethan said. "And describe it for you. It's beautiful and . . . restful. I know it won't last. But for now it's a good place to be."

They said their good-byes. Shortly after that, Nick Akonos, a tall man in a flowing white shirt and pants and leather sandals, strolled out onto the veranda. "Didn't want to disturb you."

"You didn't, Nick. My call is done. Thanks again for making this fantastic villa a safe house for us. I had to get out of Athens quickly, and I figured I'd be sleeping out under the stars in a field somewhere. This is almost too good to be true."

"I want to do more. Much more."

"Be careful what you promise. We Remnant people are a pretty needy bunch!"

Nick laughed. "Well, they are all inside and ready to hear from you. There must be close to two hundred, filling up every corner of my place. Every night, a new bunch. It's a good thing I am a man of means. The authorities think because I am wealthy that I'm just throwing big parties. And that meeting where you spoke down along the harbor last week, someone tried to count and said there were more than two thousand who happened to show up. I don't know how this is happening." He grabbed Ethan by his shoulders and gave a bigger laugh. "But it's a miracle. Especially the way the crowd had already disbanded by the time the Global Alliance police showed up."

"Yes," Ethan said. "God's stirring the hearts of men and women, and boys and girls, around the world. It's a battle between darkness and light." He reached and clapped Nick on the shoulder. "I'm glad you're part of the light."

□□□

LAS VEGAS, NEVADA

Dillon Ritzian finished the last bite of his cheeseburger and wiped a blotch of ketchup off his Hawaiian shirt as he walked down the Vegas Strip, basking under the neon light from the marquees overhead. He had his Allfone to his ear; he'd put a call in to his contact, but now he was on hold.

A couple of prostitutes approached him in tight micro skirts, but he waved them off. On a better night he would have paid for an all-night party, as long as he was sure his girlfriend, Darlene, wouldn't find out. But things being as they were, Ritzian wasn't flush. Maybe soon.

A large man who looked like an American Indian sidled up to

him as he walked by and made a few obvious references to a drug buy. Ritzian was sad he had to dismiss him too. Still, he had a flicker of hope.

I could be rolling in the cash pretty soon.

Henry Bender answered the call on the other end—a gruff-talking guy with a voice that sounded like a hacksaw cutting metal. "What can I do for you?"

"You can tell me what your guys need. Then I supply it. Then I get rich. That's more or less what I got in mind."

"Don't we all," Bender growled.

"So I'm taking orders," Ritzian said brashly. "What'll you have?"

"My people want two things."

"Just two? Is that all?"

"Why don't you shut up and listen first. When I tell you what they want, then you can play the part of the big-talking gas bag."

"Fine. Shoot."

"They want the control codes and the passwords to get inside the tech support files in the mainframe computers at the administration building. Open access to digital roaming."

Ritzian stopped walking. He stopped fussing over the ketchup stain on his shirt. "That's pretty heavy."

"You're the big talker. Time to put up or shut up."

"Listen, I've given you data before. I can do it again. I was the electrical whiz kid for Triple T Construction over at Bluffdale, remember? But I'm gonna ask for a whole lot of money."

"Don't worry. They've got it."

"What's the timeline?"

"Like, a week ago. Get the picture?"

"Yeah. Okay, I'll see what I can do."

Ten seconds later Ritzian made another call. This time to the bet makers in Vegas. "Good news," he announced. "I'll be getting you the money I owe you, real soon."

"Okay. And here's your good news," the man on the other end replied in a monotone. "Now your kneecaps won't get broken."

Ritzian tried to laugh, but the loan shark on the other end had already hung up.

◻◻◻

NEW JERSEY

While Dillon Ritzian tried to exude a confident air as he strolled down the Vegas Strip, in New Jersey Henry Bender was placing a call of his own. Overseas.

At the other end, in New Babylon, Iraq, Ho Zhu picked up his Allfone in his massive office. Against the backdrop of stone archways and the sounds of fountains gushing water from the eaves of the palatial headquarters, he waved his finger over the one-way video option, and Henry Bender's face showed up on his little screen. Only then did Ho speak. "Did you get the information?"

"I met with my source, and I think he can get it."

"This is a rush."

"He knows that. I'm pushing him."

"Is he discreet?"

Henry Bender took a second before he answered that. "I'll make sure he keeps his mouth shut."

Ho asked, "This man was involved in the construction at the Utah data center?"

"Very deep. Has top-level security clearance. Worked with this defense construction company that dropped cable and connected the computer lines there at the National Security Agency's complex in Bluffdale. He was involved in the sync control between the nerve center in Bluffdale and the other surveillance centers through the country and around the world—the four NSA facilities, including the main one at Fort Meade, Maryland, and the connections to all the defense satellites. Links to the CIA, Pentagon, even the White House. And the connections to several listening stations in England and Australia and a bunch of other countries. All of them tied into Bluffdale. All of them wired to something they call the main matrix out there in nowhere's-ville in Utah. And this yahoo, this Ritzian guy, is the one who ended up tying a lot of the hardwire together."

"This isn't just about the hardwire!" Ho Zhu screamed. He collected himself. "I want the codes and the passwords. Don't you understand?"

"Sure I do. Nothing to worry about," Bender said in his gravelly voice. "And I told him all that. But Ritzian has been telling me something about the system there in Utah that you need to know."

"Explain."

"He says that even if he gets you the codes and the passwords, that's not enough. He says the system is impossible to break into from the outside. Some kind of electromagnetic field or something that would stop any hacker located *outside* the walls of the facility at Bluffdale. Has to be done *inside* the walls. The only other way would be to locate the underground—"

Deputy Chancellor Ho Zhu interrupted him. "Never mind about any of that," he said as he straightened where he stood. Now he smiled. "That won't be a problem."

TWELVE

HYDE PARK, LONDON

In the northeastern section of the park near Marble Arch, in the famous speaker's corner, a preacher in a tattered tweed jacket and pants with a patch on the knee was poised on top of a short stepladder. He was preaching in front of a wrought-iron fence. As he delivered an impassioned sermon, his backdrop was a row of trees and beyond those, the fine marble buildings of the Shrewsbury Business Park area. A crowd of nearly two thousand had gathered around the preacher. And the numbers were still growing. As he spoke, his booming voice carried unaided by a megaphone or sound system.

An English bobby with nightstick in hand stood a hundred yards off. As he studied the scene, a Pakistani Global Alliance patrol commander in a blue helmet tried to make a point to him, but the bobby kept gazing off at the swelling crowd and finally interrupted. "I've never seen the likes of this, I haven't," the bobby told him. "All manner of crackpots and homespun philosophers regularly show up and try to get an audience. A few dozen onlookers show up to hear them. An audience of fifty or sixty would be a rare occurrence. But to see thousands like this is astounding. These Jesus preachers have been getting these kinds of throngs ever since the disappearances occurred."

The Alliance commander snapped back, "I need to remind you of Global Alliance directive number PS458. Jesus groups are declared to be a risk to public order. A dangerous religious cult. Mass suicide. Very bad. And very dangerous. Even taking the children with them. Premeditated murder."

"If the King's Bench here in London were to hear the evidence of what the Global Alliance is claiming about the disappearances and all those *supposed* mass suicides," the bobby fired back, "in a court of law, the whole case would be thrown out. Mass suicides? Really . . ." There was ridicule in his voice.

The Alliance commander looked insulted. "Your King's Bench and your Parliament and your prime minister are all under the Global Alliance now. You're living in the past, Officer. But then, perhaps you are one of these Jesus people. Maybe I should arrest you too?"

The bobby took a step closer to the commander. "I'll not be threatened. And I am not about to lift a finger to arrest this group as long as they are peaceful."

"Very good. We don't need your help."

As the commander spoke, a long line of blue Global Alliance vans began to race up to the curb of the park. A moment later Alliance officers armed with riot shields, shotguns, rubber bullets, and teargas launchers began pouring out. The preacher saw what was coming but he was not deterred. His voice rose. "These disappearances are the proof of the Rapture—that God has taken His own, the followers of the Lord Christ, to be with Him," he shouted. "But even so, it was not too late for me. After I realized what had happened—my Christian wife disappearing before my very eyes and me left behind— I fell to my knees. I understood then all her talk about Christ and the Rapture, that it was all coming true. So I confessed to God that I was a sinner. Believing in what Jesus did on the cross for me. And declaring that He is the Son of God, who came to give us eternal life if we will only believe in Him and receive Him. And even though I don't have much from the world's standards, I have this priceless assurance—that regardless of what the world or the devil might throw at me, nothing can separate me from the love of Christ."

A small army of Global Alliance commandos were getting ready to charge. The commander had a bullhorn and was ready to give the warning.

The preacher thrust his hands forward to the crowd. "Won't you join me in bowing before the King of kings and Lord of lords, and acknowledging and receiving Him right now? Forgiving your sins . . . putting His Spirit in you . . . making you a new creature in Christ . . ." He stepped down off his little ladder and bent down to a kneeling position on the ground. At first there were dozens who followed him in prayer. Rapidly there were hundreds and soon nearly two thousand.

A small handful in the crowd who looked at the approaching blue line of helmeted Alliance commandos decided to bolt from the crowd. But the rest remained, kneeling, praying, and weeping.

And then there came an announcement from the commander that they had to disperse immediately. The crowd stayed on its knees.

Ten seconds later the order was given, and the Alliance forces began to charge toward the group.

□□□

In his office at 10 Downing Street, Prime Minister Derek Harrington watched the scene in Hyde Park unfold on his private video feed.

"Horrifying . . ."

The aide next to him remained silent.

"Magna Carta," Harrington said. "The great legacy of English liberty. All of it is on the verge of being trampled underfoot. By international thugs. How could we have allowed it to get to this?"

"How?" the aide responded. "Adoption of the Global Alliance Treaty, Mr. Prime Minister."

"But this is a peaceful assembly . . ."

"Not according to the Alliance, sir."

"The British Commonwealth has lost hundreds of thousands of workers from its labor force—America even more, in the millions upon millions—as a result of the Rapture."

His aide jerked his head around when he heard the prime minister of England actually use that word: *Rapture*. It was a dangerous word. People using it could be labeled. And with it came surveillance and suspicion. Then bad things followed.

"Industry and commerce grinding to a halt," Harrington said. "Economic chaos everywhere . . ."

Harrington wheeled around to face his aide. "I want you to contact the White House. Try to arrange an immediate teleconference for me with President Hewbright on the secure line. I am going to put a stop to this."

The aide turned to face his boss but he didn't move. Not until the prime minister let loose and began shouting, red-faced, "I tell you, the sun is not going to set on the British realm! Not on my watch!"

TH1RTEEN

CRETE, GREECE

Ethan March took in the friendly face on the screen of the 3-D video recorder. It was good to see his friend Josh Jordan again. But he had to wave his finger over the Pause function, just for a moment, so he could stop and digest what he had heard in the video message from his former mentor. Every once in a while he had to take a moment to mentally absorb that this was really happening. That he had been thrust into the very beginning of the final war for the souls of the human race, and as far as the millions of members of the Remnant worldwide were concerned, he had the intimidating rank of general, it would appear.

Ethan sat in his bedroom in the villa of Nick Akonos, still holed up in Crete, avoiding the Global Alliance forces and the dragnet they had laid for him in Athens. During his stay with Nick he had been expecting a call confirming a meeting with Jo Li in Hong Kong.

While he waited for his next move, he'd made good use of the time, teaching the hundreds of new Jesus followers who regularly made their way to Nick's elegant estate. They were hungry for information about Christ and the Bible. But they also pleaded for insight about the prophetic significance of the alarming events that swirled around them: the collapse of whole nations and their economies and the meteoric rise of this strange, tyrannical new world order—the Global Alliance. Against the backdrop of those dizzying events, Ethan repeatedly conducted two-hour teaching sessions from the Bible, trying to answer their questions, though he never felt adequate for the task.

Nick was a kind, generous man, a self-made multimillionaire in the travel business who had proven to be a friend in need to the Remnant, and especially to Ethan. But despite Nick's hospitality and the satisfaction Ethan felt in encouraging the ever-growing flock of Jesus followers, he still felt the crushing pressures bearing down on him, making him feel as if he were trapped in a metal compactor. He remembered the days when his mentor Josh would withhold clandestine information from him until the very last moment. He'd resented being shut out, until he eventually learned that Josh did it for Ethan's own safety.

Now that shoe was on his foot. He didn't want any of these eager Christians to be privy to information that could get them arrested or tortured, or worse. Ethan had heard the stories about the Global Alliance moving Remnant members into "Jesus Ghettos." Then they started disappearing. A few showed up dead.

But one of Ethan's pressure points, the meeting with Jo Li, was settled. Earlier that day he had received a call from a Hong Kong contact for the underground entrepreneur, giving Ethan an address and the name of Jo Li's Hong Kong representative. Ethan's small suitcase on the bed was already packed. He traveled light. Soon he hoped to have a way for millions of Jesus Remnant folks to buy necessities and provide for their families.

But then, there was Ethan's second pressure point. The bigger mission. And the most dangerous one of all.

As Ethan studied Josh's face on his video recorder, he could see that Josh had recorded it in his apartment in Tel Aviv. On the screen, Josh was smiling and seemed relaxed, even though the subject matter he was discussing was beyond intense, beyond anything Ethan could have imagined back then. Ethan moved his index finger over the Forward prompt on the screen, and Josh's face came to life as he spoke.

> Ethan, now that I'm up here after the Rapture and you're still down there, and the beginning of the end has started, you need to remember the endgame of the evil one: he wants every human soul under his control. The Bible gives us a glimpse of that and how he is going to do it. First, unification of all government, all religion, and all of the world's economies. We've gone over that. You'll remember when I was still down there with you, I was beginning to see this with the worldwide currency, the CReDO, followed by the mass BIDTagging of citizens in every nation, supposedly for security purposes.
>
> But you have to be prepared for what comes next—the cruelest tactic of all. The truly demonic one.
>
> Remember what Revelation 13:14–15 says about the first part of that ploy. There will be a communications marvel of unparalleled proportions. Those who "dwell on the earth"—the inhabitants of the entire planet earth—will be ordered to "make an image to the beast." So just think about your ancient history for a minute.

Joshua stopped and wrinkled his brow a bit. "Ancient history—yeah, never your favorite subject, was it, Ethan?"

Ethan guffawed. True enough. He practically had an allergic reaction to it.

"But by now, I'm hoping that you've followed my advice on reading Josephus, the famous Jewish historian. And a few of the Roman commentators. And more important, the writing of the early church fathers."

Ethan waved a finger at the screen, forgetting for a moment that this wasn't a live Allfone video call with his friend. "Hey, Josh, you'd be proud of me. In the last two-plus years after you and your family and all of the other believers in Christ got raptured, I've actually dug into all of those books—"

But Ethan was jarred back into reality when Josh cut in and kept rolling on the video. "Remember? In ancient times, physical idols were constructed by pagans who believed the idols were invested with the divine powers of the gods. The Greeks had their statues."

"Acts chapter 17," Ethan spoke out loud to the empty bedroom, thinking back to his meeting up at Mars Hill in Athens when he'd recounted the New Testament story to Gikas about Paul and the Greek philosophers.

But again, on the video screen Josh was plowing ahead.

I don't think that prophetic verse in Revelation is talking about people making idols out of wood or stone. That's a first-century kind of idolatry. I think it's referring to the kind of advanced technology that would have been unthinkable before the second half of the twentieth century, and only feasible in the twenty-first. Look, Ethan, my expertise and my training at MIT and the DOD was in lasers and aeronautics, not virtual imagery. But my prayer is that God will bring some brilliant people to you who can help you stay ahead of the curve on this and slow it down. Even though you can't stop it, maybe there's some chance to use it to your own advantage.

To get the truth out to mankind. The evil one intends it for evil, but God can use it for good.

"Already on it," Ethan said quietly to the screen. He gave a smiling nod to his friend's face. But Josh's eyes now began to narrow as he explained what to expect.

"But there's also that other prophetic part in verse fifteen: 'And it was given to him to give breath to the image of the beast, so that the image of the beast would even speak.'"

"Right," Ethan said, nodding to the screen, his voice rising. "What's your take on that?"

"So a second beast, the false prophet, is somehow involved in the casting of the image of the first beast—the Antichrist—around the world. A global system of visual communication, instantaneously, to every sector of the planet."

"I'm tracking you, Josh. And I have an idea on how they are going to do it."

"But, Ethan, don't forget this: the worldwide visual communication of the image, that's only half of the story. Then comes the real nightmare for the human race. We see it in the rest of that Scripture verse. Something hideous and unimaginable . . ."

A polite knock on the closed bedroom door. Ethan straightened in his chair. He pressed his thumbprint to the upper quadrant of the screen and Josh's face disappeared; the video machine went dark. "Come in."

Nick Akonos opened the arched wooden door and stood in the doorway. He glanced over at the suitcase on the bed. "Leaving? So soon?"

"Yes."

"Do you know *when*—" He quickly smiled and corrected himself. "I mean, *if* you'll be coming back?"

Ethan shook his head. "I can't predict."

"Unlike the prophets," Nick added with a chuckle.

"Right," Ethan replied. He smiled. Nick had been a great host. His time on Crete had been a welcome retreat.

But in the back of his mind he still heard the voice of his mentor, Joshua Jordan . . . and thought of the terrors that were yet to come.

FOURTEEN

LEIDEN, THE NETHERLANDS

Pack McHenry had traveled across the globe to the Dutch city of Leiden in a mad rush to connect with Professor Fin Luxendorf, the sixth holder of the secret Internet code card issued by ICANN. Pack needed to get Luxendorf on board before he turned up missing or dead like five of the other computer experts who also held parts of the doomsday key code.

Luxendorf wasn't in his office at Leiden University, so Pack left his name and cell number with the secretary. Later that day Pack received a callback. It was the professor.

Pack was in no mood for subtlety. "You don't know me, but I know who you are. I am a former United States government agent, and I think your life is in danger. It has to do with your sensitive position with ICANN."

Luxendorf fell into a good thirty seconds of silence. The only thing audible on the other end was his breathing. Finally he spoke. "You mentioned something about my 'sensitive position'?"

"I did," Pack replied.

Luxendorf made a noise, like he was trying to clear his throat. "Can you give me specifics?"

"I am talking," Pack said, "about your little club."

There was a nervous titter at the other end. "Oh, you mean my Internet poker club with a few of my ICANN associates."

"No. Not that," Pack responded. "I'm talking about your membership in the elite Club of Seven."

For a second or two Pack thought the line had gone dead, because the breathing at the other end seemed to have stopped.

Finally Luxendorf began to probe. "Are you with the Dutch police?"

"No."

"Who are you?"

"I can't elaborate. But I can tell you that you have something in your possession that certain people want to get their hands on very badly. They are willing to take drastic measures to obtain it."

Pack was convinced that Fin Luxendorf knew exactly what he meant. The law professor became agitated. "Whoever you are, this is bordering on harassment, which is illegal here in the Netherlands."

Pack was unperturbed. "The law will be of little use to you, Dr. Luxendorf," he replied calmly.

"I'm calling the Dutch authorities."

"I already did," Pack shot back.

"Give me a name."

"I can give you the names of the investigating detective with the Dutch police, and his commanding officer as well. But that won't do you any good."

"And exactly why is that?"

"Because I contacted them two days ago when I arrived here in the Netherlands. Yesterday they informed me that they could do nothing. They only offered to turn the whole affair over to the Internet Security Agency of the Global Alliance. If they do, I can guarantee what will happen."

"And that is what?"

"Absolutely nothing."

Pack could tell Luxendorf was mulling it over on the other end. Finally the professor said, "Give me your Allfone number. Let me consider this. I'll call you back."

"Not to rush you, but you'd better make it quick. We'd like to keep you alive."

□□□

U.S. CAPITOL BUILDING

Washington, D.C.

In the Capitol Building caucus room a small tangle of senators huddled together, arguing in senatorial style—stopping just short of outright anger, yet standing toe-to-toe and raising the ante with political threats uttered clearly in "outside voices." It was the preeminent issue of the day: what to do about the stonewalling posture of President Hewbright. He had consistently refused to acknowledge or implement the Senate's ratification of the Global Alliance Treaty. The reason for the adoption of the treaty in the first place was clear to everyone: a white-knuckled fear of economic collapse if the U.S. failed to join the new world government. As taxes in the United States skyrocketed from a last-ditch attempt to pay for the increased number of nationalized programs, every business in America—from the small mom-and-pop ones to the huge multinational companies—kept cutting back, creating staggering unemployment rates that now held at twenty-six percent.

This, coupled with the loss of America's international credit standing, fueled the fear that the United States could no longer hold its head up in the world. America was bankrupt, and in quiet voices around Washington the policy wonks predicted a total collapse into chaos—and not just the kind of riots that had already broken out in Chicago, Detroit, Los Angeles, Dallas, and Philadelphia, but something much worse. Violent revolution and overthrow, if not from within, then surely with the prodding of enemies from without.

The majority leader in the Senate, Senator Atchison, had a personal dislike for President Hewbright anyway, but now he was furious at Hewbright's opposition to the treaty. Of course the majority leader knew the new Global Alliance was filled with forces that hated America—but he'd always been a firm believer in keeping your friends close and your enemies closer. That's what he kept telling himself and his colleagues, at least, even though he treated Hewbright as the real enemy and the Global Alliance as the true friend.

Now that President Hewbright had recently given his public defense to the American people for his refusal to allow the U.S. to join the Global Alliance despite the Senate vote to the contrary, it was Showdown at the OK Corral, Washington style.

Majority Leader Atchison was waving his finger in the air as he addressed his small group of fellow senators. "The survival of our nation depends on what we do here. If we do not take this step against Hewbright, we will go down in American history as the most despised of all traitors and cowards."

"And some of my constituents would say," another senator intoned with a troubled look, "that this treaty will itself cause the *end* of American history."

"Then why did you bother voting for it?" the majority leader blustered.

"You know exactly why: the pressure brought to bear on every one of us. And I come from a battleground state, come next election."

A junior senator jumped in. "It has to start with the House. That's what the Constitution requires."

Another senator quickly countered in a sardonic tone, "Constitution? Now help me out here—which document is that?"

A few of them couldn't help chuckling nervously. But it died quickly as the stone-cold realization settled over them that they could be sounding the death knell of constitutional rule.

Atchison raised both hands as he tried to close the discussion. "True. It has to start with the House of Representatives. Impeachment of a president always starts there, but it doesn't end there. It ends right here, with his trial in the Senate. So we need both chambers racked and stacked and in a straight line on this. Which is why we need to hear the latest dispatch from the special envoy of the Global Alliance. Otherwise known as the Senate's number one unregistered lobbyist."

"Speak of the devil," one of them whispered and motioned to the other end of the crowded room where a smiling, straight-backed, middle-aged Jessica Tulrude stood confidently shaking hands with several senators.

More chuckling from within the group.

"I think our petition is about to be answered," Majority Leader Atchison announced with a smile. "And by a former president of the United States, no less."

Tulrude was shaking hands with a senate staffer, but her eyes simultaneously wandered over the room until she spotted her target. In an instant she was striding right over to the majority leader. She gave him a crushing handshake and excused herself from the rest of the huddle as she whisked him over to a quiet corner.

"Breaking news," she said. "I've just finished a meeting with the Speaker of the House. I think we've finally got sufficient votes in the House of Representatives to file articles of impeachment against Hewbright."

"So it's game on," Senator Atchison replied.

There was a smug look of certainty on Tulrude's face. "Gird your loins. This is going to be a kicking and screaming bout. Extreme cage-match fighting. No Queensberry rules."

"Jessica, I didn't know you were such a fight fan," the senator said with a laugh.

"Politics . . . extreme fighting . . . ," she said with a chuckle. "They're both blood sports, aren't they?"

The majority leader eyed her closely now, knowing the rules of quid pro quo. "And if impeachment is achieved in the House, then in return I suppose you still are looking for—"

"Full Senate support," she cut in, "for me to be appointed as the permanent world regent over Global Alliance Region One—the U.S.A., Canada, and Mexico. The other two nations are already favorably inclined to appoint me. I just need the home team here in the U.S. Senate to back me as well."

"You know how this works," the senator said. "No one's squeaky clean. Not really. It's just a matter of deciding whether the dirt is manageable."

Tulrude was nodding. She tried to muster a smile.

"Now, there is," the senator said with a tone of reflection, "still that matter of a dead president. And all those rumors about your complicity as vice president spread over AmeriNews. Whispers about your personal physician overdosing President Corland during treatment for his medical condition. Mind you, I don't believe a word of it, Jessica."

Tulrude flamed into a controlled burn. "Of course not. Come on. He didn't die until months later. In a nursing home. His blackouts had been getting worse. Let's get real."

"And then," the senator added, "there's the apparent suicide of your physician, which conveniently stopped any further criminal investigation dead in its tracks. By that I mean convenient for you, of course. That's what some people are saying."

Jessica Tulrude's reputation for controlling her fury was being tested. There was a little twitch to her mouth, and the skin over her face tightened. "Those rumors about my personal doctor when I was vice president are old, tired news. I can't control the naysayers. What's important is that AmeriNews is an ulcer on the skin of the American media. I think it's high time to cut them out like a wart. As a news service it's been on life support ever since the disappearance of all of the right-wing Jesus freaks, including the crazy Jordan family that used to run it. AmeriNews is simply a dangerous influence. A journalistic atrocity. The American people desire better."

Majority Leader Atchison held out his hand to seal the deal with Tulrude. "That's a discussion for another day. Today we have a bigger mission: the beginning of the end for President Hank Hewbright and his dangerous, self-righteous presidency."

FIFTEEN

LEIDEN UNIVERSITY

Leiden, The Netherlands

Something was wrong. Pack McHenry felt it in his gut. He glanced at his Allfone watch to check the time. He stood in the glass-enclosed vestibule outside the law school auditorium where Professor Luxendorf's next class, the Law of Internet Technology, was scheduled to begin in five minutes. His students were already starting to parade into the class. Pack wondered if Luxendorf would make it to their agreed rendezvous. When the professor had called Pack back, he'd said yes, he would meet with him, but he insisted that it be a very public place. Specifically, outside the law school lecture hall after one of his classes. He'd invited Pack to come early and sit through the class if he liked. Pack had taken him up on the offer.

The former CIA clandestine operations chief ran his fingers through a few unruly strands in his salt-and-pepper hair, then checked the time again. Students now streamed into the classroom in droves. But no Professor Luxendorf. Pack touched the security imprint icon on the face of his Allfone and spoke into it. The voice audiogram verification flashed *Voice ready.*

Pack spoke into his watch. "Please video call Dragon Lady."

It rang twice, and then the face of his wife, Victoria—a classic platinum blond and still beautiful at age fifty-two—flashed onto the dial of his Allfone. She smiled. "I see you're still using that terrible speed-dial name for me. Pack, dear, *reeeeally . . .*"

"Honey, we may have a problem. Are you somewhere near Luxendorf's house?"

Victoria was already on it. "When I didn't get confirmation from you ten minutes ago that the meeting was in progress, I drove over here. I'm just pulling up in front of his little cottage right now. Lots of pretty tulips in the front garden, by the way. Give me a sec."

Victoria's image was replaced by the words *Video off.* A few minutes went by before her face appeared again. She whispered, barely audible. "I'm inside. I zapped the digital lock on his front door. My keypad meter tells me that someone eventually got in through the lock before me, but it was someone who didn't know the code."

"Oh?"

"The lock memory says that they tried multiple variations before they hit the correct code. Probably using a portable clue randomizer. These guys weren't here just to steal a big-screen web TV or heist the silverware, that's for sure. I've got a bad feeling."

"Be careful, Vicky."

"Always. Just remember, dear, I have that innocent, helpless look that always fools the bad guys. But I've also got my semiautomatic with me. And as you will recall, at the shooting range, between the two of us, I'm the better—"

She stopped talking. Pack tensed and began to walk farther away from the lecture hall, which was now filled to capacity but with no lecturer, as the din from student conversation reached a dull roar. "What is it, Vicky?"

"They've sacked the place. Stuff all over. I have to find out where Luxendorf was hiding it."

"Have they exited the house?"

"Oh yes, they're gone. Besides, I uploaded the digital code history from the electronic door lock. It showed that it was last shut from the outside. Give me a minute, dear."

She disappeared again, but for two minutes this time, while Pack paced rigidly. The class in the law school was getting restless and noisier. A few students started walking out of class.

Then, "Okay, Pack. Luxendorf kept it in a safe on the wall, behind a painting. Gee, poor guy. Could he have been any more predictable?"

"Is it still secure?"

"Hardly. The safe is wide open and empty. No signs of forced entry."

"Which says something bad about the fate of our law professor."

"I'm going into another room," Victoria said. "Looks like his study."

One more minute before she described the inevitable. "Pack, I've located Professor Luxendorf. He's lying on the floor. He's been murdered."

□□□

SOMEWHERE IN THE PACIFIC

Ethan March stood on the deck of a Greek cargo ship, courtesy of Nick, the international travel guru. The most discreet way to cross an ocean, particularly for a wanted man like Ethan, was still the old-fashioned way: by ocean-going freighter. He anticipated a series of jokes from his associates about his taking a "slow boat to China" now that he was on his way to Hong Kong, hopefully to a meeting with Jo Li.

The moon was out and nearly full, huge in the black night sky, sending a narrow trail of light to gild the waves of the ocean. Ethan enjoyed a rare moment of peace and quiet. But his mind continued on rapid fire.

That night he had received a call from Pack McHenry explaining all about the killing of Dr. Luxendorf, ICANN code cardholder number six. He'd asked Pack the obvious question: "What's the motive behind this?" The intelligence veteran didn't have an answer.

So Ethan decided to call one guy who might. He had forgotten about the time change. A few minutes later he had a sleepy Chiro Hashimoto on the line. It was dawn in the Yukon and he had rousted Chiro from his bed.

"Chiro, Ethan here. I've got a question for you. Let's assume that someone wants to shut down the Internet. Completely. From one corner of the plant to the other."

Chiro yawned on the other end. "Uh . . . okay. So why are they doing it again? To make some technical correction? Purging some kind of global, exponential virus?"

"No, let's assume it's nothing like that."

"Well, are they trying to destroy the Internet? Nihilistic attack on all the networks?"

"No, I'm sure they're not. These people are after the ability to shut the Internet down, then reboot it again."

Chiro fired back the answer. "Oh. Well, that's easy, then. They're going to reprogram the Internet for another use. Sort of like upgrades to your Allfone or your AllView device. You know, like they used to do to computer laptops in the old days."

"'Another use.' Like . . ."

"Well, the web has been used up to now pretty much as an open-ended, interactive kind of communication network among people around the world. Receiving information. Transmitting data. Back and forth between people and entities. Two-way communication. I've been thinking about our project, watching what is happening with Alexander Colliquin's Internet research in New Babylon. If Colliquin is the one behind it, then I can think of one reason to take down the Internet and then reboot it again."

"Which is . . ."

"Changing its use into a *one-way* communications and personal stimulus-and-input network. Global behavior modification. He would need a massive rebooting if he wanted to reach the entire human race with that kind of system."

Chiro fell silent. Ethan knew his friend's mind was running down some kind of digital maze, putting together a scenario. After almost a full minute, Chiro added, "I've been preparing our communications center up here to counter, or maybe even hack into, Colliquin's new imagery network. But I've had to keep it loose—open to a couple of options. Our intelligence about his plan has been coming to us in tiny little bits. But now . . . with what you're telling me . . ." Chiro went silent again for a few seconds. "If he were to reprogram the web with a behavioral-stimulus kind of program and his people connect it to the global BIDTag grid . . . Then once he rebooted the Internet . . . it would put Colliquin in control."

"Meaning . . . ?"

"Control of everyone, Ethan. I am talking . . . *everyone*."

SIXTEEN

NEW BABYLON, IRAQ

The setting was deceptively calm. At a large semicircular table in the center of the cavernous chambers of the World Parliament of the Global Alliance, ten regents sat in their executive chairs, warmed by the glow of environmentally perfect lighting. The tone of the meeting in the great hall of white stone trimmed in mahogany had been perfunctory and smoothly administrative. But everyone in the room knew that a crisis was underfoot. The worldwide economic depression had created a frantic urgency behind the creation of the World Parliament in the first place. Nations were desperate for a financial fix, and Alexander Colliquin's new governing architecture was hailed as a lifeline thrown to a drowning world just in the nick of time.

Nine of those present were permanent representatives of their respective international regions—each region comprised of numerous nations and in some cases an entire continent. Yet one of the regents was there by temporary appointment—Jessica Tulrude, who represented Region One, the North American sector. The universal wisdom was that the inclusion of the United States into Region One, thus joining it with Canada and Mexico, was crucial to the long-term survival of the Alliance.

Alexander Colliquin had been authorized as chancellor of the Alliance to make Tulrude's temporary appointment. It fit, he said, into the category of "emergency circumstances." Colliquin had determined that the dispute between President Hewbright and the Senate over America's membership in Region One of the Alliance qualified as that. None of the other regents had the desire, or the stomach, to dispute Colliquin's move. Under the rules, though, Tulrude's temporary appointment could last for only six months, and at this point there were only two months left. Something drastic would have to be done to break the deadlock in Washington and bring the U.S. into the fold.

Of course, when Tulrude completed the term of the disabled president Virgil Corland, but then failed to capture the White House in her own right when she was trounced by Hewbright in the next election, Colliquin's closest advisors tried to dismiss her as a flawed geopolitical asset. They wanted someone else as regent. But not Colliquin. He had a particular skill the others did not: a deep understanding of human motivations, failings, and temptations that empowered him to see into the hidden things, the secret, shadowy parts of people. And he had seen into Tulrude. He alone recognized that her election failure had wounded her, but not fatally, and made her more dangerous to her opponents. And more loyal to Colliquin. On the other hand, only Colliquin and a very few others would ever know that in the final analysis, Tulrude was not the most important chess piece on the board. The ultimate endgame did not really depend on Jessica Tulrude, but would in fact require another.

Colliquin was settled into his throne-like chancellor's chair, which was off to the side and set above the regents' table, where he was bathed in a golden spotlight of his own. A moment later the secretary of the World Parliament began to read the motion currently on the floor for a vote.

> Be it resolved that, in light of the defiance by the president of the United States to the rule of law, the Global Alliance and all the nations therein shall impose economic sanctions against the United States of America and shall refuse all trade, economic support, loans, or loan guarantees to the same and shall freeze all American assets held within the Global Alliance until such time as the United States shall formally and irrevocably enter the Global Alliance in accord with the vote of the United States Senate.

The secretary then called for the vote. Seven affirmative votes were needed for a sanction. Colliquin remained confident, even though Canada had wavered up to the very end.

The little lightbulbs in front of each of the regents flashed on. Eight greens, one more than needed. However, two of the lights burned red. Alexander Colliquin glared at the *no* votes. They came from the two regions that included England and Australia.

Colliquin growled under his breath. "England and Australia. Always those two. And Canada . . . My god, they almost voted with them."

When the session ended, Colliquin strutted out of the Parliament chambers and into the back of his Bentley stretch limo. It would take him to the chancellor's palace in the center of the one-hundred-square-mile compound known as New Babylon. The area had become a global capital of lavish white stone Alliance government buildings, gleaming skyscrapers housing a thousand of the world's largest international commercial headquarters, and the five-hundred-acre

One Movement All Faiths Center, the universal headquarters for the world's religious faiths headed by bishop Dibold Kora.

Some quiet objections had been raised in the beginning by a few countries over the New Babylon name, given its historical connotations. So the official name for the capital was changed to New World City. But in private conversation Colliquin still clung persistently, almost obsessively, to the name New Babylon, and he insisted that his personal staff do the same.

Chancellor Colliquin had experienced a technical victory just now, but it wasn't complete. He simmered as his limo eased down the long two-mile lane leading to the circular drive and twenty-foot-high brass-engraved entrance doors of the chancellor's palace. He tapped the microphone function on the ostrich-skin console next to him and yelled, "Pick up the pace!" to his driver.

An armed security detail met Colliquin as he rushed in through the burnished front doors that were decorated with reliefs of mythic Babylonian sphinxes. Once he was up in the personal penthouse that adjoined his executive working suite of offices, he summoned Ho Zhu, his deputy. By the time Ho arrived, Colliquin had cooled a bit.

"Congratulations, Chancellor," Ho began, "on the vote today for sanctions against America—"

But Colliquin cut through the pleasantries. "How close are we in preparations for the computer data center for our global network link?"

"Henry Bender, my New Jersey contact, says he's close to getting—"

"I don't want names!" Colliquin shouted. "No names of your contacts, ever!"

Ho gave a short half bow and picked up where he'd left off. "We are close to getting the passwords and codes for the Utah data center's central command operating system."

"We need them in days, not weeks, and certainly not months."

And Ho bowed again.

As he lounged in his sofa chair, Colliquin rubbed his thumb over the back of his big ring. The ornate piece of jewelry bore the image of a ruby-eyed solid-gold serpent swallowing its own tail. "And what about Hewbright?" he asked.

"Regent Tulrude assures me that the House will impeach the president, and the Senate will convict him and remove him from office."

Colliquin stopped fingering his ring and stared Ho in the eye with an exasperated expression. "No. Not that. I mean the *other* thing."

"Oh yes, our default position. It's all in place. Our White House person is on standby."

"Then there's only one more area of concern."

"Yes, Your Excellency?"

"The Remnant. They are poisoning our influence in most of our Alliance nations, like a toxin. Their numbers are spreading. So we need to increase our pressure on their global leadership."

"Yes, Chancellor."

"And I'd like to have my office updated with photos of the key Remnant leaders . . ."

"Certainly. As soon as we resolve a small computer program glitch."

"Glitch?"

"A few have had their facial metrics loaded into the onboard computers in our drone-bots, but for some reason we have been unable to download the metrics back into our system to print photo arrays."

"Are you telling me our drones can recognize them from the sky, but we don't have pictures of them here on the ground?"

"I am afraid that is true. But for only a few of them."

Colliquin fumed. "Please tell me that Ethan March's photo has been distributed to every Alliance outpost on the planet."

"Before our drone program was expanded, we handed out hard copies of his photo to a few bounty hunter groups. Since then we've gone digital, and we just assumed we could retrieve all the images back from the drones. But I'm afraid he's one of a few whose images can't be downloaded due to the glitch—"

"What kind of operation are you running? Solve this computer problem! I want Ethan March. You do remember him? The protégée of Joshua Jordan. Public enemy number one. Start with him. He's at the top. Whatever it takes. Strike the shepherd first. Then we go after the sheep."

SEVENTEEN

HONG KONG

When Rivka stopped by her little efficiency apartment to check on Meifeng, she found her still in the middle of one of her school lessons. The former call girl was now being tutored in some basic classes by a local member of the Remnant, a retired teacher Rivka had hired.

"Doing okay?" Rivka asked as she stood in the doorway.

Meifeng's face was full of life, and she had color in her checks now that her body was no longer laced with drugs from Chow, her former pimp. She brightened, looked up from her book, and smiled. "Doing swell, Miss Riv."

"Fine," Rivka said. "I'm stopping by the market. Be back in a jiffy."

After Rivka left her apartment, she took a meandering route through several alleys and backstreets and cut through the lobbies of two hotels. She never took the same route on her short travels to the little corner market. Just a matter of habit from her years as a former Israeli spy.

The little grocery had a good supply of fresh fruits, vegetables, and fish. She was looking over a tray of celery, noodles, and watercress when she heard a familiar voice. And when she did, she momentarily forgot the rest of the items on her shopping list.

"So, are you inviting me to dinner?"

She turned to face Ethan March. He was grinning back at her. Ethan added, "You always could make a really great chop suey. In fact, as I remember it, that was the last meal we had together."

Rivka tried not to brighten too much. "You're right, it was. My place in Tel Aviv."

Ethan raised an eyebrow. "I thought you were going to look me up. At least that's what Jimmy Louder told me back in Athens."

"But then I changed my mind," she shot back. "I decided to let you chase me instead. It's a girl thing."

Ethan looked surprised. "So that's why you think I'm in Hong Kong? To chase you?"

"You're here, aren't you?" She smirked.

"Well, I'm actually here on business," he said, hiding a smile.

"You mean visiting this market at the exact moment when I'm here. A grocery that I just happen to frequent on a regular basis— something you learned from a local Remnant member you pumped for information yesterday after you arrived on the island. You mean that kind of business?"

Ethan chuckled. "Okay. I give. I'm duly impressed. Look, I know this market is run by one of our people, so let me sign the barter slip for your groceries. It'll go on my tab."

Rivka's eyes lit up. "Great. If that's the case, I'll change my menu— I'm going for the whole lobsters and rare fish."

The two of them had a good laugh, and Ethan took her basket and followed her around dutifully while she finished her shopping. After that, they started strolling back to her apartment, which was when the mood changed. Rivka started talking about their common mission. "So you're here to see Jo Li?"

Ethan rolled his eyes. "I see the underground rumor mill is alive and well. So much for confidentiality."

"You don't expect me to forget everything I learned in the Mossad about intelligence gathering, do you?"

"Well, I know a few things about your activities too. Like the fact that you met with Hadley Brooking, the English solicitor, trying to locate Jo Li."

"Ex-solicitor. I now wonder whether his office might be a front for Jo Li."

"The point is you should have consulted with me before you met with him."

Rivka bristled. "I knew you were hunting for Jo Li. And I was already here in the area. I was doing fieldwork for you." She added, "And you're welcome, by the way."

"I think you should have talked to me first. My mission here could have been compromised."

Rivka stopped in the alley they found themselves in and whirled around to face Ethan. "Hey, this is me, Rivka, remember? You and me. We were almost . . . well, I'm not sure what we were. But it was a whole lot more than friends."

"That's true. But it's also beside the point," Ethan said with a tone that was getting firmer. "We are trying to maintain some kind of command and control. Some structure to the Remnant."

There was no anger in what Ethan was saying, and Rivka could see that. It was something else, and it had to do with Rivka, and it surprised her, though she didn't know why. She wondered why all of a sudden she had a strange desire for the old Ethan—the guy she used to know, the man who always had a touch of wild unpredictability about him. But then, that harkened back to a time before Ethan, and then later Rivka herself, had committed their lives to following Christ, before the inner spiritual revolution that took place in both of them that had changed everything. Of course she never wanted to go back to that, not since having experienced the overwhelming reality that God loved her and that He had a plan for her.

So, if all that was true, why all these messed-up feelings about Ethan? Rivka needed to sort that out. She reached out and grabbed the bag of groceries from Ethan's grip. "Thanks for the help," she snapped. "But I can take it from here."

Ethan tried to put a patch on it. "Okay, Rivka, I'm sorry. It looks like I blew it." He studied her, but she didn't soften. "Why do I think I just lost a dinner invitation?"

Rivka wouldn't look him in the eye, instead gazing down the alley while she spoke. "Ethan, I'm sorry if you think I went rogue on this Jo Li thing. Just trying to help. So . . . anyway, maybe you and I should skip the interpersonal stuff and stick strictly to business."

"Or, on the other hand," Ethan shot back with a half smile, "maybe we can do both."

Rivka shrugged, threw him a quick wave good-bye, and turned to leave with the bag of groceries in her hand. Ethan called out to her, offering to walk her home for the sake of her safety, but she simply shook her head. She moved quickly down the alley without turning back, and then slipped into the back door of a small laundry shop, just one more sidetrack for the benefit of anyone who might be trying to follow her.

Rivka excused herself with a few words of apology in Chinese as she bumped through the steamy room full of confused laundry workers and out the front door. She picked up the pace along Hennessy Street where the pedestrian crowds along the boulevard of shops thickened, then into a lobby of a hotel, down the stairs into the parking garage, and then out onto a back street. At one point she thought she sensed something behind her and immediately turned, ready to drop her bag and defend herself if necessary. But there was no one there, so she did a one-eighty and continued on her route.

As she headed back to her apartment, she kept going back in her head to her conversation with Ethan. Her meeting with him had put her on an emotional carnival ride. She was surprised at how painful and confused she felt. Sure, she knew he had made a valid point. Before meeting with Hadley Brooking, she had given a quick thought to trying to connect with Ethan to clear it with him first. But she'd decided against it, telling herself that it was easier to ask for forgiveness than for permission, particularly given the difficulty in tracking Ethan down. But that prompted another thought, and it plagued her now.

Okay, but, girl, you never really got to that "ask for forgiveness part," did you?

Rivka was striding along the familiar streets and alleys of Hong Kong on a kind of mental autopilot by then. She had turned from a small street onto an alley that provided back entrances to a row of restaurants. She passed the rear entrance to a men's clothing store, where a tailor stood in the doorway smoking a cigarette with his measuring tape slung loosely over his neck. He glanced at her blankly as she walked by, then tossed his lighted butt down, crushing it with his foot as he eyed her, and slipped back into the clothing shop.

She turned left down another dirty alley lined with garbage cans and Dumpsters. On the left was the back door leading to an Indian café. On the right side of the alley was a buzzing neon light over a rear entrance advertising a "girl bar."

Somewhere in the alarm center of Rivka's head, the first alert started ringing. But it came too late. She recognized the cocktail bar.

What was I thinking?

She halted and reversed direction. Which is when she saw two large men approaching her, one with his hand in his suit coat.

Rivka wheeled back around. The door to the cocktail lounge on the right flew open, and a man with a billy club ran out and stood in the middle of the alley, blocking her way. After him came Chow. He hobbled on a cane, scooted clumsily out of the bar and into the alley. His other arm dangled to his side, a clip-loaded Chinese semiautomatic clutched in his hand.

"Hello, Rivka, darling," Chow grunted. "I knew I'd see you again."

She half turned and saw the two men behind her were now about ten feet away. They both stopped, as if on cue, at a point about six feet from her.

"Sorry," Chow said with a grin, "but no kickboxing today. I warned them to stay out of your kicking distance."

"Good idea," Rivka said. "Now that the introductions are over, I would like you to let me pass."

"Be glad to," Chow said. "Just tell me where you've got Meifeng hidden. Then I'll let you go."

She slowly lowered her grocery bag to the ground, but her eyes never left Chow. "Not as long as I'm alive."

"Okay. If you insist . . ."

"I've settled up my life with Christ," she said. "I know where I'm going. Do you?"

"Sure," he said with a laugh. "Back into my girl bar, after I shoot you in your pretty face."

But the back door to the Indian café had just opened. The men noticed that and turned. Out from the unlit shadows of the entrance a man's voice came booming out. Rivka recognized instantly who was speaking.

"Chow, you really know how to treat a lady."

"Who's there?" Chow screamed. He raised his gun toward the darkened back door and prepared to squeeze the trigger. "Who's there?" he yelled again.

The darkened entrance to the Indian eatery lit up with a muzzle flash. The bullet from the shot blasted through the palm of Chow's shooting hand. He dropped both gun and cane and squealed in pain, stumbling to his knees as Ethan March jumped out of the darkness and into the alley, a handgun in each fist.

"It's me," Ethan called. "Her date tonight." He aimed one of his guns toward the guy who was starting to pull his own weapon from his suit pocket. "Drop it or I won't be shooting at your hand."

The tough guy in the suit pulled out his weapon and let it fall to the greasy concrete. Rivka pulled in a shaky breath. Ethan kept the two thugs in his sights while he grabbed Chow's weapon, and then those from the tough guys too.

Ethan then ordered the goons into a nearby Dumpster. With looks of controlled fury, they did as he asked. Pulling his backpack open, Ethan grabbed a piece of nylon zip tie and secured the Dumpster lid shut. "I still think zip ties are the world's greatest invention," he said with a grin to Rivka, who had overcome her shock and was keeping watch over a moaning Chow. "I used one to secure a broken cockpit door during a test flight once. Call me crazy, but I still carry them with me."

Ethan now turned to Chow. "Broken hip. Shot-up hand. Chow, you're not doing well as a criminal. Why don't you try doing something honest?"

Chow whimpered and clutched his bleeding hand. Ethan asked him, "Yes or no—is Jo Li part of the crime syndicate? The Triad?"

"No, man," Chow groaned. "Why don't people believe me when I tell them? I wanted inside Jo Li's operation. A lot of other guys in the Triad did too. The guys who ran the gambling joints, the pimps, the sellers and pushers, everybody. But Jo Li won't work with any of them. He's just a business guy, that's all."

"I'll call you a medi-ped," Ethan said, referring to the local EMTs on bikes "They should be here in a few minutes." He hit the Red Cross icon on his public Allfone and tapped the Emergency Response key. "There. They should be here in a few minutes."

"Don't forget about the GPS function on that Allfone . . ." Rivka started to say.

But Ethan had already dropped his public Allfone to the pavement and was now crushing it with his boot. He flashed a smiled to Rivka as he picked up the pieces and tossed them into another Dumpster.

After tucking his own guns into the pockets of his cargo pants, Ethan grabbed Rivka's bag of groceries that still stood upright on the ground. He quickly whisked her through the back door of the Indian restaurant, past the kitchen, and out the front door to the street.

"You know, I'm really looking forward to your chop suey tonight," he said with a grin. He reached out with his free hand and took Rivka's. "Can we pick up where we left off?"

EIGHTEEN

EAST WING OF THE WHITE HOUSE

Washington, D.C.

Hank Hewbright had decided to meet with his vice president, Darrell Zandibar, in the upstairs personal residence rather than in the Oval Office. Hewbright had begun to question the degree of security even in that area. Besides, it was nice from time to time to have a visitor up in the residential apartments of the White House. With his wife, Ginny, having died from cancer a few years before the election, Hewbright was the first president since Grover Cleveland to enter the White House without a spouse.

He had been on his knees at the side of the living room sofa, praying, when the security buzzer sounded Zandibar's arrival. The voice of Secret Service agent Kevin Arnold came over the intercom. Arnold was the agent who worked the closest with Hewbright on a daily basis. "Mr. President, the vice president is here to see you, sir."

"Buzz him in, Kevin. Thanks."

A minute later the vice president was in the room. After a firm handshake between the men and some small talk, Hewbright apologized that they hadn't seen much of each other. Privately he knew that each man harbored suspicions about the other, and this meeting would be as good a time as any to clear the air.

Zandibar launched in immediately about the news that was now 24/7 on every media outlet around the world. "When the House votes tomorrow, it seems all but certain they're going to approve articles of impeachment against you."

Hewbright managed a smile. "That's what I've been told. Although politics is never certain. It's always been more art than science."

"I'm sure you've done a rough head count for votes in the Senate," his VP said. "They seem locked into a guilty vote to remove you. I'm sure your lawyer has already told you how they're trying to expedite this. A blazing-fast Senate trial, now that the Alliance is threatening to crush this nation with a worldwide economic boycott." Zandibar paused and added, "You've made a, well, *interesting* choice, by the way, going with Harry Smythe as your defense attorney for the trial, rather than your White House counsel. Harry's getting a little old and a little tired for a case like this, don't you think?"

Hewbright shook his head. "No," he replied. "Harry's the right man for the job." Then he shifted the subject. "I was just told that riots have broken out along the Magnificent Mile in Chicago after the news of the potential boycott against the U.S. Several people are lying dead near Water Tower Place. This country is being shaken to its core."

"Which is why," Zandibar shot back, "I think the two of us should keep in closer contact through this chaotic time. We need, you and I, to keep talking through your decision to stonewall the Senate's vote on the Global Alliance Treaty. And you need to reconsider your executive order. Just think about it for a moment—your executive order directing the Pentagon and every federal agency to resist cooperating with the Senate's vote to bring us into the Global Alliance. We need to deal with the facts as they are. And the facts are that the Senate ratified that treaty, and the Alliance is anxious to bring America into their fold. Your decision makes us an isolated island surrounded by an ocean of trouble."

"And you know my position on that," Hewbright snapped back. "The Senate alone doesn't have the constitutional power to dissolve this Republic. So am I to ignore the illegality of that vote? Stand by and watch our borders disappear and our Constitution get shredded and place us into the hands of international masters?"

Then he went right to the point. "Darrell, are you ready to lead America if I am removed?"

"I'm not looking for the presidency," Zandibar said. "Not yet. And certainly not that way."

"But are you ready?"

"That depends."

"On what?"

"Your trust."

"If I'm out," Hewbright said, "will that matter?"

"To me it will." Zandibar tapped a finger on the arm of the couch where he sat. "I know you've cut me out of some of your higher-level strategy meetings."

Hewbright didn't hesitate. "True enough. I've had some concerns."

"About?"

"Loyalty. You forget: one of the perks of the presidency is access to intelligence. I know that two weeks ago you and Jessica Tulrude had a private meeting in her suite in the Hay Adams Hotel. Why didn't you share that with me?"

Zandibar took a few seconds before responding. "I didn't think I needed to. Frankly . . . I just wanted to hear what she had."

"Against me?"

"Yes. I know you are an honorable man, Hank. An honest man and a patriot with a great vision. But I just didn't know—"

"Whether she had some dirt on me that I had been hiding?"

"I had to make sure."

"And?"

"Actually, the whole thing was a joke. Tulrude kept going on and on with the same tired line against you—your efforts to block America from joining the Alliance. What she called your 'sick addiction to an outdated view of the Constitution.'"

"Oh, that," Hewbright said with a smile. "You mean that old yellowing piece of parchment paper that I pledged to uphold, with my hand on the Bible, when I was sworn in as president?"

Zandibar nodded and looked thoughtful, as if he was trying to choose his words cautiously. Then he said, "In any event, there was nothing there, Hank. I'm sorry I doubted you."

"You don't need to apologize," Hewbright said. "If you're telling the truth."

"Hank, if you let me, I will do everything in my power to defend you and protect your presidency. But you need to let me in on your strategy. Let's remember, I am still president pro tem of the Senate."

"But once the Senate removal trial against me is commenced, the guy sitting up there in the big chair won't be you. It will be Chief Justice Straworth from the Supreme Court. He'll be presiding. The man appointed to the Court by Jessica Tulrude as payback, no doubt, for his having done some favors for her when he was back in the Senate. I suspect the whole thing will be a rigged trial."

"You mean, *if* the trial commences," Zandibar added.

Hewbright studied his vice president. Darrell Zandibar was a brilliant man. Top of his class at Harvard Law. A successful New York federal prosecutor and a young rising star in the Senate when Hewbright picked him as his running mate. But he often wondered what he really knew about the other man. What could a person truly know about a man until the testing time came and the pressure mounted? Or when the sweet siren song of temptation floated in? What was it Shakespeare had said about screwing your courage to the sticking place? Or, better yet, the command from God to Joshua in the Old Testament as the journey across the Jordan River and then the entrance into the Promised Land was about to begin, and all those bloody battles to follow. It would be the command for Hank Hewbright as well: to be strong and courageous and to fear not.

The clock was ticking for Hewbright's future. He knew that. And he had a sense that it was not just his political future. There was more at stake than that. During the last election cycle, on the eve of Hewbright receiving the nomination of his party, there had been an attempt on his life. He knew it was part of the job, though he was a little surprised there hadn't been more assassination attempts, more near misses, during his presidency. But now he harbored the firm belief that his current term, and perhaps even his life, could end dramatically and soon. He believed right down to the hollow of his gut that there were not only enemies outside, but also an enemy presence lurking inside his own house. And there were very few people he could trust with that information.

As Hewbright walked Zandibar to the door and then closed it behind him and turned, alone, back to his solo vigil inside the White House, he was convinced more than ever before that the time to cross the Jordan River was at hand.

NINETEEN

CHICAGO, ILLINOIS

The rioters had come from the ranks of the homeless, the unemployed, and the hopeless. Some of them were armed. They had barricaded the entrance doors and taken over the first few floors of the exclusive shopping mall high-rise at Water Tower Place and had set fire to several of the shops. On the ground level, with the help of the police, the fire fighters dodged bullets and tried to get their ladders in place to reach the fire that sent flames out of the broken glass in the tall semi-circular windows over the entrance to Macy's.

A few blocks away, in the backseat of a cab that was slammed in the middle of horn-blowing, dead-stop traffic, Bart Kingston was making a call to Dr. Terrance Radameyer, a retired professor who used to teach digital image forensics. His condo was along the Lake Shore, not far from there.

Radameyer picked up the call. Kingston spoke quickly. "Doctor, I'm sorry I'm late. Caught in traffic."

"Yes, I know. The riots. Terrible. Are you all right?"

"I am. But I'm going to bail out of this cab and go it on foot. Be there as fast as I can."

Kingston hung up and tossed his taxi fare over the seat to the driver, then jumped out of the cab, briefcase in hand. In little under an hour, after dodging police squads that were on their way to Water Tower Place, he made it to Radameyer's tenth-floor condo. It was a large, classy place with a nice view of Lake Michigan.

As they sat on the couch, Kingston noticed that Radameyer had the little compact AllView device on the coffee table that he had couriered to him.

"I notice you didn't want to talk over the phone," Kingston began.

"Well, my late wife was a psychologist. She used to tell me, 'Sometimes there's a healthy side to paranoia.' What you and I are about to discuss right now, this is potentially very dangerous stuff."

"We're agreed on that," Kingston said solemnly. "I'm sure you know about the international law that outlaws even the possession of this kind of material."

Radameyer raised both eyebrows. "That gave me pause at first. But then, Mr. Kingston, someone has to be willing to find out where the truth lies—no matter where it happens to be found." Radameyer reached out and waved a finger over the Start icon on the little screen and it lit up. "So, Mr. Kingston, I take it you want to know my reaction to this video material marked as 'raw footage' from the archives of the Global Alliance news network."

"Exactly," Kingston said. "It supposedly shows large masses of dead Christians, with crosses or clutching Bibles, scattered in groups, lying on the ground in enormous numbers, and all in remote locations."

Radameyer reached out and touched the Pause icon, then turned to Kingston. "I don't think I saw this footage at the time when it was first played on the web television news stories. But I obviously read about it later. Everybody did. Telling the story about millions and millions of Christians spontaneously migrating to remote locations. Deserts. Wilderness areas. And then committing mass suicide, all at the same time. Those were the headlines. But being a forensic expert who has testified in court about faked video images over the last thirty-five years—two hundred and three times to be exact—I have developed a certain amount of skepticism when stories don't add up. My first question was: Where are the bodies?"

Kingston nodded. He had made the same point himself, many times.

The retired professor explained the counterargument. "But then the Alliance officials said that many of the bodies were detected to have dangerous biological contaminants and had to be buried in mass graves immediately. A public health hazard, they said. Of course they refuse to tell anyone where these supposed mass graves are located."

Kingston wanted to pursue another angle. "On the other hand, you'll notice, Dr. Radameyer, that the footage of all of the supposed mass suicides were outside of the United States. In other words, in countries under Global Alliance control. No real attempt to document any alleged mass suicides in America. When this news hit, the only press mention of alleged U.S. suicides among Christians was a handful of still photographs of some bodies on farm properties, lying on barn floors, supposedly somewhere in the plains states. No location was ever given. I'm betting that those photos were lifted from police files on actual suicides of a few of those poor folks who took their lives after their farms went belly-up—decimated by a combination of drought and of course the bankrupting of the whole American economy courtesy of some terrible decisions in Washington over the years."

Kingston pointed to the little video player on the coffee table.

"The problem is, as logical as those explanations are, it isn't enough. I'm after hard evidence—facts—that prove definitely that the Global Alliance news feeds were fraudulent in the way they tried to portray the disappearance of Christians."

Radameyer swept his finger over the Forward icon and the news footage flashed on the screen. Then he set the Elapsed Time button at a specific point and fast-forwarded the footage to that spot. "Okay," the professor said. "I've picked the most dramatic depiction that was aired by the Global Alliance News Network over web TVs all over the world. This piece of footage was shown more times than any other. And when I dug a little further, I learned that it had more hits on the Internet than any other news story that year."

But then Radameyer hit Stop on the screen and stood up. "I think, to give you a better picture, I'd like to show you this on the bigger screen in my study."

He led Kingston into his library. It had only one wall lined with books, and the rest of the bookshelves were lined with cases of videos, DVDs, MP3 cartridges, and little cartons of megapixel zip drives all carefully labeled and alphabetized. He had an ultra-wide computer screen on his desk. The computer was already on and humming, and in less than a minute he synced the little video player with his computer. Then he hit Play.

On the screen was the familiar footage. Kingston had seen it many times. And he had heard people remark how it seemed to explain—at least to some extent—the bizarre disappearance of so many Christians.

Hundreds, perhaps thousands, of bodies lying together in a field in various postures. Many of them grasping Bibles and crosses. Their faces twisted in the final grimaces of death.

"This is the footage I was referring to," Radameyer said. "Now, let me show you a close-up."

He brought the view into a close-up of a man on his back, his eyes staring straight up, clutching a Bible. Next to him a woman in a scarf, also staring out blankly. "This is where there has been artificial image rearrangement—fakery." He brought the image even closer, to where just the eyes of the man and the eyes of the woman were visible in two separate viewing panes on the screen. "I applied a mathematical formula—standard stuff for people in my area of study—to the light refraction you see on these eyes. Taking into consideration their position next to each other, and in reference to a supposed common light source, what kind of specular highlights—in other words, the glint in the eye—should they have had? I have concluded beyond a reasonable doubt that the man's position was real, but the woman with a cross around her neck was inserted into the photo artificially. Obviously for dramatic effect, to show these were Christians who were dead. This footage is doctored. Now this is pretty hard to detect unless you know what to look for. But I also found some other, more obvious signs of fraud."

Kingston perked up. "Like?"

"I found six examples in this footage of image cloning—where the shot of a small group of bodies was pasted repeatedly into distant sections of this group photo of bodies—to inflate the size of the group, to make the mass of victims look larger. It was done smoothly, mind you. Well done. But obviously tampered with."

"If it was that obvious, why did they do it?"

"For the dramatic effect, for one. And also, as both of us know, these images were flashed over web TV sets, and the footage that the Alliance broadcasted had an imbedded no-copy matrix. So viewers only had a short time to view it. And unauthorized possession or examination of Alliance news footage is . . . Well, you know the penalties."

Kingston grinned. He knew he had hit pay dirt. Now that he had begun his own walk with Christ and spent time reading the New Testament, he knew what had really happened to pastor Peter Campbell, his friend in Israel who disappeared with all those others.

The man had spoken to him so many times about Christ and His Second Coming, and the Rapture of His church that would happen before that—before the great and awful Tribulation.

The unbelieving, skeptical world—all of those who had been fed a monstrous and hellish lie about why millions of Jesus followers had suddenly vanished—needed to hear this.

"This is impressive," Kingston said.

"But there is something else," Radameyer continued. "The news report and the raw-footage identification both indicated that these photos were supposedly shot in a grassy field in Canada. But they couldn't have been."

"Why?"

"Look closely here and see if you can see something interesting in this grotesque field of death."

Kingston stared at the screen as Radameyer brought the image of the bodies closer and closer. Until at last Kingston saw it.

"A butterfly. On the chest of one of the corpses."

"Not just any butterfly. I checked it out. It's a Freyer's Purple Emperor. Fairly rare. Found in the former Soviet-bloc countries. Especially Romania. And the grass types in this field match the geological descriptions of the Romanian countryside."

"Romania," Kingston muttered.

"That means something to you?"

Kingston felt a sudden shiver. He shook it off and explained. "A number of years ago, when Alexander Colliquin was rising to power in the United Nations, a story broke through AmeriNews, the news network that I work for now, about Colliquin and about his criminal behavior back when he was a small-time local politician in Romania. The reports were that he had ordered the gassing of a group of Christian villagers who had opposed him. Dr. Radameyer, I believe that's what we're looking at. The victims of Alexander Colliquin. That's why he would have had access to this footage and could provide it to the

Alliance News Network to use it as a lie to explain the disappearance of Christians. What an evil sick-o he is."

Radameyer clicked off his computer. "So, Mr. Kingston, you have my opinions. And as long as I stay put here in the U.S. and this nation doesn't join the Global Alliance, I guess I would have a fighting chance to avoid prosecution under international law for possessing this news footage." He took a minute to stare at the floor. "I suppose you will want me to sign an affidavit, describing my scientific findings?"

"Better than that. I want to videotape you telling the world exactly what you just told me."

Radameyer thought about it for a few seconds. "I've come this far. So I guess I'll do it."

As Kingston reached out and shook the expert's hand, his stomach growled and he thought about dinner. "Can I see if any of the restaurants around here are delivering, even with the riot at Water Tower Place? It'll be my treat."

Radameyer smiled. "There's a great little Italian place, Vini's, only a block from here. I think they'll deliver. Make mine shrimp linguine with marinara."

Kingston nodded. "And while we're having dinner, I've got another question for you."

"I thought I answered them all for you."

"Not this one."

"Shoot," the retired professor said.

"If the footage was fake—and you know that it was—and you know that the official explanation from the Global Alliance about Christians killing themselves in a mass suicide is hogwash, then here is my question to you: How do you explain the vanishing of millions of followers of Jesus? Doesn't all of this prove the accuracy of what the New Testament says? What is written there about Christians being caught up in the clouds with Jesus Christ, in the blink of an eye?"

Radameyer stood up and made his way over to a cabinet drawer to retrieve a menu from Vini's, handing it to Kingston. "You can make your choice for dinner and then call them. The telephone number is on the front." The beginning of a smile broke over his face. "Meanwhile, I'll be thinking about your question."

TWENTY

HONG KONG

Ethan March had found a temporary home in the high-rise pent-house of Zhang Lee, a wealthy real estate broker who had recently come to faith in Christ. Rivka had first connected with him a few months before when she heard about his becoming a Jesus follower, and since then she had held regular Bible studies in his opulent suite. The place was spectacular, full of Yongzheng Dynasty vases and original oil portraits by Wu Zuoren. Now that Ethan was in town, Rivka had arranged for him to stay at Mr. Zhang's place.

It was midday and Ethan was sitting on a small outside porch off the living room. It had a reflective privacy screen around it that would block any snooping drone-bots from spying down on the occupants. Ethan still had a good view of the cluster of skyscrapers and residential towers that surrounded the affluent Asian Crown apartments where Zhang's residence was situated.

His Bible was on his lap, and he had just turned to chapter six of the New Testament book of Ephesians, where he was pondering again the principles of spiritual warfare. He began to read: "Finally, be strong in the Lord and in the strength of His might. Put on the full armor of God, so that you will be able to stand firm against the schemes of the devil."

But then it happened. Without warning, everything in his field of sight fled. And then the vision appeared. The same as before, and yet slightly different this time. Yes, there was the same handsome face that was quickly replaced by the horrible image of the beast. But now it came more into focus. In the visions before, the image had been like an artist's quick rendering, a charcoal sketch of a horrific face that moved and breathed and seemed to be a thing alive. But this time the image morphed into something like a finely wrought oil painting—a detailed portrait of hatred incarnate, with red eyes and a gaping mouth that dripped with the blood of its victims. Judging by the increasing amount of detail now in the image, the time of the fulfillment had to be getting closer.

And there was something else too, reflected within the eyes of the beast. Within those eyes Ethan could see the bodies of his victims strewn everywhere, murdered and martyred. And Ethan knew at that very moment who they were. They were the souls of those who would be slain because of the Word of God, and because of having testified boldly to the world about the saving grace of the God who had delivered His only Son, Jesus Christ, to be a living sacrifice and a ransom for many.

In an instant the vision was gone, just as quickly as it had come. Ethan dropped his head into his hands. He wept for the darkness he knew had come into the world, and for the unrestrained evil that was yet to come.

He felt a gentle hand on his shoulder. Looking up, he wiped the tears from his eyes and saw Rivka watching him with a searching, comforting expression.

"One of your visions?" she asked.

He cleared his throat and pulled himself together. "Not my visions but *His*," he said. "I know God gives them to me for a reason. But I search the Bible and read it and study it, and yet I still don't know why He has decided to deliver these images to me."

For a few minutes Rivka simply stood next to Ethan with her hand on his shoulder, and the two of them silently gazed out over the metropolis of Hong Kong spread out below them. Then she said, "Could any of us really have understood how we'd end up being caught up in the beginning of this? This terrible, last night of the world? The birth pangs of the Tribulation . . . But here we are, you and I." Then she looked Ethan in the eye. "And by the way, Ethan, aren't you the one always quoting your hero, Joshua Jordan? That 'the real choice before us is always simple in the end . . .'"

Ethan finished the sentence. "'The choice between faith and fear.'" He looked out over the city of Hong Kong and out even farther to the harbor and the ocean beyond. Then he added a thought. "And I know what the Bible says—that faith is the substance of things not seen, the evidence of things hoped for. So I have to trust God and His Word, especially about those things not seen, and then do my part in dealing with the things that *are* seen, even if it means I have to witness the world falling into flames and beginning to blow apart."

He suddenly broke out of his dark mood, looking at Rivka with a glint in his eye and flashing a big grin. "But there's something else I need to get off my chest: I really can't understand why I let so much time go by without trying to connect with you. What an idiot I am! So listen carefully. Because I can't tell you how really good it is to have you near me again."

A little chime sounded on Rivka's wrist Allfone watch. She tapped it. "Sorry, but duty calls. Your video conference call is about to start. You should come inside."

□□□

IN THE UTAH DESERT OUTSIDE THE NATIONAL DATA CENTER

Henry Bender, the former New Jersey mob enforcer, didn't like getting his silk suit dirty, but he didn't have much choice as he knelt down in the sand of a ridge about a mile away from the outside perimeter of the U.S. government data complex at Bluffdale. He was looking through a high-powered pair of military-issue binoculars, complete with an internal digital camera. He surveyed the massive series of square, windowless buildings, each of them the size of the buildings at Houston Space Center. Bender was snapping pictures of the buildings, and also of the fully armed guard towers that were mounted every hundred yards along the perimeter of the high razor-wire fences. A road circled the complex, and two armored military Humvees cruised in a slow, routine surveillance around the property.

Dillon Ritzian sat next to him in the sand, swatting flies. "I told you, Henry, this place is well guarded. And I told you about all the stuff you're not even seeing—the infrared cameras they got and all the human-sensing devices planted all around this place. Geez, I'm sure they've already spotted us up here. I'm not really excited about the possibility of having the feds bust me on espionage charges."

"Cool your jets," Bender grumbled. "No one's coming after you. So are the control codes and passwords back in the car?"

"Yeah, in the contractor's notebook I left on the seat. Everything your IT guys will need to access the computer algorithm that randomly changes the daily passwords every couple of hours."

"And so, when my people are finally on the inside of the data center, they can quickly access the entire network? I'm talking Internet, cable, telecommunications, satellite, the whole enchilada?"

"Sure," Ritzian said. "After that they can control everything the U.S. government has linked together here in Utah—their NSA spy satellites, aerospace data, global surveillance, a couple of million facial recognition video cameras throughout the country that are watching us, the tracking of RFD chips imbedded in everything under the sun, all of their Internet scanning surveillance that follows everybody . . ."

"And they can also track everybody's BIDTag laser imprint, right?"

"That's the biggie, sure," Ritzian replied. "Look, whoever controls this place here in the desert is going to control data on every person and their movements and on every person's contact with every other person. You know this could get scary, actually . . ." He scrunched up his face like he'd just thought of a problem that needed to be explained. "But you know, to do that your people have to physically get into the buildings down there." He pointed down to the complex that was the size of a small city. "And the security on the outside of the buildings, hey, it's nothing compared to the stuff I saw in the schematics about the internal security inside the building. There's only one other way to hack into the computer system without actually entering the building—"

But Bender was starting to stand up, and he cut Ritzian off as he did. "You know something, Dillon," he said, brushing the sand off of his suit, "you and your schematics are only a backup that my people may not even need. They really aren't worried about security."

"They're not?"

"Naw, they're not."

"Why not?"

Bender smiled. "Because when the time is right, we're betting that they'll be able to stroll right into that place. And when they do, the doors are gonna swing wide open."

□□□

HONG KONG

On the video screen in Zhang Lee's penthouse, Ethan could see, in several quadrants of the screen, the multiple faces of his compatriots from different posts of the Remnant located in far-flung parts of the world. From Jerusalem there was Rabbi ZG. Chiro Hashimoto and John Galligher were video linking from the Yukon Territory. Two members of the Roundtable were on the call, sitting in the big living room of the Rocky Mountain lodge that had formerly belonged to Joshua and Abigail Jordan: retired senator Alvin Leander and "Fort" Rice, a former Idaho Supreme Court judge who had seen his wife vanish in front of his eyes during the Rapture as they sat together in their Boise home. As the man in charge of the media project of the Roundtable, Bart Kingston, the publisher of AmeriNews, was joining the video feed from his office in New York City, along with his editor-in-chief, Terri Schultz. Pack McHenry, who was video calling from Rome, was online too.

Ethan called on Bart Kingston and asked him to summarize the findings of Dr. Terrance Radameyer. Kingston gave a short overview of his meeting with the video forensics expert in Chicago and then jumped to his conclusions. "He says unequivocally that the Global Alliance media network footage showing an alleged wave of mass Christian suicides was doctored stuff. Every bit of it."

"Did you get him on tape saying that?"

"Of course," Bart said with a chuckle. "I wouldn't be much of a journalist if I didn't."

Alvin Leander had a question. "How do we get this information disseminated to as many people as possible?"

"We're working on a distribution idea," Ethan said. "Sorry to keep you all in the dark about the different moving parts in our plan, but for safety's sake, none of you will know all of the components, just the ones that relate to your sphere of influence. Except for me, of course."

"I just hope," Judge Rice said, "we succeed. Since the Global Alliance has taken over, our ability to counter the worldwide lies has been disheartening. Of course, we still have our AmeriNews information service on the web, until they shut that down too."

But Terri Schultz in New York broke in. "Judge, I still believe that people, when they get the truth, are going to see the light. Bart and I, and the staff here at AmeriNews, are fighting like crazy against the global news conglomerate controlled by the Alliance. Like our founders, I believe that God is in the business of intervening in the destiny of nations. Before it's all over, I think we're going to see God's hand in the mass media business as well."

Ethan was the only one who knew the big picture, and he couldn't afford to jeopardize it by informing others. Not yet, at least. But he couldn't help smiling at Terri's prediction.

Then Pack weighed in from his end. "Six out of the seven members of ICANN's international Internet Club of Seven who hold the fate of the global web in their hands have been assassinated or else have gone missing. Which means that someone is now in possession of six out of the seven smart cards that contain the codes to restart the entire global Internet communications system if it all goes down. There's only one smart card left. And it contains the final part of the code needed to accomplish that."

"Who has that last smart card?" John Galligher asked.

"A guy by the name of Dr. Boris Kasparovich. He used to teach at the Polytechnic Institute in Moscow. But they say he recently retired. Address unknown. I've got Victoria working on tracking his location down."

"Then he's as good as found," Galligher shot back. "Hey, Pack, by the way, it must be nice having a wife who's smarter than her husband."

Pack guffawed loudly at that.

"So, next step," Ethan explained. "Pack will close in on Dr. Kasparovich as soon as he's located, and he'll explain the dilemma he's facing and then offer him personal protection."

"I'm not sure I understand the significance of this bit about restarting the Internet," Kingston chimed in. "To me, it seems to be one of those issues where I say to myself, *So what?*"

"Here's the 'so what,'" Chiro said, jumping in. "Bad guys make the Internet go down. They take it over for malicious purposes and then want to reconfigure it. But to do that, the bad guys need to boot it back up. That's where the seven smart cards come in."

"What kind of malicious purposes are you talking about?" Bart asked.

"Up to now," Chiro explained, "the Global Alliance has merely been using the global technology of the Internet for things like their worldwide broadcasts of the One Movement."

"Yeah," Galligher said, jumping in. "I caught one of the sermons by that Bishop Dibold Kora character. He was saying things like, 'All will be well . . . Peace and security will be yours . . . Enlightenment is on its way.' It reminded me of the messages in my fortune cookie at the Golden Wall Chinese restaurant. By the way, it took Chiro and me forever to finally locate a good Asian takeout place up here in the frozen north."

Galligher switched gears. "Which reminds me, Ethan, about something. I mean no offense to my good buddy Chiro, but exactly how long do I need to serve my jail sentence up here on the outskirts of the Arctic Circle?"

Ethan shook his head. "John, you're an important player. Chiro needs your protection. I have a feeling that some very bad actors are going to want to get to him if they find out where he is. Especially if they figure out how he's built his cyber relay station up there to logjam a worldwide communications takeover."

"Okay," John said, "I read you." He turned to Chiro, who was sitting next to him. "Okay, partner, I guess that means I'll have to continue traveling forty-five miles just to get my General Tso's chicken."

After cracking a joke about Galligher's "deep-fried diet," Kingston returned to his question for Chiro. "I still don't think I have an answer. About these 'malicious purposes' that the Global Alliance has planned for the Internet."

"When they shut it all down," Chiro replied, "then they can boot it up and repurpose it for something very evil. Very sinister."

Kingston nodded. "So the plot thickens . . ."

"How *sinister* are we talking?" Terri asked.

Ethan answered that. "The means to manipulate human behavior. Near absolute power over human life and death."

Everyone paused for a few seconds. Rabbi ZG finally broke the silence. "We know the Word of God. And we know what it has declared about the wickedness of the Babylon that will arise during this time of tribulation on the earth. And we know that it begins with these words: 'The Revelation of Jesus Christ, which God gave him to show his servants what must soon take place.'"

Then the former Orthodox rabbi added, "In your hearing today, friends, I believe the Lord is beginning to fulfill His Word about the despicable sins of the Babylon. We are nearing the end of the world as we know it."

More silence.

Senator Leander spoke up. "Maybe I can't tell what the whole picture is going to look like. I leave that to men wiser than I. And some of them are on this video call. But one thing I can do: I can usually recognize a puzzle piece when it's sitting on the table right in front of me. So, my friends, here is one big piece for us to consider: the word I am getting from my sources on Capitol Hill is that President Hewbright, a great American patriot and a sturdy man of God, is in deep trouble. And I am also told that the news about this will be breaking any minute. And if President Hewbright goes, then

America is certain to be dragged into the Global Alliance. And if that happens . . ." His voice began to break, and he had to stop for a moment in order to collect himself so he could continue. "Then the United States of America, the nation that men and women have given their lives, their fortunes, and their sacred honor to protect, will soon cease to exist."

TWENTY-ONE

U.S. CAPITOL BUILDING

Washington, D.C.

The Speaker of the House of Representatives, a party opponent of President Hewbright's dating back to Hewbright's days in the Senate, was taking big strides into the chambers of the United States Senate. He held a large leather folio to his chest as he was followed by a contingent of congressional supporters.

The sergeant-at-arms of the House stepped in front of him, and the group came to a sudden halt. The Senate chambers with all senators present fell into a dead silence. The House sergeant-at-arms then made an announcement in a voice that boomed through the Senate. "Ladies and gentlemen of the Senate of the United States, the Speaker of the House of Representatives desires to address this honored body."

At the opposite end of those historic chambers, sitting in the high chair of the Senate that belonged to the president pro tem, and situated under the seal of the United States of America, Vice President Darrell Zandibar's face was expressionless. He spoke. "The Senate acknowledges the Speaker's presence and invites him to speak."

The Speaker of the House marched down the aisle until he was in front of the podium in the well of the Senate. He turned to address the members, and his voice began to rise as he spoke, reaching a crescendo of bravado. "The House of Representatives has this day voted to issue articles of impeachment against President Hank Hewbright, and I hold those articles in my hand." At that point the Speaker lifted his arm up to display the big black folio. "We impeach the president for conduct both grievous and illegal. For behavior unbecoming the presidency, for acts that imperil the welfare of America, and for acts of treason in his repeated opposition to the Global Alliance Treaty, which this honorable body—the United States Senate—has openly ratified. We ask this body to commence forthwith the trial of President Hank W. Hewbright on those charges, to convict him of the same, and to speedily and forthrightly remove him from the office of the presidency. And in so doing, to remove the blight on the presidency and to halt the incalculable harm that he has caused to this nation."

After only a moment's pause, Zandibar instructed the Speaker of the House to hand over the folio containing the articles of impeachment to the sergeant-at-arms of the Senate. The Speaker complied.

"Hearing no objections," Zandibar announced rapidly, "this body is adjourned until nine o'clock tomorrow, at which time the Senate trial against President Hank Hewbright will commence."

From the expressions on the faces of the Senate members, even Zandibar's friends and the members of his own party were shocked that he hadn't tried some stalling tactic to delay the trial. Instead, Zandibar hammered his big gavel down on his desk, and the *bang* reverberated through the Senate chambers as he brought an end to the business of the Senate for the day.

□□□

IN A WAREHOUSE IN MOSCOW, RUSSIA

It was a hopeless-looking place—that abandoned warehouse off of Leningradskoye Highway outside of Moscow. The glass had been busted out of the windows, and there was an inch of dust and debris on the concrete floor. When the torture of Dr. Boris Kasparovich first began in that forsaken building, it was quickly followed by the helpless screaming of the victim. The birds nesting on the steel beams in the ceiling began to flutter around, and a few of them took flight.

Vlad Malatov now stood over Dr. Kasparovich, who was still strapped to a metal table. The former cyber warfare professor had been a tough customer, even as a sixty-eight-year-old man. It wasn't surprising. After all, he had been a colonel in the Russian army and a former KGB agent himself.

But in the end Malatov had won, which was inevitable. The Russian assassin and Ultra-Extreme Fight Match champion always considered it much easier to simply kill a man rather than force him to disgorge information. It certainly took less time. But no matter, because he had been successful in getting what he wanted from Kasparovich.

While Malatov tortured his subject, the professor had tried to refocus the conversation, even as his face contracted in pain. "You sound American . . . Are you American?" he grunted through his teeth.

Malatov didn't answer at first.

"I bet you are CIA . . . right?"

Still Malatov didn't answer.

"So . . . you're CIA, then . . . ," Kasparovich said before vaulting into a loud scream as Malatov began breaking his fingers one at a time.

As Kasparovich's eyes started losing focus and it looked like he would pass out, Malatov slapped his face to bring him around. "Yes, that's right," he finally said, answering the professor's question with a lie of his own. "I'm CIA."

Malatov smiled now. He had possession of what he came for. He fingered the little plastic card he had obtained from Kasparovich that contained his part of the Internet start-up code. He slipped the card into a little leather case and put it into his pocket. Now the only thing left for the freelance hitman to do was to wait and watch and listen for the news. Depending on the outcome of the trial in the United States Senate, he might need to arrange a flight to Washington, D.C.

But before any of that, Vlad Malatov had to finish up the bloody task at hand. He studied the battered body of Dr. Kasparovich. The man looked as if he had passed out again. Or maybe he was dead already. Just to make sure, Malatov slipped out his switchblade knife and dug it into the man's arm until the flesh started to pump fresh blood. There was no response from his victim. But the rate of blood-letting told him that the heart was still beating. He put his finger to the other man's jugular and confirmed it. The logical explanation was that he was unconscious.

Not only did Malatov know that the professor had been KGB himself once upon a time, but in fact Kasparovich had actually been at the FSB for a short while when Malatov first started as a new agent in that spy agency. Malatov was a little surprised that Dr. Kasparovich didn't recognize him. But then he realized Kasparovich had retired to the quiet life of a cyber intelligence professor *before* Malatov underwent what a few of his FSB superiors called his "extreme makeover."

Of course Malatov knew that even with his intense pain, the professor could still have been playing a game. On the other hand, when the professor asked Malatov whether he was with the CIA, Malatov had been checking very closely the iris of each of his victim's eyes. There were no visual signs of deception. The questions the Russian professor asked must have been genuine.

So now the time had come. Malatov prepared to thrust his razor-sharp knife deep into the left quadrant of the doctor's chest and puncture the heart. After that he would clean off his knife and strip off his super-thick latex gloves and then make an exit from the scene.

The old cargo warehouse had grown quiet. The birds up in the steel rafters must have either flown out of the place or for some reason grown silent. But something happened that caused Malatov to look up at the sound of the birds above him. In one large flock they fluttered out of their nests on the steel girders and began to soar out of the warehouse through the open cargo door.

Vlad Malatov stood motionless as he listened. Now there was a sound, like feet stepping on gravel—stepping carefully and quietly, but heading nevertheless in the direction of the large cargo door. Malatov clicked his knife closed and dropped it into the pocket of his fatigues. He snapped his rubber gloves off his hands and stuffed them into his other pocket as he began to sprint toward a square opening in the floor that had a bar mounted across it, with a chain that hung down to the basement level below. Fifty feet away from the bottom of the chain, there was a sewer pipe that led away from the building.

□□□

Twenty seconds later Pack McHenry stood in the open cargo door with his Beretta semiautomatic in his hand and pointing into the empty warehouse. Russian FSB agent Pavel Liztokoff was right behind him with a riot shotgun. But Malatov had disappeared.

Pack spotted Dr. Kasparovich strapped down on the table and

raced over to his side. He put his finger to the doctor's neck to see if he was still alive.

But Dr. Kasparovich blinked open his eyes, and even though the pallor of his skin was a ghostly white from the pain, his voice was clear. "Don't waste your time. I'm still here. But please unstrap me. My back and my insides are killing me. I'm not as young as I used to be. And watch my fingers; they're broken, I think."

"Where else are you hurt?" Pack asked.

"I think both lungs are punctured. And my spleen too, maybe."

"We've already called for a medical crew to follow us. They'll be here any moment. Did he get your ICANN Internet card?" Pack asked.

"I am afraid yes," Dr. Kasparovich replied. "And I ended up telling him how to use it."

Pack shrugged. "At least you're alive."

"Thanks to you," he said, grimacing and groaning as Pack and Pavel unstrapped the leather restraints. "I got your encrypted message. But not soon enough. He got to me at my office first."

"Do you have any idea who the man was?" Pavel asked.

"Yes," Dr. Kasparovich replied, gritting his teeth. "I only know *of* him . . . A new recruit at the operations division . . . Russian FSB . . . when I was about to leave . . . Name is . . . Vlad Malatov."

Pack realized the doctor was slipping into unconsciousness and elevated his head slightly as he heard the sound of the EMT vehicle pulling up outside. "The medics are here, Doctor. Hold on."

"Oh," Kasparovich replied with a voice that was suddenly weaker. "I think . . . I . . . pass out . . ."

TWENTY-TWO

HONG KONG

Ethan didn't expect a call so soon from Pack McHenry. But Pack was on the line less than twelve hours after the video conference call. At the time, Ethan was talking with Rivka and Zhang Lee in the living room of his big penthouse. When the call came, Zhang smiled and followed the established protocol and politely left the room.

"We've found Dr. Kasparovich," Pack reported.

"Do you have him in a safe location?"

"In a manner of speaking," Pack replied. "Vicky located his last known address, and with the help of my Russian FSB contact we traced him to the warehouse where he had been taken and worked over pretty bad. He's being cared for in a Moscow hospital under a security detail," Pack explained. "The bad news is that the guy torturing him obtained his ICANN key code card."

"So is there a silver lining in any of this?"

"I think so. We have a fix on the identity of the guy who roughed up Kasparovich."

After Ethan hung up with Pack, he immediately placed a call to a cell number in New Babylon, Iraq. Dr. Iban Adis, a scientist at the digital imagery laboratory of the Global Alliance, answered it on the second ring.

"Hello, Quiet Partner," Ethan announced.

"I am surprised at your call," Adis replied in a hushed voice.

"I know this isn't our prearranged time. But something has come up," Ethan said. "I need to know how things look from your end."

"Not good," Dr. Adis replied. "I think they are entering some kind of final stage in the plan."

"Why do you think so?"

"They're beginning the testing phase. Getting closer to human trials."

Ethan needed the full picture. "What else can you tell me?"

"This much I know," Dr. Adis answered. "First, the computing capacity of what we have here in Iraq at the headquarters is not sufficient to create the kind of massive digital net that the Global Alliance is trying to throw over the entire human race. They would need a much larger system. There are several possibilities for large-capacity computer systems they could access around the world, but I just don't know which one they've chosen. The only person who would know would be our chief here in the digital imaging lab. I'll see what I can find out."

"What kind of computing power are you talking about?"

"Well, as an example, I think something around the range of five exabytes of information represents the sum total of all human information accumulated from the dawn of time until about twenty years ago. That was an estimate at the time from the head of Google. This system that our lab is working on now will have to handle about three thousand exabytes of information all at once. It will contain a veritable catalog of information on every living person on the planet and will be formatted in a way that could target and locate any one particular person at any one time at any place on the planet."

Ethan sank back into the couch in the living room. Sitting next to him, Rivka was studying his sober expression. Ethan now contemplated the magnitude of what Alexander Colliquin must be planning. The whole thing seemed way too big for him. And, it seemed, probably unstoppable. After a moment of silence Ethan directed Dr. Adis, "Tell me more."

"They are bringing in many, many cages. Taking them into the secured inner lab."

"Animals?"

"Chimpanzees. A large number of them."

"So," Ethan said, "it's true after all."

"I am afraid so," Dr. Adis said. His voice had a heaviness to it.

"How long will it take for them to finish the animal testing protocol?"

"They are working around the clock. This project is moving at light speed."

"Months?" Ethan asked hopefully.

"I don't think so," Dr. Adis replied. "More like days, or weeks at the most. This is not like your FDA testing in America, where the goal is to minimize unreasonable risk to citizens. Here it is very different. There is no concern for human safety. The point is just the opposite— achieving human behavioral control, regardless of the risk."

Ethan asked Dr. Adis to keep him posted. Then he ended by saying, "Please stay safe. You are in a very dangerous position where you are. We will be praying for you."

"I will be fine," Dr. Adis said at the other end.

"You are a courageous man. We appreciate your service to the cause of freedom, and for the gospel of Jesus Christ."

"Without the strength I get from Jesus, my Savior," Dr. Adis said, "all of this would be futile."

After Ethan clicked off his cell, Rivka took his hand and squeezed it. "So, from the first call from Pack, it sounds like they got to the seventh man. And they now have his Internet card."

Ethan nodded.

"And from your second call, I take it the Global Alliance is speeding up their project."

"It's behemoth, gigantic," Ethan answered with a weariness to his voice. "I'd like to talk privately to Rabbi ZG soon."

"Anything you can let me in on?"

"Yes. I would like to ask him something: I just wonder whether the End Times situation we're in is better left entirely to God's control."

"I didn't think it was ever out of His control," she said with a smile.

Ethan chuckled at that. It was one of the things he liked about Rivka. She always seemed to be able to shake him out of his uncertainty. "Yes," he said. "Point well taken. But I'm talking about *our* role in this."

"Oh, you mean like lowering Paul down the side of the wall in a basket when his enemies were after him—the incident at Damascus in the book of Acts. *That* kind of thing that we're doing? But instead of one basket for one apostle, we are trying to launch an ark to rescue the entire Jesus Remnant from torture. Isn't that what all of this is about?"

Ethan pondered this. "I get the feeling once in a while that Josh Jordan picked the wrong guy to lead all of this. Maybe God had other plans, someone else in mind."

"I recall Moses had the same complaint," she said slyly.

"I'm no Moses."

"True. He had Aaron at his side."

"Also true," Ethan said. Then he smiled back. "On the other hand, I've got you. And I bet you're a whole lot cuter than Aaron ever was—and a better kickboxer too!"

They both had a laugh. It felt good to loosen up. Finally Ethan said, "We have to find out how the Global Alliance is going to link this global communications system together. Dr. Adis says that the core computer system won't be located in New Babylon. It'll be somewhere else. We need to know exactly where. And the second order of business—we also need to get this meeting with Jo Li underway. Our Jesus Remnant is going to need a buying-and-selling system that is outside the control grid of Colliquin and his Alliance. And it has to be soon."

□□□

SYDNEY, AUSTRALIA

The young Christian mother had her two sons ages four and six in tow with her that day. She stood in front of the small grocery store and looked in the window, calculating her chances. This little shop had been selected because she had heard it would still honor payments made with global CReDO currency accessed the old-fashioned way, from account cards, rather than demanding payment from a BIDTag laser imprint. This was crucial for her, because she had refused to be BIDTagged. It had seemed obvious to her and a few of her friends that the human skin imprints were a precursor to the biblical sign of the Antichrist prophesied in the book of Revelation. Some of her family thought she was crazy for refusing to get it and becoming a nontagger. But she was willing to endure the ridicule.

She entered and strolled through the shop with a plastic basket, picking up milk, breakfast cereal, bread, some lunch meat, and a few other necessities. It had become nearly impossible to survive financially ever since Australia had joined the Global Alliance and had begun to enforce the rule requiring payments and purchases to be made only through the BIDTag process. But she was hoping this store would be an island of refuge.

The mother brought her two children close to her as she laid the basket on the laser scan counter across from the smiling store clerk. The total lit up on a small digital screen.

"G'day," the clerk said greeting her. "Hand, please." He motioned to the BIDTag scanner that hung down over the counter like a curved flashlight. "You'll need to put the back of your hand under there," he added, pointing to the digital lens. "You've done this before, right?"

"To be honest," she said flashing a smile, "I was hoping you'd let me pay with my CReDO card instead."

The man shook his head no.

"Would you happen to be Rudy, the owner of this store?" she asked.

The man shook his head again. "Naw. Rudy's gone. Someone bought him out."

She looked at the small basket of groceries on the counter. Her six-year-old tugged on her shirttails. "Ma, are we going to get some food today?"

"Listen," the clerk said as he looked her up and down, "give me a minute. I'll check on something. Maybe I can help you out." He disappeared into the back room.

For a moment she wondered whether she shouldn't just leave the food on the counter and exit as quickly as she could. She waited for a few minutes, feeling increasingly uneasy.

The clerk popped his head around the corner. "It'll just be a few more minutes. I'm trying to get authorization for the old CReDO payment. Hang on . . ." He disappeared again. Another few minutes passed. Just as she was about to turn and leave, the clerk strolled back in. "Okay. All done. Let me see your CReDO card."

She handed it over. The clerk placed the card under the scanner and there was a little buzz. He looked at the screen on his register. "Hmmm. That's a funny one. It should have worked." He swept the card under the scanner again. It buzzed a second time. "Oh, I know what the problem is. Wow, I'm a regular codger now, aren't I? Hang on . . ." And he ducked into the back room again.

The clerk still had her CReDO card. She was getting restless and decided that as soon as he came back, she would ask for her card, forget about the groceries, and promptly leave the shop with her sons.

After several minutes a *ding* sounded as the shop door opened. She thought it was some customers, but she didn't want to look, so she kept staring ahead at the closed door where the clerk had just disappeared. The feet of the people behind her sounded heavy as they strode up to where she was standing. Her oldest son turned to look.

"Ma, it's police," the six-year-old said.

She wheeled around to see two Global Alliance policemen in light-blue caps standing just inches away. "Ma'am," one of them said. "Have you been imprinted with a lawful BIDTag?"

After a moment's hesitation she said, "I would like to speak to my lawyer, please."

"If you need to," the officer said. "But only after you've been arrested first, on suspicion of violating the international welfare law on personal identification." He clamped a set of thick nylon handcuffs on her wrists while her boys looked on in silent alarm and then burst into tears.

The officer pointed to the cross around her neck. "Are you a member of a Jesus-affiliated group or organization?"

"I am, but so what—" she began to say.

The other officer grabbed her two boys as the children began calling for their mother.

"What are you doing?" she screamed.

"Your children will be placed in the custody of the child welfare center while your case is being heard," they intoned as they began to lead them all away.

By then the shop clerk had returned to his place behind the counter.

He called after the officers, "Hey, am I going to get my reward for turning in a Jesus nontagger?"

"We'll be back to give you the digital code," the officer said over his shoulder as he dragged the mother toward his squad car. "Then you can apply for your debit reward electronically."

TWENTY-THREE

JERUSALEM, ISRAEL

Three Jewish priests—men who could trace their lineage all the way back to the Old Testament priest Zadok—crossed the Western Wall plaza. They strode toward the private entrance to the newly completed temple that loomed above them on the Mount where smoke spiraled up to the sky.

They were easy to spot, dressed in blue-and-white robes with long red sashes and their heads wrapped in white linen turbans. They were on their way to take their turn overseeing the animal sacrifices that had been reinstituted ever since Israel had been granted sole possession of the Temple Mount—part of the bargain struck between Israel's prime minister Sol Bensky and Alexander Colliquin, who had negotiated it on behalf of the United Nations and its successor, the new Global Alliance.

Since then, the temple had been carefully constructed in accordance with every detail the scholars and architects could find about the dimensions and layout of the last Herodian temple; they had scoured everything they could find in the Old Testament and in references contained in the Jewish writings—the Mishnah, Gemara, and Talmud.

On that day, the plaza below the great temple was busy. In the crowd there were a dozen young men who had just finished two straight days of partying in the brothels and the New Amsterdam Marijuana Emporium located just outside the Dung Gate of the Old City area, in the shadow of the temple. The young men eyed the priests and then started taunting them. The biggest one among them shouted, "You guys are really bizarre. And what about animal rights, hey? Maybe we ought to cut you guys up instead of letting you kill goats and sheep. How about that? And maybe set you on fire, man. How'd you like that, huh? Light you up and see if we can get some smoke comin' out of you . . ."

One of the priests, the older one, slowed down to respond, but his partners whispered to him to ignore the harassment. But the priest had to say something. "You young men should know better than to make fun of what the Lord calls holy."

"Oh, so you're holy, right?" another of the young men yelled out, and in an instant the group started striding toward the priests. Now they were within arm's length. A crowd started to form, with others starting to jeer at the priests too.

The two younger priests tugged at the older man's robe. "Come away. Come away and don't speak to them."

But the older priest would not be silenced and pointed his finger at the group of young men, nearly touching the nose of the biggest one. "Beware! Beware!" he cried out.

"Ooooh, we're scared!" one of the young men shouted back at the older priest.

In the growing melee, no one seemed to notice the two bearded men about fifty yards away, dressed in camel-hair robes, one man short and scruffy and the other tall. They quietly observed the events unfolding on the plaza.

The older Jewish priest began to recite something, shouting it in a trembling voice:

> Many nations will pass by this city; and they will say to one another, "Why has the LORD done thus to this great city?" Then they will answer, "Because they forsook the covenant of the LORD their God and bowed down to other gods and served them."

Off to the side, the shorter man in the camel-hair robe said to the other man standing with him, "He quotes from Jeremiah."

"Yes," the taller man responded. "But maybe he should have quoted what comes after: 'Behold the days are coming, declares the LORD, when I will raise up for David a righteous Branch; and He will reign as king and act wisely and do justice and righteousness in the land.'"

Now the group of young men were poking and pushing the three priests as they tried to walk away, continuing to shout at them. "We worship the weed! And we worship the whore. And every pleasure we can find. It's better than your ridiculous God."

The bigger man in the group grabbed the older priest by his sash and yanked on it until the old man tripped and fell. Several of his gang began to kick the priest while he was on the ground.

That was when a squad of Global Alliance police who had been at the far end of the plaza trotted over to the scene. When the young men saw them, they sprinted in the opposite direction. The police ordered the crowd to disperse. The two priests helped the old man up to his feet and brushed off his garments. One of them asked the police, "Aren't you going to pursue those ruffians?"

But the cop shook his head. "We're here to keep the peace. We've told you people several times to create a different entrance for your-selves so you can get up to the temple without disturbing the civilians. They have rights too."

All the while, the two men in the rough-hewn robes watched with countenances like stone. The shorter one finally spoke. "The fathers have abandoned their sons. The young men have rejected the fathers. And this is what results."

The taller man nodded. "Which brings us to this hour. The full-ness of time."

□□□

In Agion House, the prime minister's white stone mansion just off of Balfour Street in the stylish Rehavia District of Jerusalem, Sol Bensky had just finished dinner with his wife, Esther. As the servants cleared the table, both of them waved off the idea of dessert, but Esther asked for chamomile tea and Sol for some plain black coffee.

"You'll be up all night if it's not decaf," Esther said gently.

"I'll be up all night regardless," he replied. "The presence of the Global Alliance controlling us here in Jerusalem has become a night-mare. The Knesset has a number of proposals to counter this drastic stranglehold of the Alliance. I need to review them tonight."

"Who is leading the anti-Alliance movement?"

"Joel Harmon."

"The fighter pilot? The hero from the War of Thunder against the Russian-Arab coalition?"

Sol rolled his eyes. "Everyone says that. Yes, he's a hero. *Was* a hero. But to me he is simply a thorn in my flesh."

"Really, Sol? You think so?"

"A few years ago he had the audacity to bring the American, that Colonel Joshua Jordan, into my office for a meeting. Colonel Jordan ended up insulting me to my face."

"I think I remember that, dear."

"How could you possibly—"

"Didn't he quote from 1 Kings 11:1 in that meeting?"

Sol's face fell, but he waited to reply because the kitchen aide was bringing in his coffee and his wife's tea. When she left, Sol responded in a blistering voice, "Yes, the part about Solomon having many foreign women! Can you imagine the outrage?"

"I believe, dear, that Colonel Jordan was using that as a metaphor."

"I don't care what he was using it for." But a few moments later he asked, "A metaphor for what?"

"Spiritual adultery of Israel. The kind that comes with dalliances with foreign intruders and idolatry and false religions."

Sol grimaced and tossed his napkin on the table. "And you agree with the American, I suppose?"

Esther paused for a long time and took a slow sip from her teacup. She wiped her mouth demurely with her napkin and then answered him. "I heard there was another incident down by the temple today. Three priests were accosted by a group of young toughs who sound like they had been high on pot or liquor or both. I imagine those young men were probably in town to savor the delights of our fine array of sex-trade shops and drug cafés."

"Enough!" he shouted as he rose to his feet and began to head toward his study. "I am not responsible for the decadence and the depravity that has infiltrated Jerusalem."

"Perhaps you're right, my love," his wife said in her soft voice. "But if not, who is?"

TWENTY-FOUR

NEW BABYLON, IRAQ

If it had been under a big top, it would have been the world's biggest three-ring circus. Three separate gatherings were simultaneously taking place in different parts of the one-hundred-square-mile complex of buildings within Iraq that belonged to the Global Alliance. And each of the conclaves had their own ringmaster.

In the case of the geopolitical meeting, Alexander Colliquin held the position of master of ceremonies, seated in his elevated faux throne, overseeing the proceedings while the caucuses took place in different corners of the Alliance's World Parliament. He was monitoring their progress through the use of the touch screen of his wireless control panel that was set into the extra-wide arm of his chair.

There was even a kind of high-wire act taking place, performed by former U.S. president and now temporary regent Jessica Tulrude, who scurried around the hall counting votes, twisting arms, and making deals as the personal envoy of Alexander Colliquin. The global chancellor desperately needed a yes vote on the single motion on the slate for today, and he had tasked Tulrude, his political insider, to get it done.

The motion up for consideration had required the convening of a full assembly of nations. Delegates filled the mammoth curved chambers decorated with three-story-high double Romanesque pillars in each of the four corners. As soon as the caucuses ended, the ten regents from each of the ten global regions would be seated in the inner lighted ring in the well of the chamber; they would be surrounded by the larger concentric circle of the arena, populated by two representatives from each of the nations that constituted their respective region.

The motion to be debated and then voted upon was the draconian set of trade sanctions Colliquin wanted imposed on the United States. The logic behind those drastic measures was simple: it was an attempt to finally bring America to its knees, forcing the current Hewbright administration—or his successor, if he was removed from office by the Senate—to join the rest of the Alliance.

The delegates had been invited to come to New Babylon a day or two early, if they wished, so they could enjoy the theaters or the fashionable sex-trade shops in the entertainment district. Colliquin figured that might soften up some of them. But now it was down to business, and Colliquin had made it quite clear to Jessica Tulrude that she had to do whatever it took to ensure the vote.

It had taken awhile for Tulrude to work on Canada to convince their delegation to vote yes, but in the end it was accomplished. Mexico was already in the bag. Now she was button-holing the senior member of the British contingent, but he was resistant.

"Jessica, you and I have both read the Economic Commission's study," the Brit said. "It's giving a doomsday scenario for the United States if we vote for these kinds of sanctions. Really, the scope of this proposal is breathtaking—banning all trade with America, shutting off imports to its shores, including consumer products and petrol. Their strategic oil reserves could be depleted in a matter of months. The report estimates a collapse of the New York Stock Exchange and the commodities markets in sixty days, probably less. And all this while the president is facing impeachment. Good heavens, it seems clear that internal civil war could break out inside America's shores within months if you push your plan. It's rather ironic, but true, that heartless tyrants like Saddam Hussein are always capable of maintaining control for long periods of time in the face of crippling sanctions. On the other hand, legitimate democracies simply cannot."

"I see that you're just singing the tune that Prime Minister Harrington has scripted for you," Tulrude shot back. "Why don't you tell your man over at 10 Downing Street that he's making some very powerful enemies."

"I'm afraid we're rather firm on this."

Tulrude snapped back, "You just don't get it. Jolly old England is a tiny little island, and in the grand scheme of things you have a small economy and very little prestige left. Nobody cares anymore about your royalty or your past history of empire or your beefeaters in their cute red outfits standing outside Buckingham Palace."

The British delegate smiled and struggled not to smirk. "Actually, Jessica, the beefeaters in the quaint red uniforms are the yeomen of the guard—strictly ceremonial. You've confused them with the—"

"Forget the lecture," she bulleted back. "We want your yes vote today or there will be repercussions."

"The thing about us Brits," he replied in a stronger tone now, "is that we don't take kindly to threats, or to hobnail boots on the back of our necks, for that matter. We didn't take it from Hitler. And we won't take it from you."

There were very few occasions when Jessica Tulrude was at a loss for words. But this was one of them. She stammered for a few seconds, then threw the British delegate a dagger-eyed look that said, *You're a dead man. You just don't know it yet*, and stomped off.

□□□

At that same moment, twenty miles away in the great ballroom of the World Economic Convention headquarters in New Babylon, Colliquin's deputy, Ho Zhu, sat at the head table, feting a banquet for the CEOs of the two thousand largest companies on the globe. Beneath crystal chandeliers they had dined on black truffles, beluga caviar, rare la Bonnette potatoes, and Kobe beef flown in from Hyogo, Japan, while they enjoyed the sounds of a string quartet. The event had singlehandedly cleared out the world's supply of bottled 1959 Chateau Mouton Rothschild.

After dessert was served—imperial caramel gingerbread pyramid—the dignified mood changed. A spotlight at the end of the hall lit up a golden curtain, which opened to the sight of twenty-six-year-old global pop music sensation Gigi Salome, who had poured herself into a sexually suggestive leopard-skin bodysuit for the occasion. Her rock band was behind her, and together they charged into the thumping beat of her number one international hit. The business leaders applauded wildly at the surprise performance.

The usually stern-faced Ho nodded and half smiled. While the music blasted, he turned to his assistant sitting to his right. "Security has verified that all of our guests have tickets? And they have checked identification?"

His assistant nodded. "Yes, sir." Then, as he glanced at the bottles of the world's most expensive champagne flowing into crystal glasses, he added, "And we are sure that none of the media have slipped in."

After Gigi Salome finished her music set, one of five CEOs who had been carefully selected by Ho Zhu's staff to offer a toast rose to his feet and used his knife to tap his water glass next to the little wireless microphone pad on the table in front of him. The crowd of two thousand began to quiet down.

"I propose a toast." he announced. "To Ho Zhu, the finance minister of the Global Alliance, for his leadership in forging our worldwide enterprise coalition. Since the Global Alliance was formed, we have seen a global increase in GDP by almost three percent and unemployment worldwide has decreased by two-and-a-half percent. A modest beginning, perhaps, but hopeful. And I believe the trend will continue and the effects of this temporary financial slowdown will eventually be eradicated."

Cheers broke out across the great hall.

"And, as another reason for a toast to our gracious host, I further expect we will soon learn the World Parliament, which is convening at this very moment, will vote to impose economic sanctions on the United States to bring that nation to its senses so it will finally join our Global Alliance."

There was another round of cheers.

"And lastly, we toast Mr. Ho because we anticipate that the Alliance will soon be able to take control of the massive shale oil deposits that have been discovered in Israel and place them on the international market for global bidding so that the world may benefit from those oil-rich deposits."

The audience reacted with jubilance.

Then he added, "After all, why should the Israelis be allowed to monopolize their shale oil deposits? Israel has had the benefit of an energy windfall ever since their victory over the Russian-Arab coalition. For at least a period of—what has it been, six years or so now—they've been burning those lignostone weapons that the Russians used and then abandoned, along with the unspent nuclear fuel from the Iranian missile that dropped on them but didn't detonate. So the Israelis have been storing those deposits of energy. They don't need the oil as badly as the rest of the world does."

With that, the CEO lifted his glass. "To Mr. Ho Zhu!" he shouted, and following his lead the entire hall of billionaires rose to their feet and raised their glasses to Ho Zhu and to the Global Alliance. "To Ho Zhu! To the Global Alliance!"

□□□

Around the same time, in the very center of New Babylon, Bishop Dibold Kora was conducting an evening meeting of the One Movement Spiritual Council. Seventy other leaders from the world's religions had gathered with him: a few high lamas from the Gelug sect of the Tibetan Buddhists; two shamans from Gabon and the Philippines, respectively; a half-dozen Hindu priests; eighteen Islamic clerics; a scattering of representatives from various occult, New Age, Gnostic, and spiritualist groups; two Oglala medicine men from the Native American tribes and several others from indigenous tribal groups from around the world; and a full contingent of church denominational delegates as well. They were seated around a semicircular conference table with Kora at the head.

Kora announced the single order of business. "The question that brings us together is whether this body should formally petition the Global Alliance Parliament. The request would be for increased enforcement of the public safety regulation they have already passed, which lists the Rapture Jesus followers—including members of the so-called Remnant—as a menace to public safety and welfare. We have all recognized, of course, that their mass suicide cult poses a danger to the physical, mental, and spiritual health of the public. Yet, tragically, it seems that despite existing regulations, their group is growing like an unchecked virus and gaining new converts by the hour. This is a very unsettling signal. We have extended free counseling sessions to these delusional Jesus extremists so they can come to grips with their antisocial, fundamentalist urges, but to no avail. And so we have convened this special session to urge Parliament to take even stronger action to pursue them and squelch their unhealthy influence."

Bishop Kora then turned to Higga Monodostra, who sat to his right, dressed in the black robes of a Wiccan priestess, to offer a hymn of exultation to bless their deliberations. While Monodostra extolled Mother Earth and the harmony of the universe with her arms raised and a beatific expression on her face, Kora glanced down at the screen of his Allfone wrist device. He had just received an insta-memo from Alexander Colliquin.

Full vote in World Parliament taken. Victory. Sanctions against U.S.A. to commence ASAP.

It was excellent news, and Kora smiled at the breakthrough and what it meant for his own ambitions and for the Global Alliance.

TWENTY-FIVE

JERUSALEM, ISRAEL

The voice at the other end of the Global Alliance military satphone was terse. "Should we proceed to an attack point or not? We're awaiting orders. My men are ready. We're about a half kilometer away from the stadium."

The plainclothes Global Alliance detective held his satphone to his ear, peering through one of the entrance gates into Teddy Kollek Stadium to get a better view inside. Another Alliance detective stood next to him with the same view, and he was shaking his head dismally.

The detective snapped back, "How many troops did you say you have?"

"Two hundred and twenty," was the reply at the other end. "How many of these Remnant sympathizers are there in the stadium?"

It was evening and someone had clicked on the stadium lights. But this was no soccer match. In the center of the playing field Rabbi ZG stood on a hastily constructed platform and addressed the crowd on a wireless microphone. The stadium was nearly full as the detective sized up the scene.

"Well," the detective replied dejectedly, "a surprising number of them showed up."

His partner bent over and yelled into the satphone, "It holds about fifty thousand. I'm betting at least forty thousand are here. Maybe more. An assault would be craz—"

But the senior detective threw his partner a dirty look and pulled the phone away. Lowering his voice, he spoke. "This stadium is full. You need more men."

"I'm not sure we can hustle up a larger assault team on short notice. I was told this unauthorized assembly would only be a thousand or two, tops."

"That was the projection. Nothing on the web. No posters. Our intel said it was strictly word of mouth. It looks like someone guessed wrong." After a pause the detective added, "I'm going to put a call in to the base commander. Talk to him myself."

In the stadium, Rabbi ZG had been speaking about the horrors of Babylon, a biblical prophecy he said had now been fulfilled. And about Alexander Colliquin's corrupt rule over Jerusalem and most of the world through the Global Alliance.

"But there is good news tonight!" he shouted. "All who call on the name of the Lord Jesus Christ can be saved. In other words, all who will confess their state of sin and claim the benefits of forgiveness by the blood of Jesus the Christ, who shed it for us on the cruel cross, and all who believe in Him as the One who was raised from the dead according to Scripture, the only true Messiah, the Son of God, the son of David, and the son of Abraham. Scripture tells us that in the latter days God will call out from among you sons and daughters of Israel—from the twelve tribes. One hundred and forty-four thousand valiant ones who, like the apostle Paul of old, will turn the world upside down for Jesus the Messiah. Will you become one of those valiant ones tonight?"

He paused. Then he shouted, "Will you resist the political Babylon?" He recited by memory from Revelation 18:3: "'For all the nations have drunk of the wine of the passion of her immorality, and the kings of the earth have committed acts of immorality with her.' Will you defy the economic Babylon?"

He then finished the verse: "'And the merchants of the earth have become rich by the wealth of her sensuality.' Will you keep yourself clean of the spiritual filth of the religious Babylon?"

Then he shouted to the stone-silent crowd from Revelation chapter 17:

And he carried me away in the Spirit into a wilderness; and I saw a woman sitting on a scarlet beast, full of blasphemous names, having seven heads and ten horns. The woman was clothed in purple and scarlet, and adorned with gold and precious stones and pearls, having in her hand a gold cup full of abominations and of the unclean things of her immorality, and on her forehead a name was written, a mystery, "BABLYON THE GREAT, THE MOTHER OF HARLOTS AND OF THE ABOMINATIONS OF THE EARTH."

Then Rabbi ZG cried out, "God, the Almighty and Supreme Judge, has declared that this monstrous Babylon shall be destroyed. Babylon shall fall by the hand of the Lord." And he shouted out the text from Revelation 18:9–11:

And the kings of the earth, who committed acts of immorality and lived sensuously with her, will weep and lament over her when they see the smoke of her burning, standing at a distance because of the fear of her torment, saying, "Woe, woe, the great city, Babylon, the strong city! For in one hour your judgment has come." And the merchants of the earth weep and mourn over her, because no one buys their cargoes any more.

When the message was finished, tens of thousands in the audience flooded down to the front of the stadium to acknowledge their faith in Jesus the Christ.

Outside the stadium, the detective was waiting for an answer from the other end of his satphone. "Commander . . . Are you still there?"

The voice growled from the other end. "Yes. I'm still here."

"The crowds will disperse soon. Shall I give the order—"

"You mean two hundred and twenty soldiers to confront a crowd of forty—perhaps fifty—thousand?"

The detective started to reply, but the commander cut him off. "No, we will not attack. You miscalculated, Detective. Miserably."

TWENTY-SIX

U.S. SENATE

Washington, D.C.

There was silence in the Senate chambers, broken only by a single polite cough by someone up in the gallery. It was a seminal moment in the proceedings as Chief Justice Straworth considered the issue that was now pending before him. He rocked back and forth in his special, high-backed judicial chair. Before the trial, he'd had the Senate maintenance crew fetch it from the Supreme Court chambers and carry it over to the Senate. By all indications, the trial against President Hewbright under Article II Section 4 of the Constitution—the provision allowing for impeachment and removal of a president for "Treason, Bribery, or other high Crimes and Misdemeanors"—was not destined to be a long one. But Straworth had a penchant for

162

comfort, so he'd demanded his own personal executive chair—the one usually positioned dead center in the line of Supreme Court justices during oral arguments.

Or at least that used to be the lineup before that bizarre day when several justices vanished right before Straworth's eyes in the middle of the Court's Friday conference discussion about pending cases. Some people called it the biblical Rapture. But Straworth refused to let that word pass his lips. He'd even called the FBI into the Court building to do a toxicology sweep in the conference room to see if some terror group had managed to gas everyone with a hallucinogen. The Bureau came up with zero. And when the missing justices never showed up again, a few of the law clerks privately joked about Straworth's suspicions about mind-altering drugs, calling him Chief Justice LSD.

But that hadn't been the only freakish occurrence leading up to this Senate proceeding. Unlike the only other presidential removal trial in recent American history, against William Jefferson Clinton, this trial lacked the polite diplomacy that usually characterized the Senate. A global confederation of nations rising up against America, a crushing economic depression and riots in the streets—those events had helped set the political stage in Washington. The trial in the Senate was bare-knuckle boxing from the very start.

Straworth stopped rocking in his big black chair. He leaned forward, preparing to address Corbit Hibbings, the prosecuting attorney for the House of Representative managers. Hibbings was a Washington trial lawyer and the former solicitor general under former president Jessica Tulrude.

"Mr. Hibbings," he asked, "I need one clarification. It's about the procedural posture of this case. The prosecution has rested its case. The attorney for the president has moved to dismiss these proceedings on the grounds that the evidence has failed to support any Article II Section 4 charges against him. On the other hand, you argue that in these kinds of proceedings the Senate need not prove actual treason or even any specific crime against the president at all, for that matter, in order to vote for conviction and to remove him. But if that is true, then I wouldn't even have to follow the usual procedures that a criminal trial would require. Am I correct?"

Hibbings nodded and came to his feet at counsel's table. "Exactly, Chief Justice Straworth. This is not a criminal trial. Or a civil action either, for that matter. This is a constitutional trial, set out by Article II of the Constitution. As such, we don't have to shoulder the ordinary burden of proof. The motion to dismiss by the defense is sadly misplaced."

Justice Straworth directed his attention to the opposing counsel's table with a scowl and cocked an eyebrow in that direction. "Counsel?"

□□□

Harry Smythe, the privately retained defense counsel for President Hewbright, rose to address that last point. Now seventy-two, the Washington trial lawyer with his familiar shock of white hair had long enjoyed a reputation as a landmark in the D.C. legal establishment. But lately the consensus was that he was too far past his prime to handle a case of this magnitude. And then there was that other matter: the issue of his more recent clientele. There'd been a time when his gold-plated clients were culled from the U.S. Senate or from governors' mansions or even the chambers of a few federal judges accused of malfeasance.

But then he'd taken on the mean-spirited and trumped-up, though politically sensitive, criminal cases that had been brought against Joshua and Abigail Jordan. And even though the ultra-affluent Jordans were multimillionaires, he didn't defend them because they had deep pockets. He agreed to get involved because he knew that the Jessica Tulrude administration had targeted them with a red laser dot on their backs. Harry tried to keep himself at a distance from their powerful Christian zeal, focusing instead on the fact that their activities as real-life heroes and influential private patriots had put them on a collision course with then president Tulrude and her lapdog attorney general. The case against the Jordans was a partisan-tainted sham, and Harry Smythe was jubilant when it finally collapsed under its own weight.

But in Washington, taking sides and drawing lines can come with a heavy price. Harry's vocal criticisms of the Tulrude administration and his championing of the Jordan family created rabid chatter among the local lawyers as they flocked for drinks at the local watering holes just off of Constitution Avenue.

As Harry now stood at the defense counsel's table, he returned Chief Justice Straworth's frigid stare. There was bitter irony in those two men facing each other now. Straworth, a former senator, had been appointed to the Supreme Court by his political crony Jessica Tulrude, the primary persecutor of the Jordans. Now Straworth was judging the legal arguments of Harry, who represented Hank Hewbright—who had defeated Straworth's patron saint, Jessica Tulrude, in her bid for another term as president. The lines could not have been more clearly drawn.

As Harry readied himself to respond to the chief justice, a smile broke over his face. *What is it about Washington, I wonder, where picking the right friends also means you make the wrong enemies?*

Chief Justice Straworth intoned a stern reminder. "Your silence is not a proper reply, Mr. Smythe. Do you intend to respond?"

"I do," Harry replied in a casual tone. "First, I am, Mr. Chief Justice, rather alarmed at the willingness of this august body to forsake any semblance of normal legal process when it comes to this trial. Burden of proof. Standards of evidence. They have seemingly been tossed to the four winds."

Straworth's face flashed with a momentary look of internal combustion, as if he had just bitten into a jalapeño pepper. The chief justice gave every indication that he knew where Harry was aiming his darts. But he held his peace as Harry continued.

"The Senate rules for this proceeding have specifically given you, as presiding chief justice, nearly absolute autonomy in guiding this constitutional process in any direction you chose. Now that, in itself, is a curious thing—a *very* curious thing—considering the way the Senate usually guards its power to govern its own internal procedures. *Jealously* guards its own Senate rules, I might add. Practically clinging to them like an out-of-work lottery winner grasping his winning ticket."

A few stray chuckles echoed across the Senate, but Straworth continued to scowl.

"Now, why, I wonder, would the Senate do such a thing?"

Harry's question hung in the air like a toxin. His point was apparent to every astute Senate watcher in those chambers that day. Straworth was a former senator and a political opponent to Hank Hewbright. The two men sat on opposite aisles in the Senate. Apparently there was only one explanation why Senate Majority Leader Atchison and his bunch would be willing to cede absolute procedural discretion to Straworth, their former Senate colleague and a member of their political party, as presiding chief justice over this impeachment trial. They figured that they could count on him to help scuttle President Hewbright's ship.

"But just as the Senate holds dearly on to its own rules," Harry continued, "I hold on to something too, Mr. Chief Justice. And I hold on to it like, well, a Kansas father might cling to his child when he sees a tornado winding its way toward his farm. What I hold on to is the rule of law and the idea of justice. And the concept that if a president of the United States is going to be kicked out of office under Article II of the Constitution, then his misdeeds had better go to the very core of his fitness for office—rather than some spineless fear on the part of certain partisans that the political judgments of our chief executive won't sufficiently mimic the current climate of opinion in the so-called international community. When our founders forged this Constitution—under a wisdom aided by the divine sovereignty of God, I might add—they feared that external international influences could undermine the integrity of this Republic. Now it appears, in light of these articles of impeachment, that the House of Representatives and perhaps even some members of this Senate body have completely turned that notion clear around—they now fear that the integrity of this Republic may interfere with the international community and that that alone is grounds for removing a sitting president."

"Mr. Smythe," Straworth barked. "This may be the Senate chambers that we're in right now, but I will not tolerate speechmaking. Address the point."

"The point?" Harry called out, his voice ringing through the hall. "It is simply this: the Senate, in an attempt to weld the beams of our noble Republic into the hull of that ill-fated *Titanic* called the Global Alliance, has ratified a document they call a 'treaty,' and they complain that the president has refused to honor it. But that document was no such thing. That so-called treaty was in essence a declaration that would totally dissolve this Union that we call America. And for what? For forty pieces of silver from the Global Alliance treasury, with the Senate acting like some traitorous Judas? Trading our nation's sovereignty for a bowl of stew like Esau of old? Contrary to all of that, President Hewbright simply believes that this devastatingly harmful Global Alliance document *cannot* be magically turned into a true treaty by merely calling it that, much the same way that a man who has been beheaded at the guillotine can't have the damage reversed by someone renaming it 'head and neck surgery.'"

A few explosions of laughter rolled through the chambers. The chief justice reached for his huge gavel and the laughter quickly disappeared.

"Now," Harry continued, "the Senate disagrees with the president.

And that is the Senate's right. So the White House attempted to avert a constitutional crisis over all of this. And the president attempted to appeal that matter to your Court, sir—your Supreme Court—for a decision. But your Court, sir, your Court refuses to hear it. Why? Perhaps because several of its justices—men and women who had placed their faith in the Lord Jesus Christ—happened to disappear that day—"

"Enough!" Straworth bellowed. A second later he added, with a banging of his big gavel, "Your motion to dismiss this case is denied."

Harry nodded.

"Present your case," Straworth ordered.

It was now in the lap of the defense. The court watchers had predicted that Harry's case could consist of an array of law professors, designed to counter the parade of law professors that had already been presented by the prosecution. On the other hand, the betting money had the odds heavily against President Hewbright actually testifying. In Las Vegas the odds sat at five hundred to one.

Harry had one request. "Mr. Chief Justice, I will need a twenty-eight minute recess."

"For what conceivable reason?"

"For the eminently conceivable reason that the *only* witness I will be calling needs at least that long in order to get over here."

That bit of news sent ripples through the chambers.

Straworth was still visibly inflamed. "And why, pray tell, is that?"

"Because, Mr. Chief Justice, that is how long it takes to get out of the White House and over to these Senate chambers. Depending on how fast the president's security motorcade can make it down Pennsylvania Avenue, of course."

TWENTY-SEVEN

NEW BABYLON, IRAQ

The question was important enough that Alexander Colliquin had to repeat it again to his chief of international security. "Mr. Martisse, you're sure about this?"

"Indeed, sir. We've run it up and down our chain of intelligence several times, link by link, just to make certain."

"In Canada, you say?"

"Yes, Chancellor. In the Yukon Territory. We're trying now to get a closer fix on the exact location." Then Martisse added, "It looks like our global reward system is working. This delivery person responded to our public notice about payment for information on suspicious activities or the whereabouts of Remnant facilities."

Colliquin spoke up. "And this facility . . . You think this could be linked to the Remnant?"

"I think it is very possible. The delivery man contacted our public information and reward office. The whistle-blower center. He indicated that, according to the sender's packing slip on the boxes, a tourist hotel in Canada was receiving products from a company he was familiar with. A sophisticated digital and electronics corporation. He said that it looked suspicious for a Yukon tourist hotel to receive shipments from a company that produces military-grade defense monitoring and computing equipment. It turns out that the delivery man had once worked for that company. But after the global depression, he was fired and took on his current job."

"And this snitch, what does he do?"

"He drives a delivery truck now, sir."

"So could this be some kind of electronic listening station—up there in the Yukon Territory?"

"It appears to be. We put a trace on the components to the electronics company that sold them. They told us that the digital telecommunications equipment they have sold to this hotel would compete with the most advanced technology available today."

Colliquin rubbed the solid-gold underside of his large ring, feeling the tiny, perfectly designed scales along the reptilian image. "We have to be careful not to let them know we are coming . . ."

"Yes, Your Excellency. And I have an idea about that."

"Tell me."

"If we bring Global Alliance forces into the area for an all-out assault, that could tip them off in advance. I suggest instead that we use the Canadian authorities to make a casual investigation. That won't raise as much attention."

Colliquin thought on that for a while. "Fine. But watch out for the Canadians. I'm not sure they can be trusted. They were nearly the last ones to join the Alliance. Next to England."

"We do have substantial Global Alliance troops already stationed in Canada," Martisse answered. "So, when the time comes to advance against this electronic listening station of the Remnant up there in the Yukon, if indeed it is one . . ."

Noticing that Alexander Colliquin was gazing off into space, he let his voice trail off. Colliquin's face morphed into a grimace as he said something else, under his breath. "They must know . . . what I am about to do."

"What you are about to do?" Martisse asked. "What do you mean, sir?"

"Nothing," Colliquin snapped. "Get the Canadians on this. But they must be discreet. Don't let them blunder this. Or heads will roll, I swear it."

ooo

VICTORIA HARBOR, HONG KONG

It was evening, and Ethan March and Rivka sat on the third deck of Jo Li's sleek Azimut-Benetti super yacht. Jo himself sat at the varnished mahogany deck table across from them, eating canapés and sipping Dom Perignon White Gold Jeroboam champagne.

"You are sure you don't want a drink?" Jo asked.

Ethan and Rivka shook their heads.

"You know, this is sixty thousand dollars a bottle now," Jo remarked, lifting his glass to study the sparkling lights of the Hong Kong skyline through his champagne. "I remember when it was only forty thousand a bottle. But then, inflation, global recession . . . it wreaks havoc with luxury items."

Ethan smiled. "I wouldn't know about that."

Jo lifted an eyebrow. "Yes. Not many luxuries for you Jesus Remnant-type people?"

"No, not really. But that's okay. The reason I'm here is to find out more about your underground economy and your system of barter and trade."

"I know all about you, Mr. Ethan," Jo said. "You are the disciple of Colonel Jordan."

"Actually," Ethan said, "more like a disciple of Jesus Christ. But I also consider it a compliment to ever be mentioned in the same breath as brave, brilliant men like Joshua Jordan or brave, brilliant women like his wife, Abigail."

"And your people—all of these Jesus people in your group—they are how many now?"

"If you are trying to calculate the potential numbers that would be added to your financial structure, it's millions upon millions who are coming to Christ. And when they do, they quickly realize the devilish direction that the whole Global Alliance is taking, including their BIDTag system. And they wonder why it took them so long to question a world government that electronically marks the human race. Ever since the Rapture, though, people are coming around."

"Okay, so you've got impressive numbers. Which means I can make a decent profit off their transactions." Jo eyed Ethan closely. "Though I've wondered about something, ever since my man Gikas cleared you for this meeting: Why didn't you set up your own underground barter system?"

"We tried. A couple of our very sharp Remnant economists worked on it. But only on paper. They kept running into a practical roadblock."

Jo broke into a grin. "Let me guess: your Remnant people are scattered everywhere. And are being systematically hunted, of course. So you need a buying-and-selling system among your people that is both instantaneous and global. To be one step ahead of the Alliance. That means a digital scheme, which requires the Internet. But the Alliance controls every Internet transaction."

"Except for those inside the United States—the one country that is hanging on by a thread, still refusing to join the Alliance," Ethan added. "Except for those transactions."

"And the ones in my system," Jo added with a smile. "My underground digital economy. As for America, well, that thread is about to break, I hear."

"I would love to know how your system has managed to bypass the heavy hand of the Alliance."

"A magician never reveals his secrets," Jo replied with a laugh. "Didn't Harry Houdini say that? The point is that his tricks worked. And so do mine. I can only tell you that I have managed to exploit a loophole in the Alliance economic control regulations. But you can ask me anything else about my financial masterwork." He gave a sigh of delight as he gestured with arms open wide to take in the expanse of his super yacht and added, "It has obviously served me very well."

Ethan was unimpressed. "I need some assurance that your underground economy is not tied to criminal elements. Drugs, prostitution, money laundering, kidnapping, any of that."

Jo grew solemn and put his champagne glass down along with a half-eaten canapé. "I am a financial wizard. London School of Economics. And also a smart technology fellow. Stanford University. With honors. So I grow weary of that kind of question. This is no illegal money-laundering operation. Not some second-rate Ponzi scheme. Want to know the type of people who buy and sell in my economy? Business people who don't trust this new global government. I can supply you with plenty of testimonials. Others are people who think their rights have been taken away. Some are the doomsday types who keep guns and gasmasks in their basement and grow their own vegetables. Some people join my system because they are afraid. Others just think it's good business."

He abruptly stood. "I will think on our meeting today. And will give some thought to allowing your Jesus Remnant people to join my buy-and-sell economy. I must admit, I admire their courage in not getting BIDTagged. Even if I don't agree with their religion." He reached out his hand to shake with Ethan. "I will let you know my decision."

TWENTY-EIGHT

JERUSALEM, ISRAEL

Micah and his fellow Jesus followers clustered in a corner of the grounds of the Yad Vashem memorial, near the long lane of trees that had been planted through the decades in memory of Jewish heroes and their protectors.

Earlier that day the group had left Rabbi ZG's apartment in the Old City section of Jerusalem. Now they awaited the arrival of a few others—members of the core group, the most trusted members of the Jerusalem Remnant. A few thought holding a Jesus meeting in the open at the Holocaust memorial grounds was risky. On the other hand, some of the secretive places in the old Jewish Quarter were now being regularly raided. Neither the Global Alliance police nor its peacekeeping force that occupied Jerusalem had ever come up there to the memorial. The same went for the Alliance drone-bots. Micah had reliable information that Prime Minister Sol Benksy had negotiated with the Alliance to make that entire area a "no-fly/no-patrol zone."

A few stragglers jogged their way over to join the group. Micah felt his Allfone watch buzz on his wrist. He looked at the square mini-screen and noticed a message icon in the corner. It was from Rabbi ZG. He put his finger to the icon and the message appeared.

Micah, important news. Bishop Dibold Kora is giving another of his global addresses. You can get it on channel 3-Q. Started at 11.

When Micah looked at the time function on his watch, he realized Bishop Kora was already fifteen minutes into his speech. He told everyone to crowd around him as he pulled out his pocket microweb TV and tabbed onto channel 3-Q. Bishop Kora appeared on the screen, a man in his fifties with a head of curly silver hair and a smile that always seemed to be permanently pasted onto his face. He was decked out in his usual ecclesiastical dress—red velvet jacket, black shirt, and baby-blue clerical collar.

Years before, Kora had made huge headlines when he managed to forge an international coalition of the world's religions, getting them behind the Alliance's international treaty on global warming and environmental protection, declaring that the "defense of Mother Earth is the highest spiritual duty." In the wake of all that, he'd created the One Movement.

But few could have foreseen the heavy-handed legal enforcement that would follow, including international takeovers of industries in noncompliance. Even companies in Chicago, Micah's boyhood city, where he and his parents had been living before they ended up moving to Israel. But then, neither Micah nor his family could have imagined the climactic events that would follow their immigration to Israel: an ill-fated invasion of that tiny nation by a Russian-Arab League army. A war that looked impossible for Israel to defend against, until an amazing rescue occurred—an event nonbelieving journalists and pundits tried to ascribe to a mere "cataclysm of nature." That is when Micah and his parents started realizing that something utterly stupendous and supernatural was happening—something of biblical proportions.

Equally miraculous was the disappearance of millions of Christians around the world. And the troubling capitulation of Israel's prime minister to overtures by Alexander Colliquin that resulted in a covenant that promised lasting peace in Israel and Jewish control over the Temple Mount so that a Jewish temple could be built there.

It was all coming true—not only the Old Testament prophecies, but also the ones in the New Testament that Micah and his parents had been secretly studying. Christ as the long-awaited Messiah? By then it was undeniable. Micah couldn't help thinking back on all of that as he studied Bishop Kora, who was wrapping up his address on the little screen.

And so, at long last, it is here. A seminal moment in the history of this planet. A coming together of all the world's religions in a single statement of common faith. And so we have called it "Our Common Faith," a document unifying our belief and settling our former differences. A promise of an end to religious strife, bigotry, and ethnic racism. And an end to fear and mistrust. By this common faith, every one of you can become a spiritual king or queen, a prince or princess, royalty over the destiny of your own soul. Churches, synagogues, mosques, temples, and centers of worship around the world have begun to embrace it. The long journey of man and woman away from the intolerant and barbaric beliefs of the past and those dangerous, prehistoric allegiances to religious texts and books we once thought were inspired, but which in the end have only caused dissension and strife and, yes, even holy wars and bloody crusades of all kinds.

Kora reached out his hands to the unseen billions watching him.

Won't you join me? Join me in rallying your neighbors, your friends, and fellow members of your worship communities? Remember, some of our global citizens are, sadly, still very reluctant to become part of this movement. We respect that. Those who do not feel comfortable with religion are still permitted the full freedom not to join with us. But then, there are also those—the religious zealots, the cultists who preach this dangerous lie against humanity called the Rapture of the Christians—who have sought to conceal the mass suicides and mass murders of their fellow Jesus worshipers. They say they exalt life, yet they embrace death. They say they are enlightened, yet they blindly obey Bible writings from thousands of years ago. Imagine the risk they pose to peace on earth and good will toward mankind. We grant them the right to their freedom of opinion, as delusional as it is. But we do insist that they be exposed to the truth. For, my friends, imagine a world where such deluded persons can receive counseling and help and an opportunity to be healed from their spiritual disability. Please, won't you let us know who they are, so we can provide them with some information and personal help?

Kora's image on the screen was replaced by a web/Allfone address: GlobalAllianceHigherSoulReportCenter@UN.all.txt.

As Micah looked on at the screen and the web address, it was clear to him that the word *report* was not intended to be a noun, but a verb. Kora added a final thought before ending the telecast.

For those of you who care enough to share the identity of someone in this kind of need, you will be blessed with a generous contribution credited directly to your digital CReDO account. This is our way of thanking you and helping you in this time of global economic distress. Thank you. And may the Common God of our Common Creation bless you all. Have a beautiful day.

After Micah clicked off his pocket web TV, he studied the faces of his fellow Jesus Remnant members. He pointed to the screen of his little TV, but was only able to utter three words: "Blasphemies from hell—"

A distant sound stopped him from finishing his sentence. A drone-bot was cruising overhead. An instant later several dozen Global Alliance police charged at them from several directions, their weapons drawn.

Someone cried out, "They'll drag us all to a Jesus Ghetto!"

Micah's mind whirled. Colliquin and his dreaded Alliance must have betrayed Prime Minister Bensky. He turned furtively around, three hundred sixty degrees, looking for a way of escape. But found none. The police were almost within reach.

Then Micah spotted two transport trucks approaching, each with the blue-and-white Global Alliance insignia. The trucks drove quickly down the tree-lined lane toward them and slammed to a stop. Blue-helmeted police surrounded Micah's group as the drivers of the trucks got out and opened up the big double doors of the transport vehicles. It was clear what was going to happen next.

Closing his eyes and lifting his hands, Micah cried out, "Father in heaven, by the blood of Jesus Christ Your Son and through the power of the Holy Spirit and by Your matchless might, protect us this day."

The commander of the Alliance unit stepped forward and called to them loudly with his French accent, "Don't be ridiculous. Stop your silly prayers. Come with us, all of you, and you will not be harmed."

Micah took in the frightful sight: more than thirty armed men in Alliance uniforms, with their weapons poised and aimed. One of Micah's men stepped forward. Micah called out to him, "Don't do it. Our God is faithful."

The commander pointed to Micah and called out an order to the two officers standing next to him. "Arrest him for insurrection. He's a leader."

Two Alliance cops pointed their extended-clip Berettas at Micah's chest as they stepped toward him. That was when Micah felt the presence of something—or someone—brushing past him on either side from the midst of his group. Two men strode toward the Global Alliance police. The hair stood up on the back of Micah's neck as a numinous shiver came over him. There was something unspeakably powerful about these two. One was tall and magisterial, the other short and stocky with a thick neck that was hairy on the backside. Both were bearded and they wore rough robes that looked like they had been woven out of camel hair; the robes were gathered at the waist with coarse rope.

The short man held up his hand, palm out toward the Alliance forces. When he spoke, it was like the roar of a great lion, and the sound of it seemed to have a force that could stop even one of the new high-speed "qwiktrains" in its tracks.

"In the name of the Son, the Holy Lamb of God, the slain One who rose again, and in the name of the Father who is Lord of the universe, I command you: you shall not pass!"

As the stranger in the coarse robe spoke those words, a shimmering wall of fire rose up like a curtain from the ground. It created a barrier between the Alliance police and Micah's group.

The commander screamed for his troops to commence firing. All of the barrels of their guns burst smoke as the troops let go with a volley of gunfire aimed directly at Micah and his Jesus followers. Micah winced, half closing his eyes. He was about to be executed. But when nothing happened, he opened his eyes again. He saw, in the curtain of fire, the bullets hanging in midair, then melting into little globs and falling to the ground.

The short man in the rough-hewn robe wasn't finished. He balled up both of his fists and then in one motion tossed his hands forward, fingers open, toward the squad of slack-jawed Alliance police. The entire group of armed men were lifted up into the air and blasted fifty feet back, where they then landed onto the ground in a tangled human heap as if they had just been dropped to earth by the force of an EF-5 tornado.

The two men in robes turned to face Micah, and the tall one pointed down toward the Old City below, where Rabbi ZG's apartment was. Micah nodded, understanding exactly what was meant even though it had not been spoken in words.

"Yes, I will take you there," he muttered, still numb from what he had just witnessed. He looked over his wide-eyed group, all of them staring in shock and disbelief.

Leading his followers, Micah strode down the hill toward the Old City; as he walked, the curtain of fire continued to surround and protect the entire group of Jesus Remnant followers as the stunned troops on the ground began to regain consciousness.

The two bearded men strode solemnly and silently behind Micah.

It was then that Micah remembered something, and as he did a shivering sense of awe overcame him. He remembered the words of Rabbi ZG and the Bible prophecy he had spoken of. Now Micah was certain of it.

They're here.

TWENTY-NINE

U.S. SENATE

Washington, D.C.

President Hank Hewbright sat in an ornate wingback chair that had been brought into the Senate chambers specifically for his testimony. The chair was positioned on a slightly raised platform so the chief justice could have a clear, unobstructed view of the witness. And the witness could look up and see Chief Justice Straworth.

Hewbright, during the direct examination conducted by attorney Harry Smythe, had given a long and detailed explanation of his decision to issue an executive order to all branches of the military and to every federal department and agency following the Senate's vote ratifying the Global Alliance's so-called treaty. His order directed the Pentagon and those federal agencies to "resist cooperating with both the spirit and the letter of the Global Alliance document that was approved by the Senate, and that wrongly purports to a lawful treaty, and that the Senate wrongly presumed to have been within its jurisdiction and powers to ratify."

Everyone knew the president's reasons and the constitutional and legal basis for his decision. But now, in cross-examination, prosecuting attorney Corbit Hibbings submitted Hewbright to a withering battery of questions, most of them designed to extract admissions from the president that he had full knowledge his decision—even if it was constitutional—to buck the Global Alliance might end up causing the financial collapse of America because of the Alliance's retaliatory worldwide boycott. That he knew his decision might even risk a civil war breaking out in the nation's streets as a result.

"And you," Hibbings called out in a powerful voice, "were willing to place the fate of this nation on an altar of high principles—your personal principles—at the risk of destroying the very nation that you were sworn to protect?"

"These are not just my personal principles," Hewbright replied softly. "They were shared by others."

"Oh, you mean the Founding Fathers, I presume?"

"Yes, every one of them, I believe."

"So your defense here today, in this trial, is that your principles were shared by a small group of men who have been dead for two hundred years, some of whom held slaves and didn't see the benefit in granting the right for women to vote? You mean those men?"

"Not just them," Hewbright replied.

"Then who?" Hibbings boomed out, loud enough that his voice reached the gallery. "By all means, name names, Mr. President."

The president paused. And then he looked to his lawyer, Harry Smythe, who smiled and nodded to his client. Hewbright was ready to answer.

"Here in the Senate there is a procedure—we all know it—called *special orders.* The ability, sometimes late at night, after the regular business of the Senate has been completed, for a senator to place on the congressional record some additional thoughts. Many times those comments are preserved when there is only that single senator present, talking in these chambers, and the audio taping system of course is recording it all."

"We all appreciate your recollections of Senate procedure, Mr. President. But I don't see the relevance—"

But Hewbright kept talking and cut right through. "And there was this one evening—I was a senator back then when it happened—and another senator was talking during special orders. I was standing in the back, and I don't think that senator saw me. Except for the two of us it was an empty Senate chamber. Thinking back to that night, I imagine that man was baring his soul a little because he felt safe to do so, entirely alone with his thoughts. I can't recall the legislative issue he was addressing at the time, but regardless, what that senator said was profoundly true. I made a point of remembering it. He said, 'The government of the people, by the people, and for the people, has one duty above all others: it must preserve the American Republic and the constitutional rule of law upon which it is founded. Because if those foundations be removed, how can our house be saved from ruination?'"

Hewbright continued, "Now I was up in the far corner, listening. That senator and I were from opposite parties. Often locked in bitter disputes. But what he said that night was true and right and it has stayed with me ever since."

Attorney Hibbings sneered. "And we are to believe, Mr. President, that this little tale about that unknown senator has stayed with you all these years and was conveniently retrieved from your memory just in time for your impeachment trial?"

"No, Mr. Hibbings," Hewbright said in a gentle voice. "Not an *unknown* senator, but a very *known* one." And with that, he looked over to the tall judicial chair at the bench above him, and into the eyes of the chief justice sitting in it. "Isn't that right, Mr. Chief Justice? Because those were *your* words spoken that night, back when you were a senator, in these very same Senate chambers."

And with that, Hewbright turned to the hall full of senators and members of the press and citizens up in the gallery. He now asked his own question. "Mr. Chief Justice, and ladies and gentlemen of the Senate, I have to ask myself: How is it, exactly, that we have allowed this nation to sink down to this miserable state of affairs?"

□□□

PARIS, FRANCE

At three in the morning Paris time, the Allfone on the table next to the bed started ringing. Vlad Malatov bolted up from sleep and reached over to tap the Receive icon on the cell.

"Who is this?" Malatov asked.

It was Henry Bender on the other end, calling from New Jersey. "I'm the newsboy. Morning paper."

Malatov glanced at the time function on his Allfone. "Talk."

"The Senate finished deliberating. My contact says they just returned to the Senate chambers and voted."

"And?"

"Failed. Two votes shy of removing Hewbright."

Malatov didn't say anything.

"A little surprising," Bender continued. "They thought it was a done deal. So congratulations, I guess, to you. Sort of like being awarded a government contract, huh?"

On the other end, Bender laughed a little at his own pun, but Malatov gave no response as he sat in bed.

"One more thing," Bender added. "This is a rush-rush deal.

There's a lot riding on this. A lot of moving pieces. My boss says that any delays—"

Malatov clicked off the call and tossed his Allfone down on the table. He stood up and stretched his rock-hard muscles a bit, and then walked over to the window of the hotel room. He had picked that hotel because it was situated within walking distance of the Gare du Nord train station, a quick, low-security mode of transportation to the first of several airports he would take. It would be a circuitous route, but necessary to shake off any snoopers who might be following him.

He looked down to the street where, on the other side, sat a McDonald's sign. The hamburger restaurant stuck out conspicuously from the Parisian architecture.

"Americans," he muttered. And then he smiled.

TH1RTY

WHITE HORSE, YUKON TERRITORY

John Galligher stood on the back porch of the vintage gold rush hotel. Chiro Hashimoto had done a nice job setting it up as a front for a major satellite/Internet control center for the Remnant, but Galligher was restless for the kind of action he was used to as a guy who tracked down terrorists for a living. He was now on a call with Ben Bolling, a former FBI colleague of his. It had taken him awhile to track Ben down.

As the two of them talked, Galligher gazed at the outline of the Golden Horn Mountain, wondering how he had ended up in this northern wilderness, particularly as a former New Yorker.

Bolling was talking. "I don't get the point of this, John. You want to know if I can renew my old connections with the Secret Service?"

"That's it," Galligher answered brightly.

"Why?"

"For the good of the order."

"Any other reason?"

"Saving America."

"Keep going . . ."

"And because Ethan March wants it."

"So this would be something for the Remnant and Joshua Jordan's old Roundtable, right?"

"Yes."

"Why didn't you say that in the first place?"

"I like to spice things up with a little intrigue. You know, surround myself with some veiled mystery."

"I don't have time for much mystery these days," Bolling said. "When I left the Bureau I wanted some predictability to my life. Something my wife wants too. And a little peace and quiet."

"Then I'm afraid you picked the wrong decade to live in. Just look at the world around you, Ben."

"Actually, I'd rather not."

"Okay, I need to tell you that this involves President Hewbright. You saved his butt once upon a time."

"He wasn't the president back then."

"No, just a presidential candidate. Now the stakes are even higher."

"Yeah. And my chances of getting close to a sitting chief executive, especially since I left the FBI, are zero to none. And by the way, that last mission I did for you, I ended up having to spin a whale of a tale to my wife as a cover story. When she found out I hadn't been on a fishing trip, but that I was trying to stop an assassination attempt, she had me sleep on the couch for a month. She told me my marital crime wasn't the fact that I was walking into danger. No, it was the cover-up. It always is."

"Really? A whole month on the couch? Helen, my ex-wife, was never that bad. Even she had a maximum of ten days for me, tops."

"Look, John, I'd love to chat, but I've got things to do."

"Sure, important stuff, I'm sure," Galligher snapped back. "Like letting the cat out and mowing the lawn."

"Actually, John, our old cat died," Ben said with a comic attempt at solemnity. "Puss 'n' Boots was twelve. Thanks for bringing up painful memories." Then he added, "By the way, since leaving the Bureau I've taken up a new hobby: I've begun collecting old battle pieces. Created my own ancient armory. You know, swords, shields, breastplates. English, Spanish, that sort of thing. It keeps me busy."

"Ben, no offense, but I've got a better idea for your spare time. What if I were to tell you that you're being called to play a role in the final chapter of God's master plan for the whole human race?"

"See, that's another thing: I think that I liked you better *before* you got religion and became St. Francis of Assisi. At least back then you didn't sermonize me."

"I only wish I didn't have to," Galligher replied, his voice softening. "But I know what I know. And now I realize the world is in a mess and everything is lining up, just like the Bible said it would. And that Jesus is coming back pretty soon on a big white horse. And that the day after the entire Jordan family and a whole lot of other people got raptured off this planet, I finally got down on my knees and really got down to business with Jesus—and yes, I admit at the time I was crying like a junior high kid—was the smartest day of my life. And for me, that's saying something. Because I was never that smart to begin with."

"Clever, John, using the old 'Aw, shucks, I'm just a dumb old FBI guy' routine."

"You know," Galligher said, "the trouble with being clever, which I guess I'm guilty of, rather than being smart like you are, is that people just chalk my comments up to witty repartee and don't listen. Even when I'm right. Which happens to be the situation in this case. About God, I mean. One of the few things I can claim to really be right about, by the way."

There was silence on the other end for several seconds. Then Ben spoke. "Look, I'll do this much for you. I'll find out who I may know that's still on the Secret Service active list. You're talking about the plainclothes White House detail, right?"

"That's it."

"I'll start making calls. May take me a couple of days," Bolling said.

"How about a day or two, tops?"

Ben Bolling gave an exasperated sigh followed by a little grunt on the other end. "Not sure about that. We'll see. Just don't expect much from me."

After Ben clicked off, Galligher strolled into the lobby of the old hotel. Bobby Robert was manning the check-in desk again.

"Say, Bobby, have you ever had a real customer in this place?"

"Yuh, two."

"Really? How'd that go?"

"One guy complained because the bed was lumpy."

"How about the other?"

"He said it was creepy that he was the only one staying here."

"Great. Well, I'm going upstairs to see Chiro," Galligher announced. He trotted up to Tron Central. As usual, Chiro was immersed in his complex of cables and hard drives. When he noticed Galligher, he rolled his chair around and greeted him. "How was your phone call?"

"Good, I think. But something popped in my head while I was talking."

"What was that?"

"About my ex-wife, Helen. I'm thinking I should probably try to touch base with her once again. You know, keep trying. Even though it's a little like putting my finger in a wall socket."

"That sounds like a good thing to do," Chiro said. "Share the gospel with her, right?"

Galligher gave a quick nod and then said, "Oh, and one other thing. I think we need to stay close to home. No more restaurant runs for Chinese take-out."

Chiro groaned with disappointment. "How come?"

"Nothing I can put my finger on. Just call it an ex-special agent's intuition, that's all. And I've had negative vibes about that express delivery guy—the one who brings those parts you've been ordering. Just a feeling about him. The Alliance is offering a reward for any information on activities of the Remnant. You never know who's after the money."

"Okay," Chiro said. "You're the boss. I wouldn't want this place to get raided. I'm very close to finishing our communications platform. Thanks for thinking about security. For manning the walls for us."

"Sure." Galligher flashed a smile. But inside his head he was thinking about a trip he'd taken once to do some sightseeing at the Alamo. The Texans manned the walls of that place too. The problem was simple math: about two hundred Texans on the inside of a small fort and fifteen hundred Mexican troops on the outside. He started counting up the couple of weapons he had brought with him to the Yukon and thinking about the half a dozen guys at most who were with him there in White Horse. Most of them had never handled a weapon, he was sure, except maybe Bobby Robert.

That's when he decided to change the channel in his head. *Get a hold of yourself, Galligher. Don't start getting paranoid just because the driver from Blazin' Fast Delivery gives us strange looks.*

TH1RTY-ONE

JERUSALEM, ISRAEL

A showdown was coming. The local Remnant members, including Rabbi ZG, all sensed it. The rabbi was thinking about that as he locked the door of his little apartment on an alley off of Misgav Ladakh Street in the old Jewish Quarter. He was lagging behind schedule that morning. The Two Witnesses, as they were now called, were already on their way to the temple area where Global Alliance troops would undoubtedly be waiting for them.

Rabbi ZG, Micah, and a few of the Jerusalem inner circle knew the two men by the code names they used for themselves when in trusted company: Tishbite is what the shorter, stocky one called himself, and Mashah was the name used by the taller one. The rabbi, an astute scholar of the Old Testament, didn't miss that; he had figured out the true identities of the men in the rough, camel hair robes. As he thought about it, it shook him down to the soles of his feet.

But as Rabbi ZG turned the key in his door to lock it, he heard a noise and turned around. Half a dozen Global Alliance police were hustling up the steps toward him. A plainclothes detective was still down on the street level, and he shouted up to him, "You are under arrest, Rabbi. Please do not resist."

"I will not resist—" Rabbi ZG began to reply, but couldn't complete his sentence because the first two Alliance cops in the front of the gang grabbed him and threw him to the ground, binding his wrists behind him.

The detective from the Alliance strolled up the stairs to the porch and bent down in a crouching position to address the rabbi where he lay on his stomach. "I need some information about your two friends."

Rabbi ZG didn't reply.

This time the detective shouted it. "Our sources tell us you are in collaboration with these so-called Two Witnesses. Where are they?"

Rabbi ZG's voice was calm. "If you have eyes to see and ears to hear, your question will be answered soon enough."

The detective stood up quickly. "Enough with the riddles. Take him out of here."

□□□

On the Western Wall plaza, a massive crowd of more than ten thousand milled around. The word had spread through Jerusalem that the two men who had summoned a miraculous wall of fire up at the Yad Vashem memorial were going to appear at the foot of the Temple Mount.

Pockets of protestors appeared too—the Neo-Pagan Association with more than two hundred of its members from their headquarters in the Morasha section of Jerusalem; a couple dozen homosexuals who had come from the Man2Man Love Club on Aba Sikra Street near the Herod family tomb; about five hundred members of the Anti-Colonialist Union for Global Unity who happened to be in town for a conference; a large contingent of local leaders of the One Movement; and assorted activists from animal rights groups and creation worship networks.

No one actually saw the Two Witnesses appear. But when they were spotted, the mob began to spontaneously push and shove back in order to create a space for them, as if a bomb had been discovered.

In the middle of the plaza the Two Witnesses at first stood still. Then they began to walk in tandem, as if in a slow ceremonial dance, in a circle along the outer reach of the space that had been cleared for them. As they walked along, the crowd stumbled backward in a wave.

Then the Two Witnesses stopped in their tracks. Tishbite, the shorter man, spoke first, his voice tough and coarse like the camel hair robe he wore.

As the Lord lives, I am the man of God. And I speak the Word of the Lord. And I speak to you, who are fathers and mothers. You have forsaken the souls of your children. You have allowed them to wander aimlessly. Without truth. You have poisoned them with the lies of the evil one and allowed them to follow after false gods, filthy pleasures, and vile entertainments, craving words that tickle their ears but leave their hearts empty. You have failed to teach them the true meaning of love because you have not taught them that God Himself is the Author of love, having given His Son, Jesus, as a ransom for many. You have failed to teach them truth, for Jesus is the Way and the Truth and the Life, and the Word of God is truth. You love your dogs more than your sons and daughters. Your own children have fallen into the pit and yet you will not rescue them.

And you, the sons and daughters of this generation, you have dishonored and disgraced your fathers and mothers and cursed them to their faces and ridiculed their teachings, and you have played the fool because you have made yourself the measure of all things, and you boast in your own pride of life, not knowing that your measurement is nothing and your pride will come to nothing, and that your golden youth will perish like the grass of the field. Beware—a reckoning is coming. The Christ, the Holy One of God, who is Jesus, is coming again, and He will rule with righteousness when He comes.

So, you fathers and mothers, and you sons and daughters, seek wisdom that can be found in Jesus Christ, the Son of God, the Alpha and the Omega, the First and the Last. You have sinned and fallen from a great height. But there is only One who can catch you. His name is Jesus. The One who died for your sins and rose from the grave victorious in this very city. This same Jesus who is salvation for all who call on His name in faith and who believe that He is the Resurrection and that He gives the waters of eternal life.

Then the taller witness called Mashan began to speak. When he did, even though his voice faltered and there was a strange thickness to his speech, his words burned like a fire, as if his words were spoken from the top of some ancient and holy mountain.

Do not let your hearts be stubborn and hard. I have seen what terrible things can come of a hardened heart. It was true for the pharaoh of Egypt, and it is true for you. Open your hearts to the Word of the Lord while it is still day. For the night is coming fast. And when it comes, the Light will be hard to find. But you shall know that the Lord is God. You may know it, if you seek Him with your whole heart and bow before His Son, Jesus, who is your rightful and eternal King. But if you do not, you shall still know that the Lord is God, but then it shall be by the hard and fearful tests that will be delivered to you.

From outside the plaza came the sound of a voice over the loudspeaker. It was commanding the crowd to disperse. On the outer edge of the pavement, a Global Alliance commander held a wireless microphone to his mouth. In a cold, amplified voice he told the mob they had ten seconds to clear the area.

The crowd started to break apart in a sudden melee, running in every direction. But as the plaza cleared, the Two Witnesses did not move. Standing in the center, they turned slowly to face the commander, who was some two hundred feet away and who had marshalled a hundred and fifty soldiers with automatic weapons to stand behind him. Some of the Alliance soldiers were shaking their heads, nervously looking for some way out of the charge that now seemed inevitable. The commander ordered the Two Witnesses to lay flat on the ground so they could be arrested, telling them that they were guilty of violence against the Alliance and if they resisted, they would be shot.

Mashah cried out to the commander, "Be warned! If you seek to harm us, then by the power of the Living God, you shall see this day the terrible power of His right hand."

The commander turned to his troops. "These men are armed with advanced weaponry. They're dangerous. You will commence firing on the count of three. One . . ."

"This day," Mashah boomed, "your souls shall be required . . ."

"Two . . . ," the commander yelled.

"And you shall know that the Lord is truly God . . ."

"Three!" the commander bellowed. "Commence firing!"

Faced with the order, more than thirty Alliance soldiers dropped their weapons and began to disperse. A dozen more dropped to their knees or covered their faces with their hands in prayer.

But the weapons of the rest of the Alliance troops exploded with a massive volley, aimed at the two men who stood alone in the center of the plaza.

When the smoke cleared, the Two Witnesses were still standing.

Tishbite took a step in the direction of the troops. His voice had the ring of ages past, and it echoed through the plaza. "O Lord, the God of Abraham, Isaac, and Jacob, today let it be known that You are God in Israel, and that we are Your servants, and that we obey Your word. So answer me, O Lord, that this people may know that You, O Lord, are God, and that You desire that the hearts of the people be turned back to You again."

The troops were now charging full speed across the plaza toward the Two Witnesses with orders to fire again. When the soldiers reached a range of deadly accuracy, Tishbite stretched out his hand. The automatic rifles in the first flank of Alliance troops became as hot as molten lava. The soldiers dropped them to the ground and cupped their hands as they screamed in pain. The charge came to a confused, disorganized halt.

The commander yelled again over the loudspeaker for the assault to continue. But now more than half of the soldiers dropped their weapons and ran in all directions. The commander screamed his orders again. Finally the diminished flank of remaining soldiers began to charge once again on the two men.

Tishbite raised his hand up toward heaven. When he did, something appeared way up in the sky. There came a flashing glimmer of red illumination, like a fiery bolt of lightning, followed by a chest-pounding wave of thunder, as if the earth were cracking. Then came a deafening roar as the sky lit up and a funnel of fire appeared and fell down on the advancing military force.

In an instant—less than a second—the small number of remaining Global Alliance troops that were still charging, and the commander as well, were burned into hollow shapes where they stood. A wind from somewhere began to blow across the plaza, and the ashen remains of the soldiers and their commander scattered like dust in the sudden whirlwind.

TH1RTY-TWO

HONG KONG

Ethan had a sense of foreboding that evening as he sat with Rivka on the outside porch of Zhang Lee's high-rise penthouse in Hong Kong. "I've been trying to call Rabbi ZG," he said, "but he's not picking up."

"You wanted to ask him about negotiating with Jo Li?" guessed Rivka.

"Right," Ethan replied. "I'm a little conflicted. On the surface it looks like a good deal for our people. Helping them get the necessities they need in an economic system that keeps everything under radar. Away from Global Alliance surveillance. But I don't know how much I can trust this Jo character."

"Would you like some woman's intuition?"

Ethan laughed. "I thought you weren't into gender stereotypes," he said, teasing her. "After all, you're a kickboxing ex-member of Israel's spy agency."

"And also a woman," she added, "who does happen to believe that God gives some of us women a special sensitivity about people. So, do you want to know what I believe?"

"Sure."

"I think Jo Li was willing to tell you anything you wanted to hear."

"And that's based on what?"

"A gut feeling."

Ethan wasn't convinced. "Maybe Jo's underground Internet economy is God's way of providing for His people in a time of crisis. Like manna from heaven when the Israelites fled out of Egypt. Or the loaves and the fishes."

"Except that God didn't use a criminal in either one of those situations."

"There's no evidence that Jo's a crook."

"The world is in the middle of a global depression. And that guy is cruising around in a fifty-million-dollar yacht. Come on, Ethan . . ."

Ethan couldn't help smiling. There it was again, just one more thing he liked about Rivka: she was willing to challenge him when she thought he needed it. And frankly, Ethan knew he needed it now more than ever. He had been elevated into a position of leadership because Joshua Jordan told everyone that if the Rapture happened first, then Ethan ought to take over the leadership of the Roundtable and spearhead a global resistance against the evil empire he saw rising up. But the weight of that responsibility felt like a three-hundred-pound barbell had been dropped on his shoulders.

Rivka was still waiting. She wasn't going to let it rest. "Okay," she said with a smile, teasing him in return. "Captain, my captain . . . What say you to my last point?"

"What do I say? I guess I'll meditate on it, pray about it, and then . . . well, we'll see."

Before Rivka could respond, Ethan's Allfone vibrated and he picked up the call. Rivka bent down and gave him a peck on the cheek before slipping inside.

The call was from Jimmy Louder. Ethan was glad to hear from him. "How are our people doing in Cyprus?"

"I haven't made it to Cyprus yet."

"Why not?"

"I stopped over in Jerusalem first to check on our group of Jesus followers. That's where I am now. And I'm glad I did. Something's happened to Rabbi ZG."

"Where is he? I've been trying to call him but he isn't picking up."

"The Global Alliance arrested him. They have him at some unidentified location. Ethan, things are really popping over here. The same day as his arrest the Two Witnesses were preaching by the Temple Mount and Alliance troops fired on them. Some of those soldiers were turned into ash when the Witnesses got through with them."

Ethan quickly tried to process what he was hearing.

"I've talked to Micah, ZG's right-hand man in Israel," Jimmy continued. "We decided that someone needs to approach Prime Minister Bensky about this. There's a political guy who Micah thinks has inroads to the PM. The Alliance has been running roughshod over basic human liberties over here. It has to stop. Nobody's safe."

"True enough," Ethan said. "Though I think at this point the question isn't just about safety. It's about courage." He thought about something. "But who am I to lecture you about courage? Sorry about that."

Louder laughed that off with a snort. "Hey, come on, Ethan, are you kidding?"

"Who's your entrée to the prime minister?"

"A member of the Knesset named Joel Harmon."

When he heard that, Ethan brightened. "I know that guy. He

helped Josh and me once when we were in a really tight spot in Israel. A former IAF pilot. Politically connected. Great choice. Keep me posted."

Ethan clicked off the call and gazed out over the Hong Kong skyline, trying to sort out what he had just heard. He stayed there until Zhang Lee poked his head through the door to the porch and announced his personal chef had prepared a fabulous dinner and that it was waiting for them on the table.

Lee, Ethan, and Rivka sat down and enjoyed a fine meal of prawn dumplings, steamed *suimai* with crispy noodles, and a long conversation. Zhang talked about his history in the real estate business and the uncertainty created by the transfer of power that took place when China took the wealthy island back from Great Britain.

Ethan wanted to know Zhang's opinion about something. "Why did China, now a world power, decide to go along with this Global Alliance idea? They joined without a fight. No fuss."

Zhang nodded. "The Chinese are infinitely patient. They've joined, all right. But Beijing is biding its time, waiting for the right moment to make a power play."

Rivka asked him something too, about the transfer of the island back to China. "I had a meeting recently with a former English solicitor here in Hong Kong by the name of Hadley Brooking. He was here on the island when it all happened. Do you know him?"

Zhang thought for a moment. "Doesn't he rent an office over on Hennessy Street?"

She nodded. "That's the one."

"Yes. I actually handled the sale of that office building. Mr. Brooking does some import and export, as I recall."

"Is he reputable?"

"I think so. He runs a consulting business. Why?"

Rivka tossed a quick look over at Ethan, who knew exactly why she had asked it. He smiled back at her.

"Oh," Rivka said, "I was just doing a character check on Mr. Brooking, that's all."

When dinner was finished, Ethan accompanied Rivka down the elevator to the ground floor. He mentioned the Hadley Brooking issue, and Jo Li too. "I like the way you don't give up," he said.

"You mean," she said with a laugh, "that I'm like a dog on a bone regarding this deal you might be working with Jo Li?"

"I wouldn't say that. I just like the way you're committed to our doing the right thing. One of the things I love about you."

She smiled at that. "Well, if it makes you feel any better," she said as they stepped out of the elevator, "it sounds like Hadley Brooking checks out. And even that low-life Chow says Jo is legit. And meanwhile, on my side of the ledger, all that I have against your plan is my female intuition that something's not what it seems."

Ethan walked her through the tower lobby and outside. Hong Kong was a city that didn't sleep, and the place was still very much alive, even then, way after midnight. Cars, taxis, and motorbikes still crowded the street. A few couples strolled past them on the sidewalk, arm in arm. Rivka saw that and smiled.

Ethan remembered something about Jo's underground economy. He stopped and turned to Rivka.

"One thing I learned that's interesting," he said. "Jo Li's system is what he calls a private trading, buying-and-selling club. I asked Judge Rice to do some legal research on that. He called me back and said that Jo's system is exempt from the Alliance financial regulations. The World Parliament apparently left a loophole in the global finance law to grandfather in these so-called private financial clubs. But Jo's was the only one that qualified. Basically, he owns the loophole."

"So what are you thinking?"

"Why hasn't Colliquin closed the loophole? Shut Jo Li down?"

Rivka bobbed her head. "That's something that already hit me. But then I realized that the Alliance is only a few years old. Maybe they just haven't had time to address that one small glitch. Or maybe there's a solid reason for the loophole that we don't know yet."

Ethan shrugged and glanced at the time on his Allfone watch. "Wow, it's late. Why don't I escort you home?"

"Don't bother. I'll be plenty safe." She reached out and squeezed his hand, then pulled herself close to him. "I like you, Ethan. A lot. And it's been terrific having you around. And . . . during that year and a half when I didn't hear anything from you . . . I just wondered if we would ever get together. That was very hard for me."

Ethan could see that she was tearing up. He pulled her closer and gave her a kiss. "I'm sorry about the silence when we were apart. Everything that happened—the whole Jordan family gone in a flash, the whole world getting turned upside down. And me there in Israel, feeling pretty much alone, trying to figure things out by myself."

All of a sudden Ethan felt the urge to say something straight out of his heart. Reckless, perhaps, but in a good way. *This woman is so amazing. Why don't I just pop the question right here? I can look for a ring later. Get down on my knees here on the sidewalk. In front of all the passersby. And ask her . . .*

But he didn't. Instead, he said again, "Hey, you sure you'll be okay?"

She nodded and patted his face with both of her hands. "Good night, Ethan. Sweet dreams."

Making his way back inside, Ethan went directly to his bedroom in Zhang Lee's penthouse and closed the door. As he lay on the bed, he was still thinking about Rivka. He knew that he loved her. *Yes, like crazy. I need to pray about this. But the way I feel about her, I really, really want her to be my wife. And soon. Before life gets in the way again.*

Ethan glanced at the satellite clock on the bedside table. *Never enough time.*

He knew that there was one more thing to do before he could catch some sleep. He turned on the video log from Josh. He had been slowly working his way through it, but he still had about a third of it to go. He was tired. He decided to catch just a few minutes of the log.

On the screen, Joshua looked preoccupied. His face was more worn than Ethan had recalled. Josh was talking about the practical needs of those coming to faith in Christ. And the need to prepare for a particularly terrifying form of tyranny.

For Ethan, that message seemed providential. Josh was quoting the admonition of Jesus that His followers should be as innocent as doves and as wise as serpents.

That serpent reference, Ethan thought, was exactly what he needed to hear. The need to be practical about the ways of the world while still being morally upright. It was a difficult balance, no question about it.

Ethan rubbed his eyes. They burned with fatigue. He was increasingly convinced that he needed to seal the deal with Jo Li while there was still time. And at least that would solve one of the two great burdens he was dealing with: finding a financial system to safely provide for the basic survival needs of his Remnant group of Jesus followers—the millions of them around the world. Those numbers that were growing exponentially.

But the second problem still plagued him as he felt himself drifting off to sleep: Sure, Chiro had created a digital substation tucked away in the wilderness of the Yukon to help counteract Alexander Colliquin's plan for some kind of digital takeover of the world's web communications networks. But even with his Japanese cyber genius helping him, that wouldn't be enough. Alexander Colliquin's audacious technology plan was still too sketchy for Ethan's forces to attack. How did one fight a shadow?

It was clear that it would come down to Dr. Iban Adis, Ethan's inside source at the Alliance's digital imagery laboratory. Adis needed to dig into the engineering details and then slip that information to Ethan.

Finally, Ethan gave himself an order. *Okay, stop the gears in your head. If you don't shut down your brain now, you'll never get any sleep.*

Thankfully, the admonition worked.

TH1RTY-THREE

THE WHITE HOUSE

Washington, D.C.

During that day's press conference, Hank Hewbright's victory in the Senate had been touted by his press secretary as a major vindication of the president's leadership. But privately Hewbright knew that he was wounded prey and the wolves were circling. He had a conversation with William Tatter, his CIA director. That's when he realized his enemies had something even bigger in mind than just his impeachment.

His meeting with Tatter in the Oval Office happened without notice. Tatter showed up without an appointment and told Hewbright's executive secretary he had some urgent information for the president and that it couldn't wait.

"Mr. President," Tatter started out, "I was contacted by a former agency asset. An insider. Someone who has some intelligence information that may shed some light on the plans of the Global Alliance." Tatter spoke plainly. "Does the name Pack McHenry mean anything to you?"

Hewbright shook his head.

"He's our source. He works as a lone ranger now. But he has credible information that there have been a series of coordinated assaults against a small group of seven Internet experts who collectively hold a key code for the world's wireless Internet matrix. I've had our analysts track this. We have verified it ourselves from field reports."

"What do the key codes do?"

"Restart the web in the event of a catastrophic event."

"What kind of event?"

"It could be anything, ranging from a global nuclear war to a geophysical catastrophe that knocks out the world's communications networks. Or perhaps a worldwide cyber attack of unprecedented sophistication. Or maybe something that we haven't thought of yet."

"It sounds ominous, but vague."

"Mr. President," Tatter said, "I'm telling you everything I know. Except for two additional facts. First, Alexander Colliquin is putting huge resources toward some kind of technology development, the details of which are still a little uncertain. From what we can tell, it looks like a wireless communications conduit to reach the four corners of the planet and everything in between."

"And the other thing?"

"He's going to need a titanic amount of computer capacity to achieve that goal. Our IT experts have analyzed that and have identified only a few sites that could come anywhere near that computing power. Qatar Telecom in India. Some of the big networks in Frankfurt and Singapore. But there's one that stands out among all the others."

"I'm waiting with bated breath."

"Our National Data Center in the Utah desert. Right here in the United States."

Hewbright was abrupt. "As long as I'm in the White House, they'll never get access to that site."

"Which is exactly my point, Mr. President. You've survived the political assault in the Senate. But an even deadlier attack may be on the way."

TH1RTY-FOUR

DIGITAL IMAGERY LABORATORY

New Babylon, Iraq

Dr. Iban Adis stood up slowly and glanced across the main hall, trying not to be obvious. All of the lab cubicles were filled, occupied by computer network engineers, digital imagery technologists, electronics physicists, and even neurophysiologists. He could see that at the far end the chief of the section was striding out of his office, and he was in a hurry. He stopped in his tracks and doubled back into his office for a few seconds and then reappeared, walking even faster, this time with a folder in his hand.

Dr. Adis, as a senior researcher, was one of the few who had access to the chief's schedule. He knew his boss was on his way to a meeting down on the first floor with an electronics vendor from Germany.

But Dr. Adis' staff position also gave him access of another kind. He could access the secondary computer in the chief's office, which was situated on a separate desk in the corner, in order to sync data. At first he thought it was a little laughable that his computer had not been networked with instant sync ability, particularly because he was often tasked to coordinate data from very different parts of the project. But then he thought about it and realized the great opportunity to retrieve the computer data that Ethan March needed.

Adis had only been a follower of Jesus for a little more than a year. But he was certain of two things: First, the minute he bowed before Jesus Christ and received Him into his heart by faith just as his precious wife, Farrah, had done a year before that, he realized his life would be in peril, just like Farrah and all of the other Jesus Remnant people. And second, he knew his employment as a senior researcher at the Global Alliance tech lab was no accident of chance. The reality of God's sovereign control of human events excluded that option. From time to time, when his faith flagged and grew weak, he would secretly regret working at the lab. But then he would feel like a coward for having those thoughts. He knew he had to steel himself to the task that God had given to him. No, this was no coincidence. He was in this position, like a Caleb in foreign territory, to be a spy for the people of God.

Adis slowly walked through the labyrinth of cubicles until he neared the chief's office. From the other end of the hall it looked like the chief had left his office door unlocked. Now Adis could see that the door was ajar and the light was still on. He tried to look calm as he opened the door and stepped in. He knew there were video cameras in two corners of the office.

The secondary computer was on and the screen was lit up. Dr. Adis sat down and took one quick side glance through the glass door. No one was outside. He scooted up close to the screen so he would block the cameras from viewing the data he was accessing. He put his finger to the authentication pad and then input his password. Then he gave his name out loud and the screen flashed *Voice command authenticated.*

To sync data as part of his job he usually entered the site labeled *Peering Coordination Data Portal.* But that's not what he wanted now. He was after something much more sensitive than that, but he would have to finagle a back-door entrée to get into the program he really wanted. He touched the icon Deep Properties. Then he configured a false code that suggested a problem with the data portal. The program asked if he wished another source for the same information.

Adis glanced at the glass door and noticed that one of the neuro-physiologists, with a thick file of charts under his arm, was chatting with a colleague. Adis froze in front of the computer screen. Finally the two men went on their way.

He resumed, giving the audible commands, trying to locate the potential site for the lab's global data core. "Locate all scenarios from all files for facilities with maximum exabyte capacity." And another one. "Retrieve universal binary code mandate for all subjects."

He glanced over at the glass door again. The area was still clear. Two menus were on the screen. He gave the verbal order: "Search now." Ten seconds elapsed, but the two searches were still pending. More waiting. Almost sixty seconds.

"Hurry up," he murmured to the screen in front of him. Then two reading panes lit up on the screen. He did some keyword scans. He knew what he was looking for, but he just couldn't find it.

Adis spoke the command for the entire directory. The list of potential digital computing sites under consideration by the Alliance began to cascade down the screen. Opposite each was a computer capacity rating estimate. He went to the biggest number and looked at the name and its location, and then typed it into the insta-memo function of his wrist Allfone.

He closed out that reading pane and then went to the other, an absurdly long string of computer code. He moved his finger to read down the strings of code, then stopped and examined one string in particular. A very short two-digit number followed by a letter of the alphabet. He quickly tapped the three characters into his Allfone, followed by the words *hexadecimal value*. After that, he tapped the words *Binary aka base 2*, followed by ten binary characters.

Lastly, he gave the remaining search term verbally, but tried not to say it too loud, so it was almost a whisper: "Abstract of neuron testing protocol for subject compliance."

The computer spoke back to him. "We are unable to process your audible command. Do you wish to disable audible command system and convert to manual commands?"

Adis knew that would take too much time. He glanced at the time sequence on his Allfone. The chief had been gone fifteen minutes so he had to hurry. He spoke louder. "No." Then he said the command again. Now the screen filled with data, even quicker than he expected. When he read it, he was stunned. In a voice full of astonishment and horror, he found himself muttering out loud to himself, "Sweet Savior, we are nearing the end . . . and how close Your coming must be."

The computer spoke back. "We are unable to process your audible command. Do you wish to disable audible command system and convert to manual commands?"

"No, thank you," he replied. Then he tapped the citation to a Bible verse into his Allfone, followed by the long binary code he had retrieved, and finally hit the encrypted function on his Allfone, directing it to his wife, and hit Send.

There was sound by the door. Dr. Adis swung his chair around, but as he did he tried to poise his right hand over the Delete Search History button on the screen, hoping that his finger had found the right part of the screen, as he looked in the opposite direction to see who was at the door.

It was the chief, with folder in hand. His face was cemented into a look of disdain as he studied Adis. "What are you doing?" he asked loudly.

Adis, with his hand still on the screen, touched what he hoped was the right icon to delete any history of his last computer search. "Well, sir—"

Before he could answer, the chief stepped up to him and shoved him aside, causing his chair to roll away. The chief glared at the screen, which Adis could still see from his position. The history of his actual search had been deleted and the screen now read, *Peering Coordination Data Portal*. It was the usual kind of inquiry Adis was authorized to log into the computer. He exhaled quietly.

"You should get permission from me first before you access the program," the chief said.

"I'm sorry," Adis replied. "But I have accessed it many times without permission . . ."

The chief roared back at him, "Because I was always in the room. That is implied permission. No more access when I am out of the office, is that understood?"

Adis nodded. Then he asked nonchalantly, "How did your meeting go?"

"A waste of precious time. The German rep was unprepared to explain his product details. After a while I sized him up. Undependable. So I cut him short and sent him on his way."

Dr. Adis rose to leave the office, but the chief was blocking the door, and as Adis approached he didn't move out of the way. He kept talking, and as he did he gazed into Adis' face as if he was searching for something, some clue of vulnerability. "You know, I'm a good judge of character. Most scientists lack interpersonal skills. They cannot see deeply into a person. On the other hand, I can." He continued to stare into Adis' face. "The slightest flaw. The hidden secrets. I find them out." A flicker of a smile broke over the chief's face. "But of course, I can also detect the positive things in my staff too."

Adis grinned. "Well then, I hope that bodes well for me in my next salary review."

The chief dropped his smile, and Adis scurried past him and exited the office on the way back to his cubicle.

TH1RTY-F1VE

WHITE HORSE, YUKON TERRITORY

John Galligher happened to be gazing out at the street through the big picture window of the hotel when he noticed the white police vehicle with the RCMP—Royal Canadian Mounted Police—insignia on the door as it pulled up to the curb. There were two officers in white-shirted patrol outfits sitting in the front seat. The officer behind the wheel said something to his partner and then stepped out of the vehicle, snatched his black patrol cap off the dash and donned it, straightened his black bulletproof vest, and, with his hand resting on his sidearm, turned to survey the front of the hotel.

Galligher quickly strode over to the registration desk where Bobby Robert was leaning over a book and whispered, "We've got company. Get Chiro down here immediately and tell him to lock up the cyber stuff."

Bobby Robert tapped a quick text into his Allfone for Chiro and hit Send.

When Galligher wheeled around, the Mountie had entered the lobby and was checking out the place.

"Good day to you," the officer said with a booming voice. "I'm Captain Morganthau. I'd like to talk to the person in charge, aye?"

"He's on his way," Galligher said and strolled up to the officer. He extended his hand to shake. "I'm John Galligher." The Canadian cop just looked at his outreached hand and didn't reciprocate. So Galligher responded with an attempt at lightening the mood. "Yeah, I remember that trick. The old invisible handshake. That's a good one."

Bobby Robert was silently shaking his head.

"I need to speak to the person in charge," the officer announced. "*Immediately.*" This time he sounded a little perturbed.

A voice floated down to the lobby. "I'm right here." Chiro was making his way down the spiral staircase.

The officer pulled a piece of paper from his pocket and glanced down at it. "We've received a request for investigation from the Global Alliance. Need to check this place out."

"That's okay. Very much okay," Chiro said with a tremor in his voice.

Galligher could see that the little computer genius was nervous so he made another stab at jocularity. As he spoke, he motioned over to Bobby Robert with his long, braided hair and then over to his Japanese computer genius friend and then pointed to himself. "So, Officer, did you ever hear the joke about the Indian, the guy from Tokyo, and the Irishman who couldn't lose weight?"

The officer stared at Galligher. At first he said nothing. But after a moment, a smile appeared in the corner of his mouth. "I've heard about the *Odd Couple*. You know, that old movie. So what does that make you guys—the *Strange Trio*?"

John Galligher exploded with a belly laugh. But Chiro and Bobby Robert were still staring like a pair of deer in headlights.

"Hokay," the officer added, "I'd better check this place out. Need to see one of the rooms."

"Which one?" Chiro shot out with a distressed look.

The officer strolled up closer to Chiro. He flashed a relaxed look. "You pick."

Galligher interceded. "Just follow me," he said and grabbed a key off the board next to Bobby Robert. The officer followed him up to the second floor, where he unlocked one of the bedrooms that actually had the look of a place where someone could sleep there for the night.

The officer looked around and nodded to Galligher, who locked the door behind them. They made their way back down the staircase to the lobby, where the officer strolled over to a cabinet that hadn't been dusted. "Looks like you need maid service here," he said as he put his finger down on the top of the cabinet and swiped a swirl in the dust.

As the officer slowly stepped toward the front door, he added something else. "These Global Alliance people are pretty insistent. I don't know how long they're gonna be satisfied with my report. They may end up making a visit here themselves. And if that happens, it won't be the friendly kind, you know what I mean, aye?"

He glanced at each of them, then threw a half wave and disappeared through the front door.

"What was that about?" Chiro asked.

Bobby Robert was shaking his head. "This is not looking good."

But Galligher stepped over to the top of the dusty cabinet. After he studied what was in the dust, he smiled. "On the other hand," he said, "we may have more friends than you think."

He tapped the top of the cabinet where the Mountie had drawn in the dust with his index finger. Clearly outlined was an ichthus, the Christian symbol of the fish.

ооо

KNESSET BUILDING

Jerusalem, Israel

Jimmy Louder and Micah, Rabbi ZG's right-hand man, sat across the desk from Joel Harmon. The member of the Knesset appeared relaxed in his spartan-looking office in the MK chambers building of the legislative complex. Harmon, an ex-fighter pilot who at thirty-nine still had a boyish look about him, seemed cordial, casual, and understanding. They had talked at first about their common connection—Joshua Jordan—and the bond of friendship that had developed between them when Joshua was living in exile in Israel.

But then matters shifted to the subject of the mistreatment of Christians by Alliance forces in Jerusalem and the incident that had just occurred in the shadow of the Temple Mount.

Harmon seemed to be in the clutches of a tough political dilemma. "With the death of a number of Global Alliance troops on the plaza," he said, "this has now escalated to a level that is politically unmanageable."

"And the Jesus Remnant people are being blamed for that?" Jimmy asked.

"Of course!" Harmon shot back. "The Alliance is saying that those so-called Two Witnesses used some kind of stealth weapon. And they're part of your group, aren't they? Preaching the same message? Babylon is calling this an act of war. And considering the fact that Jerusalem is under the international control of the Global Alliance as part of the rotten treaty struck between our PM, Sol Bensky, and Alexander Colliquin, they may actually have a point. Tragically, I'll admit."

"What happens," Micah asked, "when the Lord God sends you two messengers, like the two angels sent to Abraham who were on their way to Sodom and Gomorrah? Their message was pure truth, yet their mission was also a very stern one—and even a scary one. When that happens, Mr. Harmon, isn't it time to choose? Do we stand with the Lord, or against Him?"

Harmon countered, "Micah, first, you're assuming that God has sent these two men. And I'm just Joel, thanks," and there was a flicker of a smile.

"I was there when it happened," Micah said with passion in his throat. "I saw it all. It was fire, falling from the sky. The right arm of God."

Jimmy leaned forward and added something. "Joel, you and I are both pilots. We've both flown combat sorties using the world's most advanced weaponry. We know something about warfare. I've talked to people who were there that day. Witnesses say this was no military weapon. It was a supernatural event, pure and simple. And that leaves only one conclusion."

It was clear to Jimmy that Harmon was trying to be objective, to sort the problem out from a technical standpoint, conducting an event analysis, looking for the technology to explain it—typical aviator approach. He could see it in Harmon's face. But there was always that point, just as there had been in Jimmy's own life, when the laws of physics and science had to open up to something else—the metaphysics of God. When that happened, there was always that profound and awesome choice to be made.

Micah seemed to notice something too. "Joel, you and I are both Jews. The only difference is that I've already met the Messiah. He was here in this city two thousand years ago, but He's coming back. This incident at the plaza was an attack by over two hundred soldiers firing on two unarmed men. By any sane person's definition, the Global Alliance was the one committing a war crime." He paused and added another thought. "I know you are an observant son of Israel. I know you've read the Scriptures. These Two Witnesses . . . Joel, go back to the book of Malachi and read about one of those two men for yourself. And then ask yourself this: Are we rushing headlong toward that great and dreadful day?"

Harmon had a startled look, like a boy who had just realized he'd forgotten his homework assignment. Just as quickly, that look vanished from his face.

"I know your schedule is tight, and we appreciate your meeting with us," Jimmy said, wrapping up the meeting. "Here is why we came to you: we need some legal protection for the followers of Jesus here in Jerusalem. Also, Rabbi ZG has been wrongly arrested. He's done nothing wrong and he needs to be located and released. We were hoping you could bring these matters to the attention of Prime Minister Bensky."

Harmon rose to shake both of their hands, saying he could make no promises but that he would think on it and see if there was anything he could do.

□□□

As soon as they had left, Harmon strode over to his bookshelf and pulled out his copy of the Scriptures. He flipped to Malachi 4:5–6. It had been a long time since he had read it. But he was reading it now, and the full impact of that text became self-evident, so much so that he unconsciously mouthed the words aloud to himself as he read, "Behold, I am going to send you Elijah the prophet before the coming of the great and terrible day of the LORD. He will restore the hearts of the fathers to their children and the hearts of the children to their fathers, so that I will not come and smite the land with a curse."

TH1RTY-S1X

ANIMAL TESTING ROOM #5—DIGITAL IMAGERY LAB

New Babylon, Iraq

Behind the big viewing window in his command station, the lab chief stared at two of the *pan paniscus* species—the bonobo chimpanzees—on the other side of the pane of glass. One was sixteen years old, the other eighteen. They roamed freely in the little room that was furnished with a climbing apparatus, a rope hanging from the ceiling, and a few toys.

The bonobos, rather than common chimpanzees, had intentionally been selected for the experiments. First, they had been supplied en masse and for free, as a gesture of appreciation by the Democratic Republic of the Congo for Alexander Colliquin's help in jump-starting that nation's economy with the Ultra-Extreme Fight Matches and the numerous sex trade and recreational drug resorts. But there was a clinical reason too. The bonobo was an animal with a nearly insatiable desire for sex. Because of that, the research team thought that in its behavior, and perhaps even in some aspect of its brain functioning, this type of chimp was the closest match to twenty-first-century humans.

The test subjects, both males, were numbered 137 and 138. One of them, 137, had been given a BIDTag laser imprint on the back of his right hand, similar to the type administered to nearly all of the world's eight billion inhabitants, but with a few modifications.

At first, the little matrix within the invisible laser imprint on the chimp's hand had contained a QR code typical of the ones used for imprinting and tracking the human race. When it was first devised, the QR coding system for the BIDTag was based on those little black-and-white squares with squiggly lines that had been used for two decades to digitally link people to products on the Internet. But in a later experiment, the chimp's BIDTag code had been altered successfully by a wireless command sent from the chief's remote station behind the glass.

The old QR codes for human BIDTags had always been just a one-dimensional code design. Now test subject 137's BIDTag had been brilliantly converted, remotely, to a three-dimensional digital cube design, still invisible to the naked eye. This new cube configuration increased exponentially the amount of data that could be input into the subject's BIDTag. And a higher data capacity was critical because of the new, high-powered commands that would soon be input into the brains and central nervous systems of human subjects.

In the final phase of the project, every BIDTag of every human could be converted to the newer digital cube design from a remote source—namely, the Global Alliance's tech command center in New Babylon. Of course that was just theoretical at the moment. But once the Alliance's Iraq nerve center was linked to a site with sufficient computing power in another part of the globe, the theory would then become a reality. The Global Alliance satellites roaming the skies and the worldwide wireless technology of the Internet would then be melded into a single dazzling display of surveillance, command, and control over every square inch of the planet, and over all who lived there.

The remote reconfiguring of BIDTags was a major breakthrough. There was no reason why the BIDTags of billions of humans could not also be modified remotely, and over vast distances, in the same way as had been done to chimp 137. Painless and imperceptible, even to the human subjects themselves.

By contrast, test subject 138 had not been given a BIDTag. Amusingly referred to as the "Jesus nontagger" by the Babylon scientists, chimp 138 would be tested today too, but in a different way.

Unlike the other chimp in the experiment, Chimp 137 had been taught three commands in varying degrees. His best trick was to jump. Next best was his ability to climb on command. But he had been insufficiently trained, on purpose, to kneel on command.

The chief touched the Holographic Imagery icon on one of the four screens in front of him. The screen lit up with a map of the chimp room on the other side of the glass. Then he leaned forward to the microphone and spoke the coordinates for the part of the room where he wanted it to happen. Then he calmly said, "Launch image."

On the other side of the glass, in the chimp room, a three-dimensional image appeared in the air before the chimpanzees. Both of them sat, seemingly stunned for a second, slack-jawed. Then they screeched and fled to the far corner of the glass-enclosed room, only to find that the image was already there, waiting for them. They howled again and lunged on all fours to the other side of the room. The image was there again. They both ran to the center of the room, embracing each other in fear.

The lab chief touched the icon for the microphone feed into the room. "One-thirty-seven," he said clearly. "Please jump."

Chimp 137 hesitated.

"Jump," came the command again. This time he obeyed, but his mouth yawed open in a tortured grimace of fear and confusion.

"Now, 137, climb."

Again, hesitation at first, but then a moment later the chimp scampered up the little jungle gym.

The chief waited until 137 climbed down the playground equipment and joined his chimp partner in the middle of the room. Then he gave his third command. "Kneel, 137."

The chimp waved his arms wildly about and began to screech.

"One-thirty-seven, kneel."

But the chimp still did not kneel.

The chief touched an icon on one of the screens that read Disable Subject.

Inside the glass booth, the holographic image hung in the air above the chimp. Then the image blasted a sudden, brilliant flash. The chimp's eyes widened as the electronic impulse that had been laser-beamed to the BIDTag imprint on its hand then jolted the command up to its brain. A monster electrical impulse raced from neuron to neuron along the circuit-like maze of axons in its head and then down through the central nervous system and into the heart, where the stimulus overload seized the monkey's heart as if it had been caught in a factory press and then squeezed until it burst. Chimp 137 convulsed wildly, its eyes bugging out grotesquely as it flopped around on the floor of the glass cage. After a few last, involuntary, heaving movements, it lay still.

The chief was alone, so he was free to roar with celebration on the other side of the glass, clapping his hands and doing a little dance as he saw the fatal beauty of this process, so close to being perfected. Alexander Colliquin would be insanely pleased, he was sure of it. The scientist was certain that a huge promotion and obscene financial rewards would be showered upon him.

After he calmed down, he turned to the computer that would control the command to Subject 138, the chimp with no BIDTag. He touched the Heat Sensor icon and the 3-D image in the glass cage faced 138 and bathed it in an infrared light. The computer screen in front of the chief read *Nontagged* and instantly the *Auto Destruct* command flashed on the screen.

The electronic image in the glass booth blasted a laser beam at the chimp's head. Chimp 138 dropped to the ground for a second, but then screamed and scampered up the jungle gym and continued to caterwaul with teeth bared against the menacing image.

The chief drew his lips up tight and tensed his face, as if he himself endured some kind of invisible, psychic pain. "No, no, no . . . ," he moaned. "Not again . . ."

After a moment he pulled himself together. *Well,* he thought to himself, trying to find some kind of solace. *Until we solve this failure, we can still control the Jesus nontaggers with the drone-bots up in the air and with the droid-bots on the ground. They can still be neutralized the old-fashioned way.* Then he thought on it. And after a while he smiled. *I think I know how to fix this.*

TH1RTY-SEVEN

It took several hours for the chief to correct the flaw in the testing protocol. When it was done, he trudged out of Animal Testing Room #5 and down the hall to his office. He needed to sync his data from the last rounds of tests, so he dumped himself down on the stool in front of the secondary computer in his office and gave the command for *Peering Coordination Data Portal*. The screen lit up.

But first . . . He was fatigued from the long day's testing. And it would have been easy for him not to go the extra step: to retrieve the security data for the surveillance of his office computer. But he was a suspicious man. He couldn't be too careful.

So he made the effort. He typed in the address for the remote keyboard sensing device that he had installed a few weeks ago. Then he entered the last date someone had entered his office—in this case Dr. Iban Adis—along with the time of day that he had encountered Adis, and then entered the command for the audio sensing device that recorded and then translated key taps on his keyboard during the time frame that Adis was in his office. He drummed his fingers impatiently on the desk while his computer program analyzed and then configured the key taps left by Adis. After two minutes, a window appeared on the screen with a full description of all of the computer commands that had been entered by Dr. Adis.

The chief peered at it with astonishment. Then he muttered a single word in a guttural voice of disgust: "Traitor."

There was a cancer in the building, and he would have it removed swiftly and mercilessly. The chief spoke into his emergency console. "Security, immediately to the office of the chief of the digital imagery lab."

A voice in his console responded. "What level, sir?"

"Red alert. And come armed." He then strode out into the main room full of cubicles. Even though it was evening, the staff was buried in their work. He strolled very slowly down the aisle, glancing into the cubicles on each side. He kept walking until he came to Dr. Iban Adis, who was in the process of packing up for the night. "Hello, Dr. Adis," he said blandly.

"Good evening, sir," Adis replied. "I was just heading home." Then he added, "My wife has dinner waiting for me, I think."

"That's nice," the chief said. Suddenly there was the sound of heavy footsteps as a dozen armed security guards burst into the far end of the hall. "I'm sorry that you won't be able to enjoy it."

ㅁㅁㅁ

HONG KONG

Ethan March had planned on having Rivka go with him to the wrap-up with Jo Li. But at the last minute she was called to an urgent meeting with the doctor for her young ward, Meifeng. The former teen prostitute was suddenly showing an unexpected adverse reaction to her withdrawal from a designer cocaine mix Chow had gotten her hooked on. Ethan was impressed by Rivka's devotion to Meifeng: hard-line when the girl needed it, but always passionate about what was best for her. But more than that, Ethan kept thinking what a great wife she would make—tough and direct and amazingly resilient, yet tender and with a heart bursting with a love for God and totally sold out to the same mission that had enveloped Ethan.

As he thought about the dangers ahead, Ethan also knew that he couldn't imagine facing all of that without Rivka. Even with all of the ins and outs between them over the years, Ethan had slowly, but deeply, fallen head over heels for her. True, they didn't always agree on everything. Ethan had to smile when he thought about how the two of them viewed the possible deal with Jo Li so differently. Rivka had had lingering doubts. But Ethan had already resolved all of his.

As Ethan walked alone into the Hennessy Street office building where Hadley Brooking's office was located, he figured that it might even be for the best that Rivka was not there to toss cold water on it; after all, it was the only strategy that could provide financial sustenance for members of the Jesus Remnant as they followed Christ in a dangerous world and waited for His return.

When Ethan stepped into the little lobby of Brooking's office, the Englishman was waiting for him. Brooking shook his hand firmly and with a broad smile invited him into his inner office. Jo Li was already there, seated.

Ethan sat down next to Jo, and Brooking took his seat in his high-back chair behind his desk.

"Gentlemen," Brooking announced, "I think we all know why we are here. Mr. Jo, perhaps you can begin."

Jo Li started talking. But what he said right out of the gate was a little strange. "As I sat here waiting for you, I asked myself a question, Mr. Ethan March. The question was this: Should I describe my financial system to Mr. March or not? But I decided, yes, that I would."

Ethan didn't reply to that. Not yet. He needed to hear more from Jo and figure out where he was heading after his bizarre opening comment.

"So," Jo said, "here is the basic structure: you go to a certain website and enter a password. Your screen will say that the site is no longer in existence. You repeat the password again but with two additional characters on the login and that takes you to the first portal. That first password changes daily and we let you know what it is via a secure, encrypted site. When you're through the first portal, you enter your own private password. You have to change yours every five days. Once you're in, you can access your credit account. It's like a cyber bank account.

"Every time you do business with another member of our system—let's say you buy something from that person—your account is hit and the value that you've agreed to pay gets deducted and credited to the other person's account. There is also another private account that you can log into so you can locate other members of my underground system—or my 'private investment club,' as my lawyers call it. That's so we can qualify for the Global Alliance loophole. As long as you deal with members of the club, it all stays in my system, and it all stays private. Away from the eyes of the Global Alliance."

"A rather brilliant concept—" Brooking began to say.

But he was interrupted by a surprisingly rude Jo, who said to Ethan, "The only reason I've even told you this much is because I am proud of what I have achieved. But I am afraid that this private financial market of mine is something that neither you, nor your religious band, will ever be using."

As a black-ops pilot, Ethan knew an incoming missile when he saw one. One time a heat-seeker had hit his wing and downed him in

Syria, and he'd had to survive for three days on the ground, ducking the Muslim Brotherhood.

This comment from Jo was a missile of a different kind, but just as deadly. As he sat there in Brooking's quietly civilized office with English landscapes on the walls and brass lamps on the end tables, he visualized the incoming missile blip on his screen and he heard the heart-throbbing sound of the warning bell.

Ethan was on his feet in an instant. He said to a smirking Jo Li, "Time for me to bail out on this."

"Bail out?" Jo remarked with amusement. "Yes, of course. You were an American pilot. But you've forgotten something, Mr. March."

Ethan was already at the door to Brooking's inner office, ready to open it, when Jo finished his thought. "You are jumping without a parachute." Then Jo Li chuckled.

Ignoring him, Ethan swung the door open. Six members of a Global Alliance SWAT team stood in the lobby waiting for him. The first two lunged at him and tried to wrestle him down to the ground, but he tossed them off and tried to bolt through the rest of them, like a fullback, in the direction of the outer door. It took all six of the commandoes to force him down to the ground. They manacled his wrists behind him with computer code-secured, kryptonite handcuffs.

The team leader stepped over to Jo Li.

"My superiors at the Alliance HQ in Babylon send their warmest appreciation," he said. "Your help with capturing the ringleader of the Jesus Remnant won't be forgotten."

Jo strode over to the SWAT leader. "I don't care about 'appreciation.' What I want now is my meeting with Alexander Colliquin. As agreed. ASAP. It's called quid pro quo, by the way. In business, as well as politics, that's what it's called."

TH1RTY-E1GHT

UNION STATION

Washington, D.C.

The white marble train station held more D.C. police than usual. The clashes on the Mall and near the Reflecting Pool were still continuing between police and anti-Hewbright activists who were enraged that he had not been removed from office. The violence was now spilling beyond the edges of Capitol Hill.

That posed a challenge for Henry Bender. He had picked Union Station as the meeting place before the riots. Bender had a manila envelope containing a Civil War calendar tucked under his arm as he strolled down the aisle that cut between the waiting area for train passengers and the food and magazine kiosks. He saw that most of the cops were positioned in the huge main entrance hall of the railway station, facing the flags outside and the cab stand and the circle drive;

he assumed that they expected protestors to start pouring in from the outside. So Bender sent a quiktext to the Allfone of his contact, to let him know where they would meet.

He made his way to the buffet-style Italian joint on the other side of the train station. He grabbed a tray and picked out some stromboli on two plates and two sodas, and after paying for it, brushed through the crowd until he found the perfect table against the wall. He knew where the surveillance cameras were located in the train station, and none of them were focused on this spot.

He started eating. He was hungry and he was tempted to devour his contact's stromboli too, except that he thought better of it when he remembered how dangerous the other guy was.

Bender turned to look over the customers in the room and spotted him. The other man strolled through the crowd, stopping just beyond the buffet line. Bender didn't wave; he knew this man would already have researched him and would know who he was looking for. Bender was right.

Vlad Malatov was dressed in a dark-blue suit, white shirt, and tie, and he had a nice, close shave and a short haircut, almost military length. He spotted Bender and made his way through the tables with a relaxed smile, then sat down opposite him. Bender put the manila envelope in the middle of the table.

"Inside this envelope there is a large calendar. Stuck in between the months of November and December, you will find your credentials and badge and your transfer papers documenting your reassignment from the Miami Secret Service office to the Washington office, White House detail. No questions will be asked."

As Bender studied Malatov's face he suddenly realized that the man had taken the pains to get a good Florida-looking tan. A nice touch.

Bender glanced at the picture on the transfer papers and then looked at Malatov's face. "Whoever did your face reconstruction deserves a medal. You're a dead ringer for that Miami agent. Too bad he went missing today on his way up here to start his White House gig." He chuckled. But after a moment's reflection he asked, "So, just curious—why did Moscow pick that particular Miami agent all those years ago to be your, you know, your *facemate*?"

Malatov narrowed his eyes. Bender quickly realized it was a stupid question. Former Russian FSB agents didn't share shoptalk with civilians. Whatever the scheme had been back then to substitute this Russian for the Miami agent so many years ago, it had been abandoned. But no matter. It proved to be a beautifully useful piece in the plan today.

Bender kept talking. "Anyway, there should be no questions asked. The Secret Service has about three thousand five hundred agents. Unlike the other law enforcement agencies of the feds—FBI, ATF, Border Patrol—the Secret Service moves their agents around like they're on a shuffleboard. So your 'reassignment' won't look weird when you show up."

There was a questioning look on Malatov's face.

Bender added, "Plus, we've got an inside contact. You'll know him after you check in at the gate. I can't tell you who he is, because I don't know. All I know is that when he meets you for the first time he's gonna say something to you about deep-sea diving for buried treasure—some sunken Spanish ship off the Florida Keys."

There was a slow nod from Malatov.

"Oh, and one more thing," Bender said. "You had better time your first show-up at the White House pretty closely. I don't mean to tell you your business . . ." When he said that, Malatov's eyes flashed and Bender leaned back a bit in his plastic chair. "Look, I'm just saying, you're not gonna have a very big window of time between your initial show-up and the business you've got to get done."

Bender forked a last bite of stromboli into his mouth, washed it down with a gulp of Diet Coke, and then grabbed his Styrofoam plate and cup and stood up. "Good-bye, Agent Ted Booth," he said and then dumped his trash in a wastebasket and disappeared into the crowds.

□□□

Vlad Malatov's face tensed slightly at the mention of his new name, Booth. But it was too late now. He hadn't been part of the decision years before in Moscow to reconstruct him to look like a guy by that name who was a Miami field agent for the Secret Service. If it had been up to Malatov, he never would have picked it, considering the fact that President Abraham Lincoln had been fatally shot in the head right there in Washington, D.C., by a guy with that same last name.

□□□

Rivka had finished with Meifeng's doctor visit and the two of them had just arrived back at Rivka's Hong Kong flat when her Allfone rang. She was expecting a call from Ethan about now, but when she looked at the caller ID she saw the photo of Hadley Brooking flashing on the little screen. When she picked up, Brooking sounded flustered and rushed. He said that he was calling about Ethan, and that something had happened at the meeting with Jo Li and they needed to meet immediately, but he couldn't go into it on the phone.

Rivka's natural impulse was to demand answers about Ethan. She already had a sinking feeling. But her intelligence training kicked in. *Not over an Allfone call.* She suggested a little Cantonese café that she trusted. But Brooking said no, that he wanted to meet her down by the harbor, at the Clock Tower at the tip of the Kowloon Peninsula in the Tsim Sha Tsui section of town.

She balked for a moment. She hadn't trusted Brooking from the beginning, and now he wanted her to come alone to an area near the public pier at Victoria Harbor. She knew that Jo Li's super yacht had been anchored in that same harbor. Some disturbing scenarios raced through her head. But the worst one of all was the desperate feeling that something terrible had happened to Ethan.

Faced with no other choice, she told Brooking that she would be there, but when they met, he had to be forthright about absolutely everything he knew.

An hour later Rivka stood alone at the base of the Clock Tower that looked like an old brick lighthouse. There at the edge of the harbor, the night air was turning suddenly cool. A shiver ran down her back. She was in mid-prayer about Ethan and his safety when Hadley Brooking showed up, looking distracted and burdened.

"Over here," he said, motioning to the other side of the Clock Tower, away from a few locals who milled around.

"Where is Ethan?" Rivka barked. "What happened?"

"I had nothing to do with it," Hadley Brooking said. "You have to believe me."

"What happened in that meeting?" she demanded, her voice cracking.

"Jo Li was there. I was there. Ethan arrived. Before the meeting I was simply told by one of Jo's assistants that they wanted to cut some deal and wanted it to happen in my office. So I agreed. The next thing I know, a gang of Global Alliance soldiers showed up in the lobby, and they grabbed Ethan. He put up a fight, but they subdued him and put him in handcuffs and hauled him off. I think his injuries were only minor."

"Who called the Alliance forces?"

"I have no idea. It wasn't me," Brooking insisted.

"Why should I believe you?" she cried. "Why? And why did they let you go?"

Hadley Brooking looked her straight in the eye. "There are things about me that I can't explain yet. Let's just say that I wear many hats, and different people believe I may be valuable for different things. But you can trust me because I am here, meeting with you. Telling you this. And because, dear girl, I came alone." He took a quick look around and added, "And I am at risk right now even being here with you."

Rivka stared into his face. Looking for signs of deception. But Brooking saw that too. "You're searching my face," he said with a smile. "Dilation of my pupils, contraction of my facial muscles. To see if I am lying. Yes, I know all the techniques."

Suddenly, Rivka found herself reassessing her impression of Hadley Brooking as he continued talking. "There is a great deal that I simply cannot tell you about myself, Rivka. Just as you cannot tell me, either, about your years in the Israeli Mossad. I've done things . . . deliberately led men down the primrose path to their death. Some deserved it. Some did not. I mastered the art of calm, unperturbed betrayal. I've done extraordinarily deceptive things, and I am plagued with the realization every day that I will have to settle accounts with God over those. But you must believe me when I say this: betraying Ethan March is not one of them."

"Where did they take him?"

"I'm not entirely sure."

"You must have some idea."

"I heard a comment by the leader of the Alliance commandoes. Jo Li was talking about a meeting with Alexander Colliquin. It sounded like he had turned Ethan over to the Global Alliance as part of a deal with Colliquin. As they were leaving, the Alliance captain said that the commandoes were heading to HQ with Ethan and that he would check to see if Jo could travel along with them. What headquarters he was talking about, I can't be sure. But I think we can both guess."

Rivka blurted it out. "New Babylon."

"Jo asked, rather jokingly, I think, 'How should I dress for the occasion?' The captain replied, 'For the desert.'"

Now Rivka was left with two very disturbing questions. She wondered what kind of nightmare Colliquin had planned for Ethan. And then there was the more urgent question: she worried how a rescue team could break into Colliquin's Iraq fortress before it was too late.

TH1RTY-N1NE

ANIMAL TESTING ROOM #6—DIGITAL IMAGERY LAB

New Babylon, Iraq

Ethan March's arms were outstretched and strapped to a metal pole that hung just above him, crucifixion style. His legs were manacled to the floor. He could see a few men dressed in blue lab coats on the other side of the glass, talking together and checking instruments. He prayed silently for strength and endurance as the agony in his arms and shoulders increased by the minute. He repeated in his mind, over and over again, a verse from the New Testament. From the book of Philippians. *"I can do all things through Him who strengthens me."*

Somewhere in the back of his mind he could hear the voice of his mentor Josh Jordan. Something he had taught Ethan—something Josh had learned from his own experience in a torture chamber of his

238

own. Josh had told Ethan to focus not on the pain or the fear, but on the fact that as long as he was alive—as long as he could still breathe and think and pray and plan and, yes, experience the pain—then God still had work for him to do and therefore God would be there with him, empowering him while he endured it.

Ethan's task now was to control the natural anxiety that threatened to overwhelm his judgment—the racing thoughts about what would happen next and what this experiment was and what kind of horror awaited him. Instead, he had to focus on something else: the objective facts of his dilemma. And how that fit into the hellish agenda of his capturers. He would try to figure it out, all of it, in case by some miracle he got out of this alive. If he did, then he could use it for others. To save the rest. To help resist this monstrous evil.

But he regretted something now. If only he'd been an engineering genius like Josh Jordan. MIT graduate. A weapons inventor and designer. Then, like Josh, he could figure this all out coldly and analytically. As he hung from the metal bar by his wrists and stared through the glass at the scientists in their light-blue lab coats, he realized he wasn't Josh.

The lab engineers touched some switches and then looked at Ethan. A hopeless despair flooded over him. It was as if someone had whispered in his ear that all was lost, that God was nowhere to be found. "No!" he screamed. "Get behind me, Satan!"

The scientists paused, looked up and stared at him through the window, and then began to laugh before they resumed their work.

Now Ethan struggled to think of the verse from the book of Ephesians, written by the apostle Paul through the inspiration of the Holy Spirit. Hadn't Paul known extreme pain himself? Of course, he reassured himself. And fear. And starvation. And beatings. And sufferings. And stoning. And drowning. What was it that Paul had written?

"Finally, be strong in the Lord and in the strength of His might. Put

on the full armor of God, so that you will be able to stand firm against the schemes of the devil."

He talked to himself. *Think,* he said silently. *What was it that the members of my team told me? And what did Dr. Adis tell me about Colliquin's tech people working on a new radical form of digital imagery? He kept hinting at the possibility of a single image capable of appearing before the BIDTag of every human who received the laser code on the back of the hand or the forehead. A holographic image. An image that could command obedience. And an image that could send a data stream by laser into the person's BIDTag code to activate the central nervous system of that person, and the brain too. To capture the mind.*

He forced himself to figure out the rest. And in an instant, there it was. *Colliquin's transmission will also be capable of something else, something terrible. Thus the experiments with the chimps. If the data stream can reach the nervous system and brain, then perhaps it's capable of sending a signal—to halt the heart, or maybe to stop the lungs. A message to kill the body.*

Something clicked in the back of his mind. *Something in the book of Revelation . . . What part? Where was it? Think . . .*

It came to him. Revelation 13:15–17:

And it was given to him to give breath to the image of the beast, so that the image of the beast would even speak and cause as many as do not worship the image of the beast to be killed. And he causes all, the small and the great, and the rich and the poor, and the free men and the slaves, to be given a mark on their right hand or on their forehead, and he provides that no one will be able to buy or to sell, except the one who has the mark, either the name of the beast or the number of his name.

Was this the fulfillment, then? It had to be. Dr. Adis had said the Alliance was on the verge of finalizing a digital design for global surveillance. But that was the last thing Ethan had heard from him. After that, Dr. Adis had gone silent.

And then there was Chiro, up in the Yukon. He was ready to launch the carefully planned electronic counterstrike. Chiro had told Ethan that if the demonic Revelation 13 plan used a technological grid, it would need to modify the BIDTag codes on the hands or foreheads of all of the tagged humans to increase the capacity to receive data from the Global Alliance masters. And then, Chiro guessed, they would use lasers to transmit the data into the BIDTag codes of the humans.

Lasers—that was ironic, wasn't it? At first they were used only as blunt weapons to burn things up, but then it was discovered that lasers could be used to transmit data, and so Joshua Jordan had used them in his stupendously effective Return-to-Sender antimissile system to capture and then redirect the data in the nose cones of incoming enemy missiles to turn them around.

Ethan tried to maintain steady breathing, to regulate the pain in his arms and shoulders. *Think . . . Keep thinking . . .*

But if the plan of Colliquin and the Alliance was to manipulate the people with BIDTags, what about the nontaggers? So many of them, millions, were Jesus followers who had refused to receive the laser mark. Yes, that was it. That was the fly in the ointment, wasn't it? They couldn't be so easily manipulated. Their obedience and worship couldn't be controlled. They had to be eliminated. Destroyed.

He realized that when he was first dragged into the lab and hog-tied to this hanging bar, a scientist had stripped him down and examined every inch of him. As if they were looking for something. The scientist had used an instrument that looked like a BIDTag scanner to carefully scan his entire body. So that was what they were looking for, wasn't it? They were making sure that he didn't have a BIDTag.

That is what I am, Ethan said to himself. *The guinea pig.* Now he knew that the experiment was to see if they could remotely destroy him, or manipulate him, even if he didn't have a BIDTag.

The men in the light-blue lab coats had stopped talking. They were standing together, shoulder to shoulder, and each of them was reaching forward. It looked like they were working the computer console. Then a light flashed in Ethan's room. From somewhere he heard a faint sound. He was aware that something was in the lab room with him. A presence. He saw it out of the corner of his eye. It was coming closer. An image of something. A face. Coming closer.

A three-dimensional face now filled the room, hovering in front of him. He knew this face because he had seen it before. On the outside, the appearance of the handsome face was unremarkable. Yet Ethan had been given the power to see behind the face, to visualize the evil that would soon come upon the entire human race, and to understand that this face would orchestrate the suffering of humanity. There it was—once again, his vision.

A voice yelled out from somewhere. At first Ethan didn't realize its origin, but then he understood—it was his own voice crying out.

"Oh, dear God, the beast."

But he fought back. He yelled out what he had memorized from the Scriptures about Stephen, the first Christian martyr. He called out the words Stephen had spoken just moments before he was stoned to death: "'But being full of the Holy Spirit, he gazed intently into heaven and saw the glory of God, and Jesus standing at the right hand of God; and he said, "Behold, I see the heavens opened up and the Son of Man standing at the right hand of God."'"

But the face of the image seemed to envelope Ethan like a spider consuming its prey, and it bellowed with a powerful voice, "Worship me, Ethan March, with all your heart and all your soul and all your might."

Ethan answered, from somewhere very deep inside, the words he remembered from the Word of God, and from his servant, the apostle John. "'For many deceivers have gone out into the world, those who do not acknowledge Jesus Christ as coming in the flesh. This is the deceiver and the antichrist.'"

The image spoke again. "Those who do not worship me shall be destroyed."

Before Ethan could respond, a molten-hot laser beam blasted from the eyes of the image and found its way with surgical precision into Ethan's skull. The light beam reached deep into the interior of his cerebral cortex and into the very network of neurons there, and his mind seemed to explode with a flash of lightning. Ethan opened his mouth wide as he shook violently, groping for some way to scream, to find a voice against the horror that wrapped itself around his mind like an invisible python snake, squeezing his thoughts, crushing them. And in the darkness he saw the face of the beast. But it wasn't out there in the room any longer, not in front of him at all. For a single, horrific moment the demonic creature raised its prehistoric, winged form before Ethan and made him wonder the unthinkable: Was this horrifying beast now inside his head? In his brain?

Ethan couldn't scream or weep or speak or even find the words to pray. All he could do now was endure and believe that somehow he could overcome as he tumbled headlong, deeper and deeper, down into his inner hell.

FORTY

Alexander Colliquin was alone. He had cloistered himself inside the chapel located in the chancellor's palace. The business before him was no longer just the geopolitics of the Alliance or the bringing together of all nations—although that was on the verge of being accomplished now that the United States would soon be forced to join the fold.

Nor was this about the unification of the world's economies, though that had been accomplished as well.

This moment of Colliquin's inside the chapel wasn't really about religion either—not exactly. Although as planned, the soft, pliable metal of the world's religions had been effectively soldered together by Bishop Dibold Kora under Colliquin's supervision. Kora's arrogant boasting had to be endured so that the task could be completed. And now that too was done.

No, this moment was about Alexander Colliquin. It belonged to him.

He glanced at the stained glass wall at the end of the chapel. He had personally commissioned it from one of the great neopagan artists of Brazil. It portrayed the blooming Tree of Knowledge from the garden of Eden, where wrapped around the trunk of the tree was a red-eyed serpent consuming its own tail. Whenever he was asked by a reporter why he had commissioned that particular imagery on the stained glass, Colliquin would grin and remark, "I always felt that the real hero of that story was the Tree of Knowledge. Isn't knowledge and enlightenment something we all yearn for?"

That was his public statement. But within the very small circle of Colliquin's close advisors, it was known that the global chancellor really had a different opinion. He privately joked that he thought that the *real* hero was the scaly creature wrapped around the tree.

Now, in the flickering light from eleven huge candles on eleven gothic candle stands mounted on the altar of the chapel, Colliquin knelt down beneath the stained glass image. As he did, he ran his finger across the golden profile fashioned on the ring on his left hand—the image of the ruby-eyed serpent.

"Today," Colliquin said aloud, "your manifestations through the ages—Baal and Astoreth and Molech—are consummated in me. I am the vengeance of Cain. I am the right hand of the lord of the air, who is my god and sovereign. I am the one who has accomplished every one of the tasks that were set before me. Nothing has been left undone. I ask that I be granted your power, every bit of it. For I crave it all."

His lord answered him.

000

An hour later Ho Zhu arrived outside of the chapel, looking for Colliquin. He knew he was forbidden to enter. But he also knew that Colliquin must be inside the chapel because he could see a vague shape through the glazed glass of the outer door, set off against the flickering light of candles.

A few more minutes passed, and then the door to the chapel opened and Alexander Colliquin stepped out. But Ho Zhu noticed something different about him, and it caused him to take a step back with a startled look, as a pedestrian might halt at the sight of a menacing figure in a dark alley.

"Don't be afraid," Colliquin said in a gentle voice. "Everything is perfect."

Ho Zhu paused and gathered himself. "I have been told," he said, "that Ethan March, the Jesus Remnant leader, is now in the digital lab and is being subjected to the nontagger protocol in lab testing room number six."

Colliquin smiled at that. "Of course he is," he replied nonchalantly, as if he knew it without even being told. As if he also knew that the tipping point for his plan for Planet Earth had finally been achieved and that it was now utterly unstoppable.

□□□

Ethan was no longer in darkness. He was now in a place flooded with light. He had the strangest feeling that time had ceased, and that he had found himself in a region where schedules, deadlines, and the laws of nature were irrelevant.

All around him there was a golden illumination, like the kind that comes from the welcoming warmth of burning logs in a fireplace. At the same time, the light had the brilliance of a burning star, though there was no harshness in it and it didn't blind his eyes.

When Ethan's vision cleared, he saw that the light was coming from One who sat on a white throne and who was the source of the light itself. Then Ethan realized something else. He wasn't alone, but he was in the midst of millions upon millions of others who all stood with him before the throne. Now the One sitting on the throne spoke. and as Ethan listened to Him his heart burned within him.

The King on the throne spoke to the millions and millions about the holy fire that had burned away all of the stubble and straw from their lives—the trivial things, the worthless things, the acts done for mere show or out of secret or selfish intentions. When Ethan heard that, he had no regrets, because it was all so very clear to him now: in this place, the shiny tinsel of cheap, earthly achievements had finally been swept away like confetti, leaving at last only those things that would be truly worthy of praise—the pure acts of grace and sacrificial love and the honest, unpretentious labors that had been performed out of love for the King of kings who sat on the throne. And it was clear too why it must be that way—because, of all of the things that had ever been done on earth, only those acts that were fully true and truly good would abide forever in this realm where the ocean of Jesus followers stood before the King on His throne.

Then the King, Jesus the Christ, the Alpha and the Omega, rose from His seat with a smile and slowly stepped forward, and as He did the multitude parted for Him as He approached one man in particular.

In the crowd of millions and millions, voices began to call out, "It is Stephen!" There was cheering and applause from this human tide, and a chorus of singing burst out in countless different languages, yet they could all be clearly understood.

Jesus wrapped His arms around the bearded fellow. "Stephen," Jesus called out. His voice thundered like a thousand Niagara Falls. "You were faithful unto death. That day in Jerusalem, as you proclaimed My Truth to the mob as they picked up their rocks to dash them against your head and strike you down and kill you—even then you were faithful to Me and true to My Word. And so I give you the imperishable crown of victory."

And the millions burst into cheering that seemed to rock the rafters of heaven.

Over to his right, Ethan noticed another man, broad shouldered

and bearded, who stepped backward, looking to hide himself, as if pre-
ferring anonymity. A shorter man, slightly bald and a bit bowlegged,
with bright, intense eyes, stopped him and kept him from retreating.
The shorter man said, "How I have waited to see you honored."

"Honored?" the big man said. "Brother Paul, you deserve it, all of
it, but me? Not me. I am content."

Paul looked him in the eye. "No. Both of us had our own betrayal
against the Savior, did we not? Mine was against the Savior's followers." And with that, Paul gestured toward Stephen, who stood before
the cheering millions as Jesus held His arm around him. "I consented
to Stephen's murder." As he said it, his voice cracked.

The taller man simply shook his head, which hung low.

But the crowd parted again and opened itself to Jesus, who now
held His inscrutable gaze on the tall man, who by then had turned
himself slightly to the side. Jesus called out in a loud voice, "Simon."

The tall man froze. Then Jesus called out to him by his other
name. "Peter, come to me."

"I turned against You, Lord," Peter said. "Yet still You saved me
and forgave me. I am content with that."

There was a soft, unblinking look in Jesus' eyes as He made His
way toward him.

"I am guilty of that terrible denial," Peter insisted.

"Denial?"

"That terrible night. When You were arrested, my Lord. When
the guards had You bound I was standing by the fireside, not far from
You. Denying that I even knew You . . ." Peter's voice trembled. Ethan
could see tears welling up in the big man's eyes.

Jesus held Peter by his shoulders. "Denial?" Jesus repeated in an
even softer voice. "What denial?"

Jesus reached out toward Peter's face. And as He did, Ethan caught
a glimpse of the scar on His hand, just there, where it met the wrist—
the wound that was now healed, where He had been pierced by the

six-inch Roman spikes. With that same hand, Jesus reached out and wiped the tears from Peter's eyes. And then He said, "Your sins have been cast away as far away as the west is from the east."

Peter looked at Jesus and smiled and cried and laughed and nodded his big shaggy head as his shoulders shook with emotion. Jesus then said to Peter, as His arm clasped around the big fisherman, "I know your service to My kingdom, and your steadfastness even to death. And now I say to you, Simon Peter, well done, good and faithful servant. Well done!"

Suddenly Ethan turned in a slow circle, scanning the millions around him. Breathless now, he saw in an instant that sea of faces, all those who would be honored by Christ the King. Ethan saw the missionaries who had died from dysentery or from the spears of tribesmen in distant jungles and the humble and faithful teachers from obscure Christian schools around the world who had sacrificially imparted the gospel of Christ to tender hearts. He saw the pastors and secretaries and Bible study leaders and musicians and writers and Sunday school workers and campground preachers, radio talkers and television broadcasters, statesmen and lawyers, carpenters and brick layers. He saw tech engineers and late-night cleaning persons who with aching arms and tired feet were the last ones to turn out the lights in humble buildings that had been built on faith. He saw soup kitchen providers and rescue mission workers, and those followers of Jesus who lived out their lives in wheelchairs, on crutches, in blindness, or without limbs, and yet who still labored cheerfully in the vineyards of God to do His bidding, to preach the salvation of Jesus Christ to everyone they encountered. Ethan saw all those workers of a billion acts of unseen kindness and compassion toward the oppressed, the wanderers, the broken of body or mind, the poor, the diseased, who did it all for no other purpose than to spread the love of the Savior to those who desperately needed redemption and who sought His touch. These were the ones, the faithful, who had been saved by the blood of the Lamb of God, and now they would be rewarded by the Lamb, who was the King of kings and Lord of lords.

Just then a man directly in front of Ethan, who stood next to an attractive dark-haired woman, turned around to face Ethan. And when he did, Joshua Jordan looked Ethan straight in the eye, as they stood face-to-face. And as he did, the millions disappeared. Even Abigail Jordan, whom Ethan had suddenly recognized as she stood next to Josh, was gone too. Now it was only the two of them: Ethan and Josh.

"Be courageous," Josh said in a voice that had a calm certainty to it. He looked so much younger now, perhaps in his thirties, yet Ethan could recognize the familiar features. The stone-square jaw, the piercing eyes, the slightly receding hair, cut short.

"Don't be afraid," Josh said. "The Lord is with you. Greater is He who is in you than he that is in the world." Then he laid his hand on Ethan's shoulder and said, "Now, go. And turn the world upside down."

Ethan nodded. But as he turned to leave, he wondered, *Go where?*

He swiveled back to face Josh, but when he did he realized that he was now utterly alone. Even the King of kings and His throne were gone, and the only thing left was Ethan and the silence that had enveloped him.

"Tell me, am I still alive?" Ethan tried to yell into the milky void that was now all around him. But his voice had grown weaker and fainter, almost unintelligible. He heard his own voice, and it was barely audible as he spoke.

"I think I'm dying . . ."

FORTY-ONE

WHITE HOUSE GROUNDS

Washington, D.C.

Vlad Malatov, aka agent Theodore Booth, stood at the northwest gate, dressed smartly in his suit and tie. He pushed the button on the intercom and announced himself. A voice came back, "ID, please."

He slid his paperwork and ID through the slot in the bulletproof security booth. He knew what would come next. The security guard would cross-check the information against the NCIC and NLETS databases on the computer screen. He saw the officer tapping some buttons on the screen. Then the door buzzed and Malatov entered and passed through the body scanner.

"Okay, Agent Booth," the security guard said. "Remain here. Another agent is on the way to escort you."

Malatov waited, relaxed but focused. Ten minutes passed. Then he saw another dark-suited Secret Service agent approaching the gatehouse along the flagstone walkway. When Agent Decker entered the gate booth, he shook hands with Malatov, introduced himself, and retrieved the transfer papers from the security guard. The agent glanced at the paperwork, then nodded for Malatov to follow him back along the stone walkway that led to the West Wing of the White House.

"Transfer from Miami?" Agent Decker asked as they walked.

"Yes, sir," Malatov replied.

"Gee," the agent said, "leaving all that behind—tropical breezes, pretty girls on the beach."

"But now I can root for the Nationals," Malatov said with a grin.

"What's wrong with the Miami Marlins?"

"Everything. They came in second to last in the National League East last season," Malatov shot back. "After they fired Ozzie Guillen way back when—That was awhile ago, wasn't it? Anyway, after Guillen was gone, things suddenly went straight down the tubes for them."

"Oh?" Decker replied, slowing down his pace slightly and eyeing Malatov closer now. The doors to the West Wing lobby were just ahead. Decker smiled. "So, Washington, D.C., now, huh? Why'd you pick this place? Haven't you heard what August is like in this city with all of the humidity?"

"Why, Agent Decker," Malatov answered with a grin as he came to a full halt. "You know better than that. It wasn't my idea. The Service told me I was to be transferred. It's right there in the reassignment documents. So here I am."

"Yes," Decker agreed as he escorted him into the West Wing lobby. "So you are."

□□□

AMERINEWS HEADQUARTERS

New York City, New York

Inside the office with the title *Publisher* etched on the glass door, Bart Kingston leaned back in his chair, eyeing the enlarged digital copy on the big wall screen. The story was about to go worldwide.

Terri Schultz jogged in. "Sorry I'm late."

"I've been checking out this piece on the Hewbright impeachment," he said. "Powerful stuff."

"Thanks," she said and cocked her head like she was waiting for the rest.

"But"—Kingston continued.

"Yeah, here it comes."

"It's just that we've done several stories on Jessica Tulrude."

"Of course. And one of those was mine—the interview with the pharmacologist from NIH who checked the treatment records of President Corland back when Tulrude was his VP and swore up, down, and sideways that Corland had been given the fatally wrong medication. And then we were able to tie that to Tulrude's personal physician . . ."

"Sure, who then conveniently committed suicide before the inquiry. I remember it all too, Terri. But that also prevented us from getting any clear proof that Jessica was some kind of . . ."

"Lady Macbeth?"

"Something like that," Kingston said. "And so, here we go again, targeting Tulrude one more time."

"I think I see your point. It's as subtle as a semi."

He guffawed. "Good. I'm glad you've got it." Quickly his tone switched to the all-business channel. "Everything we write has to be nailed down. We're a very successful, but very small, digital news service. The only reason we still exist on the Internet is because the U.S. hasn't been roped into the Global Alliance yet. And the only reason that hasn't happened is because Hewbright survived the Senate trial and is still in the Oval Office. And the only reason that is the case . . ."

". . . is because," Terri said, finishing the sentence, "Jessica Tulrude and Alexander Colliquin weren't able to pull enough strings with enough senators in the Senate. But, Bart, they tried. That's the point of my story."

"And according to you, Colliquin wants Hewbright out because . . . ?"

"You've read the piece I wrote," she shot back. "Colliquin used Tulrude to try to pressure the Senate into removing Hewbright. And then he got the World Parliament to enact this brutal sanctions boycott against us just for good measure. To up the ante. Keeping the heat on the Senate in an effort to try to get rid of Hewbright."

"I don't have any quarrel with that. It's all true, and you've documented it. But then you go out on a limb—way out—and speculate about the reasons why Colliquin is trying so hard to pull America into the Alliance."

"Isn't it obvious? We have the massive communications infrastructure that he needs. Private telecommunications networks. Satellites. The NSA. The guy's a megalomaniac of the highest order. So I think it's beyond debate that he wants to control every bit of the information and communication technology on the planet. And the United States has all of the tech hardware and networks for him to achieve that."

Kingston leaned back in his executive chair. "And what's your source for all of that?"

Terri threw up her hands in exasperation. "All my sources are listed on my computer superzip. It's all there."

"I know your sources," he said in a knowing voice. His voice was firmer now, even though his face had an understanding look. "You've pieced your theory together from a few comments Ethan made during our Roundtable video conference. But you know that anything discussed in those meetings can never be used to substantiate news stories. You have to nail them down independently. That's the deal."

She sighed. There was a flicker of a smile. "Slave driver."

"Look, I'm going to run your story, but I'm cutting out all the business with your speculation about Colliquin's motivations until you get something definitive. And if you do, then we'll talk."

Terri nodded, then turned and started to exit. But she stopped at the glass door. "You know," she said, "if my name was on this glass"— she pointed to the *Publisher* title with a chuckle—"I probably would have made the same call you just did."

When Kingston was alone again he yawned and rubbed his eyes. He'd been up since four thirty in the morning, and he needed a cup of coffee. Things were rapidly coming to a head in America. He had to keep his focus sharp and clear. He knew that very soon he could be called upon to be more than just a digital journalist for AmeriNews, bucking the political system and printing the other side of the news. Once the order was given by Ethan March, wherever he was and whenever it arrived, Kingston and the whole AmeriNews office would be called upon to commit an act of global defiance.

He rose from his chair and strolled into the lunchroom, but noticed that the coffee machine was missing. Then he remembered that the electronics in the older-model coffeemaker had gone haywire. One of the interns was supposed to go out and buy a new one. But where was it? He glanced at his Allfone watch and realized it was late afternoon already and he hadn't taken a break all day. As he strode past the receptionist's desk, he told her he was taking a walk down to The Beanery Row for a latte and that he would be back shortly.

When he exited the lobby to the corridor on his way to the elevator, he saw two men in suits punching in a code on the keypad at the office next to AmeriNews. That office space had previously been for rent.

"So you're our new neighbors?" Kingston asked as he strode over to them and extended a hand.

The older of the two, with slightly graying temples, shook his hand. "We are," he said with the tinge of an accent, though Kingston couldn't place it. He looked at the new brass plaque next to the door. It read Ultratech Advanced Information Systems.

"What kind of information systems?" he asked.

"Everything you can imagine."

"Sounds . . . *advanced*," he said with a smile.

"Exactly."

Kingston excused himself and hopped on the elevator. When he reached the ground floor, he touched his Allfone and speed dialed Terri and asked her to find out anything she could on Ultratech Advanced Information Systems.

"Any particular reason?" she asked.

"Just a vague hunch. Nothing more than that, really. Maybe I just need my caffeine. "

"Oh, so sorry. No can do. We don't operate on *hunches*, remember?"

Kingston got the jab and snickered.

"Gotcha on that one," Terri said. "Fine. I'll do it. And by the way, I heard you're on your way to The Beanery Row. Can you bring me back a strawberry creamo-licous with low-fat milk and sugar-free whipped cream?"

"Sure," Kingston said, walking down the street and enjoying the outside air. "Don't forget to check up on our new neighbors."

ㅁㅁㅁ

Inside the office of Ultratech Advanced Information Systems, the older man with the silver sideburns stood in his sparse office space. He had just placed a call on his Allfone. When someone on the other end picked up, he said, "Deputy Ho, please."

He waited just a minute until his call connected. "Deputy Ho, this is Mr. Dellatar from the Global Alliance Information Security Agency. We have moved into the building in New York. I have even met the publisher, Mr. Bart Kingston. Very cordial. I don't think he has a clue."

"Very good," Ho replied. "It is imperative that the very moment the transfer of executive power is accomplished and the White House consents to America joining the Alliance, you make your forced entry into AmeriNews. You cannot afford to give them any time to damage their computers or destroy documents. We must find out who their contacts are. Their list of confidential news sources. And what they have been up to. Surprise is essential."

"We're prepared," Dellatar replied, "to capture control of the AmeriNews facility. Our office is only twenty feet away from their front door."

FORTY-TWO

SOMEWHERE OVER TURKEY

Pack McHenry didn't know whether Ethan was dead or alive. But knowing Ethan, he was willing to assume the latter, at least outwardly. And so was the team he had assembled. They were together with Pack and Victoria in the Dassault Falcon private jet now over Turkish airspace, winging their way to New Babylon. Unfortunately, they had scant intelligence about Ethan's exact location.

The revamped French jet had been freshly painted with the Global Alliance insignia on the side, courtesy of some contacts Pack had with a private air hangar at the international airport in Rome. The pilot and copilot were both former fliers for the CIA's covert operations unit in Europe.

Pack and Victoria were seated in cushy leather seats across the little table in the cabin from two of Pack's best men: Vincent Romano, a stocky muscular man formerly with Interpol, and Andre Chifflet, a tall former detective with a deceptively easygoing demeanor who used to chase down terrorists from his Paris post with the *Direction Centrale de la Police Judiciaire.*

Chifflet was looking at an enlarged satellite photo of the New Babylon complex. But he was shaking his head. "I am afraid that this tells very little, my friend. Only gives us the relative size of the palaces and buildings and the spatial relationships between them, and some data on the physical approaches to the buildings."

"Agreed," Pack said. "Those are the facts, so let's deal with them."

Romano was the blunt one and he jumped in. "Then let me give you some facts, eh? Fact one: we are a small team. Fact two: that means our effectiveness is highest in well-focused attacks. Fact three: this complex is a monstrously large area. Very complicated. Well guarded. Fact four: I'm not fond of dying. But, on the other hand, we all have our eternity settled with almighty God. So that leads me to fact five: if I'm going to die, I'd like it to be quick. But from what I've heard about this crazy Colliquin character, death for his enemies doesn't come quick. For my part, I would rather not be crucified in the Iraqi desert." He looked to the sky and added, "But pardon me, Lord—no disrespect to Your holy Son who died on the cross that way for me, a rotten sinner."

"Do we have intel on those atrocities? The crucifixions by Colliquin's security forces?" Victoria asked.

Romano raised both hands in the air. "I have very good sources."

"No one is dying here," Pack interjected. "I don't care who these Alliance orcs are who are guarding the complex. We're smarter and we have a hundred years more combined direct operations experience."

"And, all combined, a hundred years older," Romano said with a half chuckle as he looked over the group—all of them over the age of forty-five, and some over fifty. Then he tossed a look over at Victoria.

"On the other hand, some of us possess an ageless beauty, and so, Miss Vicky, my comments are not intended for you."

Pack was checking his Allfone. Chifflet called over to him. "Hey, Pack, Romano is hitting on your wife again."

"I pity any guy who thinks he can tangle with Victoria," Pack said, grinning. He noticed an incoming call from Rivka and picked it up. Rivka's voice was tense and high, near the operatic scale.

"Pack, how close are you?"

"Over Turkey. We'll be in Iraq within the hour. And you?"

"Not close enough. Had to depart from Hong Kong. Hours and hours away. I wish I was with your team."

Pack didn't say it, but he was glad she was on the slower arrival. She was too emotionally invested in the mission. She needed to settle herself. But he didn't blame her for feeling that way. There were times when Victoria was heading into some tight spots and it looked bad, and he knew exactly how he was tempted to react—with wild, blunt force that despite his years with the CIA could jeopardize everything. Rivka was no different, despite her training by the Israelis in their Mossad spy agency.

"Who's flying you?" Pack asked.

"Zhang Lee is a pilot and he's flying this mission himself. We're in his Learjet."

"You'll make good time."

"Not fast enough. So what's the plan?"

"We're looking at the satellite images of the complex right now." Rivka wouldn't let it rest. "Break it down for me."

"It's too early to give you that. We'll let you know when we settle on a plan. Meanwhile, get some rest. Try to relax."

"I'm trying."

"I understand."

"Yeah, you probably do," she said. "You and Vicky."

Pack stepped to the other end of the cabin and lowered his voice as he remembered something and decided to share it with Rivka. "We were in Budapest once. Vicky was playing the role of a double agent and was dealing with a seriously dangerous killer sociopath. But the thing was, he had some valuable information. I was supposed to intervene, just in time, after she had received the hand-off from him. But I got delayed, and when I arrived at this grimy little cold-water flat where the guy lived, I was greeted with the sight of a dead woman on the floor and lots of blood. My world collapsed. Until I turned the body over and saw that it was this guy's girlfriend. Vicky had already escaped. I still think about that."

"Thanks, Pack," she said. Her voice was soft now, and collected. "For caring. For helping. Ethan is blessed to have friends like you."

"We're going to get him back. I really believe that."

"I pray you're right. I know it's in the Lord's hands. But it's tough."

"I'll let you know as soon as we've laid out our operational plan, okay?"

After Pack hung up, he joined the others. Chifflet was rifling through some more satellite images of the complex of buildings. "On the outskirts of the new palaces and the administration buildings," Chifflet pointed out, "before the security of the complex starts with all of the new structures built under Alexander Colliquin, there are all of the old Babylonian ruins, and the earlier attempts by Saddam Hussein to rebuild them. The palace of King Nebuchadnezzar, the Isthar Gate, those things. So I was just thinking . . ."

"That those provide good cover for us?" Victoria guessed. "Or a hiding place for Ethan if he can make it outside of the complex?"

"Maybe cover for us, at least," he replied.

Pack was listening, but he was pretty sure what Chifflet and Romano were already thinking. Getting Ethan to the outskirts of New Babylon? First they had to find him. The place was the size of a medium-sized city. And then they would have to navigate their way— or more likely fight their way—through a thick layer of security.

He pointed to some of the buildings in the photograph. "One of these is the administration building. But I doubt he's there. Here is the chancellor's palace. That's a possibility. One of these structures is also his technology laboratory; I'm not sure which, but there's also a chance they could have him there in the lab facility too."

"Yes," Romano said, nodding his head. "And if that's where they have him, then you have to wonder—what have those monsters been doing to him?"

Torture? Yes, Pack was already there. But he was thinking beyond that too, and privately wondering whether at this point Ethan was still breathing.

FORTY-THREE

JUST OUTSIDE THE NEW BABYLON PERIMETER

Desert near Salman Musa, Iraq

What they had just seen was horrific. And it had sent Farrah Adis into a torrent of pitiful wailing in the front passenger seat of the little Euro car. Even though this was a flat, lonely wilderness of scrub brush, scorpions, and blistering heat, her sister Salima, who was behind the wheel of the car, still had to roll up the windows, just to be safe. She had parked her car off the highway that ran between Al Hillah and Karbala. She was afraid that Farrah's intense weeping might be heard by passersby. And then they might report the suspicious activity to the Global Alliance security forces at New Babylon.

Farrah was still clinging to the binoculars that she had used to see that scene of unspeakable cruelty. Even though the execution site and the body were within view of the highway—a deliberate ploy by Alexander Colliquin to warn the locals—Farrah had to be sure it had been her husband. Now she was sure.

Salima gently eased the binoculars out of Farrah's grip. Her sister shuddered and whimpered with grief, and Salima wrapped her arms around her.

"He is with the Lord Jesus now," Salima whispered. "And our Savior will give him the loving hugs that you cannot. Your husband is in glory now. Iban has peace and joy."

Farrah wiped her face, her chest still heaving with sobs. She tried to speak, but she choked on the words.

Salima shook her head. "Such evil. We are nearing the end of all things. Come quickly, Lord Jesus . . ."

She glanced in both directions along the highway. No traffic coming. She lifted the binoculars to her eyes and focused on the scene of the torture just fifty yards away. The two Global Alliance guards were still standing at the foot of the cross made out of steel girders. One of them was looking up at the corpse of Dr. Iban Adis that was draped up on the cross.

But the other guard had his own binoculars and he was looking right at Salima's car.

"We have to go, right now," Salima called out. "We're being watched."

Farrah nodded and wiped her eyes.

"Say good-bye to Iban, your precious, courageous husband," Salima said.

But as Salima started the car, Farrah shook her head. And she did it so fiercely that it took Salima by surprise.

"No," Farrah announced with a struggling smile. "I will not say good-bye. It is too late for that. I will wait instead. I will wait to say hello to him myself, and soon, perhaps."

Salima gunned the car north on the highway toward Karbala,

away from the disgusting city-state of death and corruption called New Babylon.

Farrah looked intently at her sister and sniffled. "And now I know."

"I am so sorry, dear sister, that you had to see that awful sight, that ugly place of execution for poor Iban," Salima said.

"Yes," Farrah added, but suddenly with a strange kind of determination in her voice. "But I know something else."

"What?"

"I know," Farrah said calmly, "exactly what I have to do now."

□□□

The Global Alliance guard held his binoculars to his eyes, watching the dusty cloud that was left behind as Salima's car headed north. Then he brought the binoculars down from his face. "More curious onlookers. These people around here must not have anything better to do."

But the other guard wasn't listening. He was still staring at the lifeless form of Dr. Iban Adis up on the metal cross. The heat had blistered and bloated the doctor's face almost beyond any human recognition. The birds and insects and reptiles of the desert had already begun to feast on his dead body over the last few days.

"Did you hear what I was saying?" the guard with the binoculars asked.

His partner looked away from the corpse of Dr. Adis and addressed him directly. "I was thinking . . ."

"About what?"

"His last words."

"Really? I don't give any thought to such things."

"I do. I think they're important, when a man is dying. What he believes . . ."

"Ramblings. Insane things, that's all."

But the other guard shook his head. "Dr. Adis looked at me. Right at me. And he said, 'Believe in the Lord Jesus Christ, and you will be saved.' That was almost the last thing."

"Almost?"

"A little later he looked up. I don't even think his eyes were focusing at that point. But he looked up and said, 'Receive my spirit, Lord.'"

His partner scoffed. "You'd better watch yourself. Don't let people think you're becoming one of those Jesus Remnant types. They're crazy."

The guard seemed to be weighing that. After a moment he tilted his head, glanced back at the corpse of the dead scientist on the cross and at the crucifixion ordered by his Alliance superiors, and then he said to the security partner with the binoculars, *"They're* crazy?"

□□□

PRIME MINISTER'S OFFICE

Jerusalem, Israel

Sol Bensky drummed his fingers on his desk. He could hear a symphonic rendition of one of Wagner's operas droning at the other end of his desktop Allfone as he waited to be taken off hold to get an answer to his question.

Across from the desk, Joel Harmon and Micah sat quietly with their hands in their laps, watching it all unfold. Micah appreciated the fact that Harmon, the young and very controversial member of the Knesset, had been willing to plead the case of Rabbi ZG. For him to have actually arranged the meeting with PM Bensky was practically a miracle. But that day in Bensky's office, to see the prime minister's reaction to the arrest of Rabbi ZG, exceeded Micah's every expectation.

Sol Bensky had even dispensed with the ordinary diplomatic

protocol and made all of the calls himself. First to the Global Alliance consulate in Jerusalem and then up the chain of command to the Alliance's special envoy to the Middle East sector in Cairo, and then to the Alliance's governing regent for the Middle East, and finally, now, to the deputy special assistant to Chancellor Colliquin himself.

Finally a female voice came on the speakerphone. "Mr. Prime Minister?"

"Yes," Bensky replied in a voice straining for control.

"So sorry to keep you waiting. And your question?"

Bensky's face flushed scarlet. "My question, twenty minutes ago, was whether I can speak to Chancellor Colliquin, personally, about the arrest and illegal detention of a citizen of Israel, known as Rabbi ZG, whose full name is—"

"Oh yes," she cut in, "no need to go on. The chancellor is fully aware of this situation. I have been asked to relay his answer to you. Chancellor Colliquin regrets to inform you that he is unable to intercede in this matter. I am sorry, Prime Minister."

□□□

NEGEV DESERT, ISRAEL

Rabbi ZG sat on the concrete floor of the Global Alliance jail that was off-limits to Israeli jurisdiction. He bled from where the guards had yanked chunks of his beard from his face. His nose, having been broken with a club, was black and blue and caked with dried blood. He had spent the last few hours praying and praising God that he was still conscious enough to pray. Thanking God for allowing him to have proclaimed the truth about Jesus the Messiah and the King. He knew His coming was imminent. The time was short. It had to be.

"Have I been faithful, O Lord?" Rabbi ZG asked out loud.

Of course he didn't want to die, but he was prepared to. How could he not be? Especially when he considered the words of Paul the apostle: *"To live is Christ and to die is gain."*

But he did wonder, in those moments on the dirty concrete floor of the jail, if it would happen today. So he closed his eyes and he began to pray again. But there came a glimmer of something—a faint light at first, that grew increasingly brighter until even with his eyes shut, he was aware of a burning illumination in the room. He tried to open his eyes to see what it was, but when he did he couldn't look straight into the light; it was like staring into the sun.

Rabbi ZG shielded his eyes, and when he could eventually make it out, he saw the source of the light. The Two Witnesses were standing in the middle of the light, there in the jail cell with him. Nothing was said for a full minute. Finally, as his eyes began to adjust to the light, he had to speak. "I need to know," he said to the two men, "your names."

Two nods came in response.

He continued, in a voice broken with surpassing joy. "In the eleventh chapter of the book of Revelation . . . your coming was foretold? To appear in the end times? During the time of tribulation? You are the two 'olive trees,' the 'two lampstands' of the Lord . . . ?"

Two nods again.

"I have not dared to ask this before," he said. "But before my end comes . . ." And then Zechariah Gamaliel turned to the tall, stately, bearded man in the rough, camel hair robe. "May I call you by your true name?"

The tall Witness smiled and nodded. "You may."

He turned to the shorter, stocky man with the fiery eyes. "And you also?"

"You may."

Rabbi ZG smiled and exhaled in one long, exhilarated breath. Then he turned to the tall man and he took another breath and closed his eyes. And when he opened them he spoke. "Moses," he said in a hushed voice.

And he looked to the shorter man, and to him he said, "Elijah."

The two men reached down and pulled him to his feet.

Rabbi ZG said to them both, "I'm ready to die."

"The Lord knows," Elijah replied with the matter-of-fact tone of a man who was absolutely certain of what he knew.

"But the Lord has a question for you," Moses said quietly.

Rabbi ZG's eyes widened, and he didn't dare speak a word. He stopped breathing.

"You are prepared to die?" Moses continued.

The Jewish scholar nodded.

Then Moses spoke again. "Indeed, you are ready to die. But with all of the terrors, and all of the trials that will soon be visited upon the earth, and with all of the aching souls of the lost who still search in their hearts for the Great Shepherd and who need to be told that they can be redeemed . . . In light of that, Zachariah Gamaliel, teacher of Israel, are you prepared also to live?"

FORTY-FOUR

THE WHITE HOUSE

Washington, D.C.

Vlad Malatov sipped coffee at the lunchroom table in Room W16, the space used by the Secret Service for their downtime. It was located directly under the Oval Office. Agent Decker had told him to wait there, that another agent would soon connect with him and begin to walk him through the White House drill, and then Decker had disappeared.

Ten minutes later Secret Service agent Kevin Arnold strolled into the room carrying a small case. One other agent was there in the room, finishing his sandwich, but as Agent Arnold walked to Vlad, the other agent wiped his hands with a paper towel, tossed his paper plate and paper napkin in the trash, and left the room to report for his detail.

Agent Arnold gave one quick glance around the room, checking for company, then sat down next to Malatov. As he did, he laid the little case on the table in front of him. He reached his hand out to Malatov and they shook hands.

"Agent Theodore Booth, I'm Agent Kevin Arnold."

Malatov smiled and nodded.

"I work very closely with the president," Arnold continued. "More than most. I'm here to walk you through some preliminaries."

"Thank you," Malatov said with a polite tone.

Arnold unzipped the case and opened it. He pulled out a standard-issue, silver SIG Sauer P229 pistol and displayed it to Malatov.

"This is your weapon. You keep the case. Your shoulder holster is in there too. There are only two rounds in the clip for now. Later I'll explain the paperwork you'll need to sign for additional ammo, including target rounds. And of course I'll be explaining the process for target practice and drills."

Arnold laid the pistol back in the case and shoved it over to Malatov. "Use it in good health," he said.

"About my schedule and the detail I'll be assigned to . . . ," Malatov began.

"I'll cover some of that today. And then more later."

"Understood." Malatov smiled and asked, "And the protocol on . . . Well, a rather embarrassing question about protocol with the president."

"He's a widower, as you probably know, but he isn't dating, if that's what you mean. He's pretty straightlaced. Religious type."

"No, not that. Something else."

"Oh?"

"About getting his autograph," Malatov said with a grin. "Getting it from him personally, I mean. I'm a big fan of his."

"Oh, I see. Yes, he's very approachable."

Malatov was pleased with that.

Arnold continued, "I'm sure that most of our basic procedures here will be similar to your last assignment. Where was it?"

"Miami."

"Right." Agent Arnold paused and studied Malatov carefully. "I was reading something about Florida recently. Maybe it was in *National Geographic*, but I can't recall exactly."

Malatov leveled an intense visual bead on Agent Arnold. "Yeah?" he said.

"Yes," Agent Arnold continued. "An article about diving for buried treasure off the Florida Keys. Men looking for a trunk full of Spanish doubloons."

Their eyes locked as the two men studied each other. Both knew that the room was full of tiny video cameras and voice recorders. Malatov arched his eyebrows with a feigned look of innocent interest. "You don't say. Diving for treasure. That sounds exciting."

"Well," Agent Arnold said, rising to his feet, "let me show you to your locker. Then I'll show you around the White House grounds."

□□□

Two floors up, in the Oval Office, President Hank Hewbright had his suit coat off and his tie loosened. He was sitting on the couch with a posture of exhaustion. At the same time his face radiated a strange expression of calm. It wasn't a look of resignation. More like a quiet acceptance of things as they really were—things that might not be changeable, despite his position as chief executive, even if he wished otherwise.

Vice President Darrell Zandibar sat across from him, looking formal and a little stiff.

Hewbright was blunt. "Darrell, I need to know if the press reports are accurate."

"Which ones?"

"I think you know. About your disagreement with me. Your saying that my administration needs to change direction on the Global Alliance issue. That we need to 'link arms' with the Alliance. I think that's the way you put it."

"That's accurate," Zandibar said.

"Then we have a serious problem," Hewbright retorted. "You're free to disagree with me—but privately, not publicly."

"The Global Alliance sanctions are crippling us," Zandibar shot back. "If we don't dial back the economic vise they have us in, we won't have much of a country left."

Hewbright thought on that. "Darrell, I asked you once, before the Senate trial, whether you were prepared to take over if I was removed from office. You said that you didn't want that for yourself. Do you still feel that way?"

"Well, Hank, you beat the Senate charges. They didn't remove you. So the idea of my replacing you—stepping in—that's all moot now. It's off the table. Isn't it?"

The president took a long, hard, burdened look at his vice president. "Unless something should happen to me, of course."

"That isn't going to happen."

"Can we be sure? For some time, the international media has been quoting you more than me. Almost daily. As if it was just a matter of time. As if the news media, the elite press that's controlled by the Global Alliance, knows something I don't."

Hewbright stood up and stretched and then sauntered over to the Resolute Desk, where he had a pile of papers he still needed to review.

Zandibar also rose from his chair, looking a little uneasy, as if he didn't know whether to excuse himself or to stay.

The president leafed casually through a few of the documents on his desk. Then he threw out a final comment, almost as an afterthought. Not based on anything except the quiet, inexplicable certainty down deep that, having defied the brutal Global Alliance thus far, his luck might be running out. "Darrell, an interesting historical anecdote—in the weeks leading up to Lincoln's death, history tells us that the city of Washington was awash with rumors about plots mounting against him. Interesting thing about that. This city never has been able to keep a secret. Not really."

Then he looked up and stared his vice president in the eye.

FORTY-FIVE

ANIMAL TESTING LAB #6—DIGITAL IMAGERY LAB

New Babylon, Iraq

Ethan March hung lifelessly from the straps in the testing lab like a
gutted animal after the hunt. The holographic image still hovered in
the air in front of him while the two lab scientists talked.

The blond, broad-shouldered lab technician with horn-rimmed
glasses was shaking his head. He was trying to explain the anomaly.
"The metrics I'm looking at show that he's in a state consistent with
death. Heart rate. Pulse. Respiration. Just nothing there. He's func-
tionally deceased. I don't think the chancellor is going to be pleased
with this. I thought the point of the experiment with this particular
subject was to demonstrate capture ability over the brain functions of
nontaggers. And to extract information from him."

The chief stood next to him. "No, I'm satisfied now with the termination option we've developed with our chimps, and now with Mr. March, our human subject. The laser-focusing technique is excellent. A direct signal to the part of the cortex that will stop the heart. But you're right. The chancellor didn't want to waste this subject on testing the termination control. What we really wanted with this human subject was a complete capture of the neuron firing process in the brain." He looked at the monitor connected to the EEG leads wired to Ethan March's skull.

"Yet, oddly, he's not flatlining," the chief said. "Perhaps he's in a permanent vegetative state." He strode over to a panel and tapped in the code for brain neuroinformatics analysis. "Let's see what thought processes are going on inside that skull. There should be no imagery or language waves."

It took only a few seconds for a trail of digital code to stream across the screen. "I'm getting something," the chief announced. "Okay, it's analyzing his brain language process." He touched the screen for the icon to decode the language portion of Ethan's brain waves.

A few seconds passed. The monitor cleared. Then the results appeared on the screen.

The chief looked, and then he looked again. He scowled. "What is this? What's going on?"

The lab tech dashed over next to him. He looked at the screen and shook his head in disbelief. It was a sentence, translated from Ethan's brain by the computer program. It read, *Greater is He that is in me, than he that is in the world.*

They both looked up at Ethan through the big plate-glass window that separated them from the testing room. The chief cocked his head as if he sensed something coming, something far beyond science or advanced technology, but that he could not have stopped in any event.

□□□

A sudden brilliant flash of light illuminated the lab-testing room, like a nuclear fission, and the big plate-glass window separating Ethan from the two men in the blue lab coats shattered into a billion shards. The blast exploded into the control room and blew the two scientists back against the wall, where they hit with sickening *whacks* and then fell to the floor, unconscious. The monitors, keyboards, digital imagery equipment, biometric instruments—everything was sparking and smoking and beginning to melt with a nauseous, toxic stench.

Hanging from his straps, Ethan opened his eyes just in time to see the holographic image that had been floating in the air before him begin to roil and ignite, as if it had caught on fire. It burst into a million digital dots until it finally vanished like a bad dream.

□□□

KARBALA AIRPORT, IRAQ

Pack McHenry had picked the Karbala airport as their staging destination for the rescue operation. It was a strategic decision, and he felt good about it. Sort of.

France had begun to expand the airstrip back around 2013 in a joint deal with Iraq, and Pack had insider relations with French aviation authorities and the *Aeroports de Paris* dating back to his CIA years. He felt confident that fact would help clear the landing of the Dassault Falcon jet with a minimum of questions. More important, they would also need to take off—hopefully with Ethan in tow—like a bat out of a bat cave, with a minimum of hassle from airport personnel on the ground.

But there was a third reason: the airstrip was less than one hour's fast drive from New Babylon. There were no speed limits, the highway was straight between Karbala and Babylon, and it cut through flat desert lands. As long as they looked out for locals with donkey-driven carts that might be in the middle of the travel lane, they would be okay. Depending again on a few other minor details, like whether they could even get their hands on Ethan and then stuff him into the vehicle, all of course without being surrounded by a thousand armed Alliance forces.

The other alternative would have been to try to rustle up a Blackhawk helicopter, drop it in really close to Ethan's place of confinement, and to zip in and out with lightning speed. All of that would have been great, except when Pack tried to explore that option, it proved harder than he expected to get his hands on a chopper in short order. And of course there was the other problem: he had no idea where Ethan was being held. Maybe it had been wishful thinking, but he knew Ethan was a resourceful guy, and he'd half hoped Rivka would receive some kind of message from him by now. But Pack had talked to her twice before landing. Each time she said the same thing and harbored the same miserable tone in her voice: she had heard absolutely nothing from Ethan.

Pack, Victoria, his two pilots, and his two special-ops guys now stood in the private airplane hangar on the edge of the airport. A French agent of the Global Alliance was checking their incoming flight plan and their impressively doctored passports and asking a few standard questions. No, they weren't bringing fruits or vegetables into the country. Their "business" in Iraq? They described it as "research at the ancient ruins at Babylon."

Pack had been assured by one of his contacts that he could trust the airport agent with *Philippe* on his nametag standing in front of him. But Pack made it a habit never to bank his life on that kind of assurance.

Philippe handed their passports back to them and passed the flight plan over to the pilots.

Pack flashed an easy smile. "Anything else?"

"Yes," Philippe said. But he didn't elaborate. He only stared.

"Is there some kind of issue here . . . ?" Pack asked, pursuing it a bit.

"Yes," Philippe replied. He had the kind of expression traffic cops usually gave drivers when they pulled them over and were stupidly asked, "Is there a problem, Officer?"

Pack pressed. "Can you tell us the issue?"

Without moving his head, Philippe darted his eyes around, casing out who might be close. Then he bent forward and his eyes softened. "You need to know, Mr. McHenry, that inside New Babylon, in the digital testing laboratory building, a general alert has been sounded. I have no other details. Thought you should know. Godspeed, sir."

FORTY-SIX

10 DOWNING STREET

London, England

British prime minister Derek Harrington had just finished his telephone conversation with American president Hank Hewbright. He tapped the Off icon on the secure Allfone screen at his desk and dropped back, deep in his chair.

Elroy Clyde, minister of defense, picked a bit of lint off his dark-blue suit. The British PM could see that Clyde was putting on a good face, an air of nonchalance as he waited to hear what Harrington could tell him about his conversation with the American president. The cabinet member was a good man and Harrington was aware how Clyde was trying to buck up under the pressure. Everyone in Harrington's government was. But the British PM also knew that things were about to get a whole lot worse before they got better.

There was silence for almost a full minute.

"The United States," Harrington finally announced, "will not be changing course. President Hewbright told me that he will continue his fight to keep America from joining the Global Alliance. Against all odds, it would appear."

"Bloody tough choice for the Yanks, I would say," Clyde responded. "Those economic sanctions are already beginning to decimate America."

"Things could change. England could take a roundabout, disobey those sanctions, and continue trade relations with the U.S."

Clyde's eyes widened.

"And perhaps," Harrington continued, "we can talk some other countries into joining us. Australia. New Zealand, perhaps. Canada— yes, definitely, I am very sure that Canada will be onboard. Who knows . . . maybe even China would start up trade again with the U.S. They're losing a major export market to the States with these sanctions."

The minister of defense touched the knot on his striped tie as he listened. Then he asked, "And Parliament?"

"I think they're with me," Harrington replied. "There's a rising sentiment over there that our linking Great Britain to the Global Alliance was a terrible mistake. I'm expecting a vote today, rescinding our agreement to the Covenant of Unity—the so-called Treaty of Alliance. As you know, I'm heading over to Parliament shortly. I'll sit there, on that green leather bench, ready to rise to my feet in the House of Lords and then go quickly over to the Commons on the very same issue, now that both houses are required to weigh in on this. My argument will be the same: that it is time to pull out of Alexander Colliquin's folly—this Global Alliance that has turned into a parade of horribles."

"Mr. Prime Minister, I have been approached by a few in our military. Top-flight generals, all of them. They are all in agreement. In view of what might happen soon—with England pulling out of the Alliance and all of that—there could be a rather nasty response from Babylon. From the Alliance. So with all that . . ."

"Yes, of course, we need to secure our defenses. Demand that the Alliance troops within our borders evacuate in twelve hours, not a minute longer."

Clyde now looked as if there was something on his mind, something personal. "There's another matter, Derek."

"You can speak frankly."

"We all think that your personal safety will be at great risk," Clyde said in a voice that became suddenly somber. "Colliquin and his deputies will almost certainly plan a targeted hit against your office. MI6 has some intelligence that Babylon has a plan to forcibly remove the heads of state of any nation moving to leave the Alliance. In light of that, the entire cabinet feels you should relocate your offices. Just for the time being. The Isle of Guernsey might be a good choice. It's not too far away, as you know. Middle of the English Channel. The Guernsey government has already said they would be quite happy to allow you to remain there, to function as PM in exile. Let you set up shop temporarily. Run the government from there if there is a large-scale attack by the Alliance, of course. Our military believes there *will* be an attack. And so does our foreign secretary."

Harrington gave a quizzical look. The bitter reality was starting to sink in even deeper. "So it really is going to come to that, is it?"

"It appears so, Prime Minister."

"And Buckingham Palace?"

"The king is fully behind our drawing the line against the Alliance. He thinks this is a good idea. 'Blast the Alliance,' he said. But he wants to stay here in England if there is an invasion. 'King and Country,' you know."

"I would feel rather like a dodger, leaving England . . ."

"We need you safe so you can make decisions," Clyde said. "Continuity in our government is paramount, I think. This will get quite ugly."

Harrington wondered about that.

Clyde cleared up the ambiguity. "I'm speaking of a *blitzkrieg* kind of ugly."

ооо

PARLIAMENT HILL

Ottawa, Canada

It could well have been a scene from the British Parliament at that very moment. Except this was the Canadian Parliament instead. But it was the same issue—withdrawal from the Global Alliance. And there was the same torrent of shouts rising up from the benches occupied by the official Opposition in the House of Commons. While England's PM was arguing to his Parliament the need for an immediate pullout by England, on the other side of the Atlantic its sister nation, Canada, grappled with the same scenario almost simultaneously.

In Parliament Hill in Ottawa, Penelope Duncan, the Speaker, desperately tried to restore order from her high-backed chair at the apex of the cathedral-sized hall. But it was rough going. The Opposition party was repeatedly bellowing, "Point of order!" The red-faced opponents of the prime minister were trying to block his ability to address the House.

Canadian prime minister Jack Laverhill had already risen up from his green upholstered chair—the traditional eleventh seat to the right of the Speaker—and was ready to address the assembly. But he knew the Madam Speaker needed to bring them into order first. This wasn't like the usual hot-button issue, where the Speaker had to wrangle members like cats. Not this time. It was more like wrestling timber wolves.

"Order, order," Duncan kept calling out.

But the Opposition party kept shouting her down. And then someone yelled out the word *traitor*.

That did it. Duncan slammed the gavel down and jumped to her feet. "Allow me to define *traitor* for you," she shouted. "A traitor would be any man or woman here who would not permit the honorable prime minister to speak on a matter as critical to the survival of the sovereign nation of Canada as the one before us at this moment."

The Opposition leader screamed, "We have already approved the treaty and it brought us into the Global Alliance two years ago. A good idea it was then, and a good idea it remains. Madam Speaker, you and the PM are now collaborating together to deny constitutional rule by dragging us through this same issue once again. The matter is settled. Let the PM retire back to 80 Wellington Street and lick his wounds. He may regret the bargain that he struck with the Global Alliance, but we don't."

Laverhill knew what was transpiring at that same moment in the British Parliament. He had placed an urgent call to England's prime minister two hours earlier, and Derek Harrington had assured him it was almost a "certainty" Great Britain would withdraw itself from the Global Alliance. Now was Laverhill's chance to try and achieve the same outcome.

The Opposition was still shouting when Laverhill began to speak. He didn't yell. He spoke at a rhetorical decibel, but nothing more. And he kept speaking until the members of the Opposition began, one by one, to sit back down in their green-tufted chairs. Finally, only the leader of the Opposition and his deputy were still on their feet, and eventually they too eased down reluctantly into their seats.

Laverhill's words now filled the ivory-colored chambers, all the way up to the high chandelier and all the way out to the cathedral windows and arches that lined the hall.

What man or woman here has never lived with regret? Which of us has not had to admit fault or folly or lapse of judgment? Or had to confess the commission of something much worse. Dare I say it? Dare I say the word in our current climate of opinion where the truth of God has been so trampled underfoot by the despots of Babylon and by their toadies, the popular press? Yes, I shall use that word. Who among us has not in the quiet moments of our souls needed to confess sin? Sin in our personal lives. And more pertinent here—sin in our public lives, because we failed to do what was required of us by our oath of office and by our moral call to integrity and courage.

A small core of the Opposition, ten in number, began to groan and jeer loudly at the audacity of the PM in preaching about such an archaic religious concept as sin. But the outburst didn't last. The other three hundred and twenty-eight members shouted for them to stop, and when that happened they fell silent.

Prime Minister Laverhill continued,

I confess that I sinned when I promoted the idea of the covenant with the Global Alliance and when I invited Canada to join it, because I wronged the nation I love by such an act. And I sinned when I ignored the quiet echoes in the conscience that had been implanted by God Almighty. And I sinned against God when I ignored the warnings in His prophetic Scriptures. I confess before all of you that I sinned when I allowed myself to be wooed by the promises of power and prestige from Alexander Colliquin. And, by the way, almost none of those promises were kept. Nevertheless, as a result of my grave error I shall call upon the governor general to seek a new leader to form a government. For my part, I shall not stand for election. I will devote myself instead as a private citizen to supporting the efforts of those known around the world as the Remnant. I will join their resistance against this lord of darkness coming out of Babylon and will embrace the mission of the Remnant in preparing the people of this planet for the coming kingdom of Jesus Christ.

There were audible gasps that swept across the hall. The Opposition party had expected a push against the Alliance. But they never dreamed of a resignation, let alone this kind of bizarre religious pronouncement.

As the members in the House processed their shock over the prime minister's confession, he gave them one final directive.

Now, as my last official act before this honored body, I urge you— I plead with you—sever all ties between Canada and the Global Alliance. Cast off any dependence that Canada may have on this abomination that lurks in the palace walls of New Babylon like a predator. Withdraw from the Alliance. And do it without delay. Any hesitation now, any lack of resolve, could be our undoing.

FORTY-SEVEN

WHITE HORSE, YUKON TERRITORY

John Galligher sat at his usual security post in the small office just behind the lobby of the faux gold rush hotel, staring at the row of little monitors connected to a complex of outdoor cameras scattered across the city. All he knew was that he was waiting for the command from Ethan any day now for them to grab Chiro's "C-Note computer"— the huge black-metal computer in the upstairs lab that Chiro kept obsessing about—and to head to their ultimate destination, wherever that would be. But until then, his job was to maintain surveillance and hope that the knock on the door from the Global Alliance the Mountie said was coming wouldn't happen soon.

When Galligher arrived in the Yukon, he had learned from Chiro that the cameras had originally belonged to the Canadian military and had been installed as some kind of defensive security system for White Horse, perhaps because it was the capital of the Yukon Territory. But all of that was before the Canadians joined the Global Alliance. After that, the military abandoned their White Horse cadet training camps and sold the camera monitoring system to the local police. The local police chief, a Remnant sympathizer, in turn had leased the entire setup to Chiro, who had also managed to rent the huge receive-and-transmit satellite dishes the military had abandoned.

A little while later the aging police chief lost his battle with cancer, but for some reason no one had dug into the fact that Chiro and Galligher and the staff that managed the little tourist hotel still had control over the city's video monitoring system.

That was just fine with Galligher, who was using it now for surveillance. He figured that if any adverse action were taken by the Alliance against the secret communications relay station Chiro had built, it would probably be land based. Some kind of ground attack. And it would likely be via the few major highway and street routes that ran through White Horse. So his camera surveillance would provide nice security.

Galligher didn't know exactly what Chiro's transmission station was supposed to accomplish, but nowadays he was trying to take orders like a good soldier, unlike his years in the FBI when he'd been a consistent maverick. Maybe he had some doubts about Ethan March's leadership, but he was willing to believe Chiro and the others on the Roundtable like Pack McHenry when they all said the Alliance's global communications strategy had to be countered somehow, and that this weird tech outpost in the Yukon was a necessary key to that.

But he was nearly dying from boredom. As he sat in front of the monitors, day after day, he found himself watching moms transporting their kids to and from school, delivery trucks on their routes, and occasionally, late at night, local kids drag racing on the part of the Alaska Highway that ran past the airport. The only promise of entertainment was the dogsled competition that started right there in White Horse that he could catch on his monitors. But that presumed he would still be there when the snows came. Galligher dreaded the thought.

Today, while Galligher glanced at the monitors, he was feasting on a haddock sandwich with extra creamy dill sauce. One thing he had learned about that part of the world: they had incredibly fine-tasting fish.

Then something caught his eye. On one of the monitors there appeared a caravan of vehicles. He zoomed in. The first two vehicles were armored troop carriers. Both of them had the Global Alliance forces logo on the side—the roaring lion with its mouth open wide and long, deadly fangs. John Galligher mused to himself, *Gee, maybe someone, somewhere, way back when, should have started asking questions about the Alliance the minute they saw that logo.*

Galligher thought that perhaps the troops were on maneuvers. But then he spotted the Global Alliance forces command vehicle and behind it a ZB D97 modified tank the Alliance had obtained from the Chinese, with a 100mm cannon on top and a 30mm cannon right next to it. Suddenly Galligher stopped chewing on his haddock sandwich. He was getting the feeling that a major assault might be on the menu. He tapped the emergency contact number on his Allfone. Up on the floor above him, in his digital communications center, Chiro picked up.

Galligher shouted, "Get ready for an invasion. I'm seeing Alliance military hardware chugging down the street toward our position."

"How much time?" Chiro asked.

"They're on the other side of town. I'd say we've got twenty minutes, to be on the conservative side."

Galligher bolted out into the lobby where Bobby Robert was poring over a magazine.

"Bobby, I think things are going to start jumping."

"What's up?"

Galligher looked down at the hunting magazine. "That's good," he said pointing to it. "You shoot. That's swell. But we've got a small army of Alliance forces heading our way. I think they want to rock our world. Call our local minutemen volunteers and tell them to get over here in fifteen minutes or less. If they have weapons, tell them to bring them. But they have to come here by the back way, the route along the Yukon River."

Bobby reached under the desk, opened a cupboard, and pulled out two long-barreled Colt 45s, one in each fist. "I've got my shotgun and my bear rifle here in the closet too," he said.

Galligher grinned. It appeared he had a new BFF. "That's a great start," he said as scenes from the movie *The Alamo* flashed in his head. Then Bobby lifted up his long Indian poncho shirt and revealed a massive hunting knife hanging from his belt.

"Okay," Galligher shot back. "That makes you Jim Bowie. So I guess that makes me Davy Crockett."

And then he had another thought, but kept that one to himself. *Which makes us both dead soon.*

FORTY-EIGHT

NEW BABYLON, IRAQ

Ethan realized that a miracle had just happened in the lab. As he hung there by his arms, cinched up with leather straps, he felt an electric surge of adrenaline racing through his body. Was that also a miracle? Wasn't God the creator of adrenaline too? It was at that point that Ethan saw the whole escape plan unfold in front of him like a videotape.

So he acted out the plan and yanked himself up to an "iron cross" position like a gymnast on the rings. Then swung his legs over his head so he could use his feet to twist the straps around his ankles, thus taking some tension off of his arms and creating some slack at the wrists. He reached for a large shard of glass from the blast that was stuck into the leather strap cinched to his left arm. Upside down,

291

he had to swing himself over to that strap, hold himself in place with his powerful left arm, and with his right hand carefully grab hold of the piece of glass. It wouldn't give; it was stuck hard into the leather. *Please, God, help me cut this strap.*

Upside down, he gingerly yanked again at the shard of glass. Still, it didn't give. Then he had a thought. *Don't pull, just push.* So he started pushing on the glass like it was a miniature saw, back and forth, back and forth. He could then feel the leather giving way. But his arms were trembling with fatigue. He wasn't sure he could do it.

And then some crazy memories started surfacing from somewhere.

Maybe it was the pain in his head. Or maybe he was dying. He couldn't tell. But the memories and the images were there, filling his head. Out of the fog of his past, as real as ever, flashing before him.

He was back in his Triple-A baseball days as a struggling pitcher. That one ball game as the starting pitcher against the Yankee farm team from Scranton/Wilkes Barre. He could see the pro scouts watching him in the stands. Ethan had just thrown a fastball low and inside to the slugger of a centerfielder up to bat. The last inning with two outs and a full count. But the batter smacked a line drive to Ethan's right side. It would have been just within his reach if in that instant Ethan had caught the speeding ball in his bare right hand. Even if he had broken a finger or two it would have been worth it—he would have won the game spectacularly, and with a no-hitter at that.

But instead he hesitated. The ball zinged past him and past the shortstop and landed perfectly with a hop past the right fielder, and the big batter made it to second base. And that started a rout. One after another, the opposing players started hitting singles and doubles and finally a home run as Ethan's pitching style began to collapse in a series of out-of-control fastballs that were followed by failed knuckleballs floating to the plate like birthday gifts to the batters. His chances of a baseball career died that day.

But now something else: the image of him training for months on that rooftop in Athens—the daily rope climbing with a fifty-pound backpack. There was a reason for that. There were no accidents. Not in God's universe.

Ethan was mentally back in that lab room again. His head was clearer now. He tried harder, holding himself by the power of his left arm and with his right pushing on the shard of glass, back and forth, in a sawing and cutting motion. Sawing and cutting. The strap was starting to give way . . .

It broke. He reached over and with his left hand unbuckled the leather band on his right wrist and fell clumsily to the floor.

After climbing through the big window frame where the glass had been shattered with the miraculous blast, Ethan could see that both lab scientists were still unconscious. He noticed that the younger guy with blond hair was roughly his size. Ethan stripped the blue lab coat off of him, removed his security card from around his neck, and hung it around his own. For good measure, he donned the guy's horn-rimmed glasses. But Ethan had perfect vision, and the lab techie must have had the eyesight of a mole because the lenses were Coke-bottle thick. That added another carnival fun-house dimension to Ethan's stumble-bum getaway.

Ethan made it to a stairwell. The lab explosion had set off red emergency lights that flashed up on the ceiling, and he could hear sirens wailing somewhere. Still dizzy, and squinting with the eye-strain from the prescription glasses, he swayed and tripped down the emergency stairs leading from the laboratory floor, trying to keep his balance against the rocking-horse vertigo in his head. The grotesque experiment had rattled his brain and left him with an off-kilter sensation that he couldn't shake.

At the bottom of the stairwell, Ethan swung open the heavy metal door . . . to the sight of dozens of communications technology staffers rushing to the stairwell at the other end of the floor. Because of the alarm, all these middle-level tech staffers were avoiding the elevator, blindly following the standard operating procedure in an emergency. Ethan used the security card around his neck to activate the elevator. He saw the Down light blinking over the elevator door. It was heading his way. A few more seconds, and then the door opened.

Ethan stepped into the elevator, still unsteady on his feet. There were three other men already there. Two of them were oversized fellows with thick necks and earbuds in their ears, and Ethan knew that they had to be security. They were on either side of a tall, handsome man in the middle. He looked familiar, but Ethan didn't dwell on it. He turned around immediately, stumbling a little as he did, and faced the door as the elevator started down.

For a moment no one in the elevator talked. Then the man in the middle with the expensive-looking suit and the five-hundred-dollar haircut started to speak. When he did, Ethan knew once again that there was an unnerving familiarity to this individual.

The man said, "I was on my way to your lab. To see the experiment for myself. What happened?"

Ethan shook his head.

One of the big bodyguards punched him in the shoulder. "Answer when you are spoken to."

Ethan slowly turned around and looked the tall, handsome man right in the eye. When he did, the shock of recognition had him stepping back. He was speechless, while inside of him a combination of righteous rage and terror shot through him like an electrical fire.

The other security guard was yelling at him now. "Answer Chancellor Colliquin, lab geek."

Ethan was now face-to-face with Alexander Colliquin. And that is when he realized something else. Colliquin's face was the image in the 3-D holograph, the one that had hung in the air in front of Ethan in the testing room and then by some hellish technology had wormed its way into his head, invading his mind and his thoughts. There was something else too. Ethan knew now that it had been

Colliquin in his visions all along—the human mask with the beast hiding behind it.

Ethan had to silently coach himself. *Hold it together. Stay cool. Don't react.*

Colliquin stared hard at Ethan, but with a detached, otherworldly expression on his face. It was as if his eyes were peering out from some dark, nameless place and didn't belong to the rest of him. Colliquin asked, "What kind of tech failure went on up there?"

Ethan swayed a bit. "Tech failure? No. It wasn't that."

"Then what?" Colliquin snapped.

Ethan cemented his features to a bland expression as he replied, "Something else. Higher than technology. Way higher."

One of the guards pointed to the side of Ethan's head. "Hey, you're bleeding from your ears. Better get to the infirmary." The other guard added, as an aside to Colliquin, "Your Excellency, no wonder he's acting stupid," and snickered.

The elevator stopped and the two guards and Alexander Colliquin swept past Ethan and out of the elevator and began to stride down the hallway. Ethan turned in the opposite direction. He had to find an exit before somebody discovered that he was the lab rat and that he had just escaped from his cage.

FORTY-N1NE

WHITE HORSE, YUKON TERRITORY

After Bobby Robert's emergency call, four local Remnant volunteers from the city responded. They had been gone for a while, working on a commercial fishing boat, but now they were back and they showed up at the hotel with hunting rifles. One of them had an ancient revolver that looked like it could have belonged to Wild Bill Cody. In the old days, John Galligher would have thought that the whole scene looked like a sick joke. Particularly when he saw the armored Global Alliance vehicles begin to rumble up to the front of the hotel.

But Galligher was a different man now. No longer the cynical FBI special agent. Not anymore. God had changed everything for him. But it was clear He was going to have to work a big-time miracle if Chiro was to keep his communications center functioning. Galligher had never been privy to the big picture—to the way in which Chiro's mass of cables and computers upstairs fit into the global scheme to push back against Alexander Colliquin's worldwide takeover, and the bigger plan to spread the gospel message throughout the disintegrating world. Because of that, Galligher may have resented Ethan for keeping him in the dark. But that was something Galligher would have to get over.

Galligher sprinted upstairs to Chiro's tech lab. He found the computer genius peering into the guts of his eight-foot-high quantum computer through the machine's two open doors.

Galligher spoke, puffing a little. "You'd better hunker down, Chiro. The guys with the black hats just pulled up."

Chiro glanced out the one window of his second-floor lab overlooking the backyard. Then he whirled around with a look on his face that was strangely optimistic, given the drastic circumstances. "Yes, but our friend just showed up too," he exclaimed. "In his red suit."

Galligher threw him a confused look but couldn't pass up the chance for a smart-aleck retort. "Red suit? Let's hope he's got some missile launchers on his sleigh."

"Go down and see for yourself," Chiro shouted, wide-eyed.

Galligher told Chiro to lock himself into his lab by closing the big metal security door they had installed to create a safe room for Chiro and his equipment. Then he charged downstairs and pulled his .357 Magnum from his shoulder holster. Bobby Robert and his four minutemen were hiding behind pieces of furniture in the lobby. The whole thing looked like an Old West shoot-out. Bobby Robert was ready for battle; he had his long black hair unbraided, a Tlinget tribal bandana tied around his forehead and war paint on his face.

"No one fires," Galligher called to them, "until I say so. And let's pray I don't have to say so. Those are my rules of engagement. Any questions?"

Everyone shook their heads. Bobby Robert threw a tense smile.

Galligher looked over this small bunch of amateurs who were risking their lives and thought about how they all counted on him. He really didn't want to screw this up now.

He strode toward the front door, praying silently as he did. *God, John Galligher here. Thanks for saving me. You hunted me down and found me and then reminded me that Jesus died for my sins. Thanks again for that, by the way. I don't thank You enough. Please keep Helen alive long enough for me to tell her about Jesus. Okay? She's my ex-wife. But, yeah, well, I guess You already knew that.*

As he stepped outside, Galligher glanced up and noticed that the sky was blue and clear. It reminded him of that movie where an Indian chief talked about it being a good day to die. Then he looked straight ahead and found himself staring down the long barrel of the cannon on the Alliance combat tank. *On the other hand, how about a good day to live?*

The Global Alliance commander was standing up in his roofless Humvee. He leaned forward and touched something on the dashboard and there came a burst of electronic feedback. Then he started speaking. "Attention, hotel occupants. This is an official Global Alliance military action. Throw down your weapons. Give yourselves up. You will be treated humanely under the international articles of the Alliance War Crimes Act. You have ten seconds to comply or we will commence firing on you as enemies of the Alliance."

Galligher wanted to say something, anything. Particularly something clever. But his mouth was dry and he had completely run out of his supply of clever. During his FBI career he had been in several gun battles with terror cells. But somehow this was different. Not just a battle against evil. His job now was to protect something infinitely good: a northern outpost that was somehow going to figure into the spread of the good news about Jesus over this entire sick, tired, beat-up planet.

He was about to say something, though he wasn't sure what, when someone answered for him. A shout came out from somewhere. "This is Captain Morganthau of the Canadian Mounted Police."

Galligher looked over to his left. Appearing from around the side of the hotel came the mounted police officer he had met before—the one who'd drawn the ichthus in the dust of the furniture. He was decked out in his bright-red Mountie dress uniform and his wide-brimmed Mountie hat, and he was riding a big black horse. Then several more Mounties, all dressed the same, and all in the saddle, came up behind him and joined him on each flank.

The Alliance commander grimaced, and even from a distance Galligher could see how ticked off he was. "Retreat immediately!" he yelled. "Or you will be treated as enemies of the Global Alliance and will be shown no mercy."

The mounted police captain shouted back, "And I am hereby ordering you to withdraw from this street and from this city. You've committed an illegal act of military occupation. Eight minutes ago the Canadian Parliament voted to withdraw Canada from the Global Alliance. Don't you know that, aye? You have no lawful authority here. If you fail to withdraw I will make sure that several of our Royal Air Force jets are given orders to direct missiles onto your position."

The top hatch of the Alliance tank opened and the head of one of the Alliance soldiers popped out. He looked frantically up toward the sky.

Galligher stood there slack jawed as he watched the Mountie, sitting tall in his saddle, practically daring the Global Alliance military to shoot first. It was *High Noon, The Alamo,* and half a dozen of his favorite John Wayne movies all playing out in front of him.

Galligher raised his .357 in the air. "And I am former FBI special agent John Galligher," he shouted. "And I am prepared to make a civilian arrest of you, Commander, if these brave Canadian Mounties should fall in the line of duty."

Somewhere, high up in the air, came the roar of a jet. Everyone on that street jerked their heads up and searched the sky. But it was only a commercial jetliner.

Time passed in the standoff. Galligher didn't know how long, but it seemed to go on forever. The Global Alliance commander was still standing up in his military vehicle and Captain Morganthau was still sitting high in his saddle. It was time for someone to blink.

Someone did.

"I am ordering my unit," the commander finally called out over his loudspeaker, "to relocate to the other side of White Horse." Then he added, "But we are not withdrawing from the city. You, Captain Morganthau, will be dealt with accordingly. That I can promise you."

F1FTY

NEW BABYLON, IRAQ

Ethan March had been running for his life, trying to sprint, but he found it hard because of his dizzy spells. He had made his way out into a parking lot not far from the digital lab building. As part of the confusion created around the palace compound after the alarm was sounded, crowds of New Babylon officials and employees were now milling outside, and a few were sitting under the shade of the tall palm trees, waiting for the all-clear sign to return to their offices. Ethan slowed his pace so he wouldn't stand out, but he was desperately searching for his next move while he walked. Then he saw it.

He noticed a white Range Rover with a Red Cross insignia on the side that was parked just outside one of the administrative buildings. A European-looking man in a white shirt with the sleeves rolled up came striding out of a building carrying a briefcase and headed toward the vehicle. He tossed a look back at the administrative building, shook his head in apparent disgust, and then began to climb into the Red Cross vehicle.

Ethan stepped quickly up to the driver's side window while the door was still open. "Can I ask you something?" Ethan said.

The driver eyed him suspiciously and nodded.

"Are you heading out of the compound?"

"Indeed I am," the man said in a crisp British accent as he looked closer at Ethan. "You sound like an American."

Ethan nodded.

The man glanced down at the ID badge Ethan had taken off the body of the big blond lab technician. "But your name looks Norwegian—Hans Jorgenson."

Ethan tried to manage a smile. He wondered if there was still blood trickling down from his ears. He had tried to wipe it clean while he walked. But he couldn't tell for sure. He began to pray silently. *Lord, tell me whether this man can be trusted.*

"So is that your name, really?" the Englishman asked.

Ethan flashed a struggling smile. "What's in a name?"

The Red Cross official suddenly broke into a smile and chuckled. "Right. 'A rose by any other name' and all that . . ." Then he nodded his head toward the sky, where the sound of a siren was still wailing. "Are you somehow tied into this mess?"

"Yes, in a way. It's a long story."

"Technically, I am not supposed to ferry passengers," he said. "On the other hand, this is a bit awkward, because I am also supposed to be involved in humanitarian work. Which is bloody ironic, because the Global Alliance hasn't the faintest idea what that word even means."

Then he took a long look at Ethan again. "But I suppose as a staff technician with the Alliance, you couldn't agree with any of what I just said."

"You might be surprised," Ethan said, moving closer to the open door of the vehicle.

The two men looked at each other for a few seconds. Then the British Red Cross worker added, "So . . . tell me something, Mr. Jorgenson. Would my driving you out of this compound constitute an act of humanitarian aid?"

"Yes," Ethan replied in an instant. "Definitely humanitarian."

The driver sighed heavily, as if he had a pretty good idea that this was not merely a matter of giving a man a ride, and that things were about to become complicated. Finally the Brit gave his decision. "All right, then. Climb aboard. Before I change my mind."

Ethan scooted around to the passenger side and climbed in.

"Where are you heading?"

"Anywhere right now."

The Englishman shook his head as he started up his car. "I was afraid you might say something like that."

As they headed down the long drive toward the checkpoint gate, Ethan noticed now that Global Alliance security guards were starting to fill the parking lot and were approaching the staff members who loitered there.

"Anything you want to share with me?" the driver asked.

"For starters, you and I have something in common," Ethan said. "Oh?"

"I don't trust the Alliance any more than you do. Probably less."

"A strange thing for an Alliance staffer to say."

"It would be . . . if I were one."

The driver glanced over at Ethan's borrowed ID and then gave Ethan a quizzical look. The driver ventured out a little in his next comment. "I had an appointment scheduled today. To ask the Global Alliance to stop blocking Red Cross aid in a number of countries. I thought at least I would get a meeting. But then I heard that our British Parliament just voted to exit this Babylonian atrocity called the Global Alliance. And it's about time, I must say. But in terms of my chance of doing any business here, that was the end of that. My meeting in New Babylon was abruptly canceled. I'm sure because of the vote in London." Something caught the driver's attention. He looked at Ethan. "You must have had a head injury. You're bleeding."

"I know."

Something must have sunk in, because then the driver added, "I'll do what I can for you."

That was good to hear. "My name is Ethan." As he reached out and shook the Brit's hand, Ethan suddenly started feeling woozy. He couldn't afford to pass out. Not now. They were pulling up to the gatehouse. But the four guards didn't wait for the Range Rover to pull up. They piled out of the little guard building, each with one hand on his side arm and the other up in the air, blocking the Englishman's car.

One of the guards, who looked like he might be an Iraqi, stepped up to the driver's side and motioned for his papers. The Brit handed them over. The Alliance guard took his time poring over them. Then he handed them back. But he leaned in through the window and nodded to Ethan. "Papers?"

The Englishman intervened. "This technician and I are on our way to an urgent assignment. We have to stay on schedule."

"And where would this assignment be located?" The guard gave a quick glance over at the ID badge that hung from Ethan's neck.

"Karbala," the Brit replied.

The guard straightened up and chortled. "I don't think you'll be making your assignment today," he said. "But you can try." Then he waved them through.

Ethan leaned his head against the headrest and closed his eyes.

"You're not well," the driver said.

"It's nothing. What do you think the guard meant by that?"

"I take it to mean they'll be searching cars along the highway. Checking closely. We may have a problem getting you very far from here." That was when the Brit pulled the Range Rover over and turned it around on the highway.

"Where are you going?"

"If trouble is waiting up at Karbala, I'll take you in the opposite direction. South, toward Al Hillah."

Ethan relaxed just a little. It looked like God was supplying another miracle. He was feeling better and better about his chances of a clean escape.

Until twenty minutes later. That's when the Englishman pulled his car over again to the side of the highway. He reached over and snatched up a pair of binoculars from the backseat and peered through them to get a better look at some activity up ahead on the highway.

"What is it?" Ethan asked.

"Not good. A roadblock. It looks like a large number of Global Alliance troops." If the Brit expected Ethan to start coming unglued, he was about to be surprised. Ethan nodded in a matter-of-fact kind of way, with a strange kind of resolve. "The Lord has brought me this far." He looked out the window to a strange collection of ancient ruins off to the side of the road and recited silently in his head a few verses from Psalm 46:

> God is our refuge and strength,
> A very present help in trouble.
> Therefore we will not fear, though the earth should change
> And though the mountains slip into the heart of the sea.

"Who are you, really?" the driver asked with an expression that was now full of searching and maybe even some deeper questions.

"Have you heard of the Remnant?"

"Ah yes, the Jesus followers."

"I am a hunted man."

"Do you have friends anywhere near here?"

"I don't know," Ethan said wearily. "But I'm hoping that some people from my group might be looking for me. Friends of mine." He thought about the friends he had. Former Mossad spies, ex-CIA operatives, retired FBI agents. His voice took on an optimistic tone as he managed a smile. "On second thought, knowing them, I would say they're probably mounting a rescue attempt."

The Brit pointed over to the ancient stone ruins off in the distance. "For the time being, I suggest you stay over there."

"What are those?"

"Uncovered not too long ago in an excavation after the Global Alliance moved in here at New Babylon. But Alexander Colliquin supposedly got nervous having archaeologists poking around so close to his government city, so he kicked them out. History says that King Nebuchadnezzar married the daughter of the king of the Medes, but his new wife was homesick for the lush gardens of her homeland instead of the harsh desert you see around you. So, as a compromise, he built a 'middle ground' for her—a lush retreat, right there." And with that he pointed to the collection of tall, interlocking stone walls in the distance that formed a kind of labyrinth. "History calls them the Hanging Gardens of Babylon. These are the real ones." Then the Brit added, "This can be your middle ground right now. You can hide behind those walls. Until help arrives for you. Let's hope . . ."

They shook hands and the Englishman handed him an extra plastic bottle of water before he left.

Ethan had a final thought for the other man. "Keep an eye out for some Westerners who might be looking for me. If you do see them, please tell them where I am. And bid them Godspeed for me. *High speed*, if possible."

As the Range Rover roared off down the highway and Ethan began the trek toward the stone walls off in the distance, he continued to feel an increased sense of dizziness and a terrific wave of head pain. His skull felt like he had been dropped on his head from a second-story window. But instead of dwelling on that, he was stuck on something else. He couldn't shake the parting words from the Red Cross worker. Yes, he knew God was with him, and that God alone would be his ultimate help. But he also had to wonder something else: whether any human help would get to him before the Alliance troops did.

ㅁㅁㅁ

WHITE HOUSE SITUATION ROOM

Washington, D.C.

President Hank Hewbright had pulled together a very small group. Just two men, in fact. He had been increasingly criticized in his own administration because he was relying on an ever-narrowing circle of confidants. He certainly could not trust his own vice president. His chief of staff had received news that Darrel Zandibar had remained in close contact with Jessica Tulrude despite his protestations claiming the opposite. Zandibar had lied about that right to Hewbright's face. Nor did the president fully trust Elizabeth Tanner from Homeland Security or Terrance Tyler, his secretary of state, or even the director of the FBI, knowing as he did how it had been infiltrated by Tulrude's people during her administration. He was confident they were still there in the Bureau.

Was he growing paranoid? Possibly. But one thing he knew for sure: now that he'd survived impeachment, Colliquin and his Alliance had every reason to mount a more aggressive kind of offensive against the United States, or perhaps even the presidency. In light of that, how could he be too careful?

He stood in front of the big screen in the situation room that displayed, with little digital triangles, the amassing of Global Alliance troops all along the Mexican border. "Their activity is always along our southern border," Hewbright said. "What's down there?"

The answer came from Secretary of Defense Rollie Allenworth. "It's close to Bluffdale, Utah."

"Our National Data Center?" Hewbright asked. "For what purpose?"

Allenworth nodded. "As you know, that data center is the core of our digital surveillance and electronic intelligence, and the repository of practically everything that our nation knows about everything. And, of course, there also is the world's most advanced computer hardware that makes it all possible."

"But it's well guarded and secure."

"Yes. It's right there on the grounds of the Utah National Guard. And we have a very strong military presence and security details protecting the perimeter. And we have intercept security all over the facility."

"Then what's the Alliance planning?"

Allenworth shrugged. "Not an internal military coup, that's for sure. You have the full support of the Pentagon and the Joint Chiefs. And I can't imagine that the Alliance military will mount a land invasion and try to fight their way up to Utah. We'd stop them well in advance of their ever getting close to the data center."

"Then what?" Hewbright wondered out loud.

William Tatter, his CIA director, spoke up. "Our intel from Babylon is that Alexander Colliquin definitely wants the data center. The question is why. Our guess is either sabotage, or conversion of the facility to their own use. It's the most advanced computing facility in the world."

"Anything definitive?" Hewbright asked.

"Not yet. But we have a reliable asset who is located just off the China mainland; he told us once that there was a person who might know more about this than we do."

"Who is that?"

"A Remnant resister. An expatriated American. Former air force pilot."

Hewbright's face lit up. "It sounds a lot like one of the good guys who's no longer with us—Joshua Jordan."

"Close," Tatter said. "His name is Ethan March. He was a protégé of Jordan's. He's Jordan's successor and the leader of the Jesus Remnant movement."

"Can we talk to him?"

"According to our contact, March had been in Athens and then relocated to Hong Kong. But we didn't have authorization to enlist him as one of our own assets. So it all ended there."

"If this Ethan March is half the man that Joshua Jordan was," Allenworth interjected, "and if he knows anything about the intentions of that crazy fox Alexander Colliquin, I say we need to bring him into the fold, stat."

Tatter agreed. "We can pursue this man, Mr. President, if you give the say-so."

Hewbright nodded. "Then I say so. Let's get Mr. Ethan March. Do whatever it takes to bring him in. Wherever he is."

FIFTY-ONE

NEW BABYLON, IRAQ

In the underground interrogation bunker beneath the main palace of Chancellor Colliquin, Mr. Martisse had been pursuing the investigation into Ethan's escape and the bizarre "accident" in the lab room. Martisse had just finished questioning witnesses, including the lab chief and his tech assistant, who had both been knocked unconscious by the mysterious blast in the control room adjacent to Animal Testing Room #6. So far, Martisse had come up with very few tangible leads.

Now a green light illuminated over the door to the concrete-walled room. Martisse stood up from his metal desk, where he had been reviewing his notes from the interrogation sessions, and strode quickly over to the door. He placed his index finger and thumb on the

ID pad. A little screen lit up with the face of Alexander Colliquin on the other side of the door. Martisse tapped the icon on the screen for the retinal-scan identification for his visitor. The screen read *Retinal scan verified, but with unexplained anomalies.*

"Hurry up, you fool," Colliquin growled through the speaker-phone on the other side. "Let me in."

Martisse buzzed him in, and when Colliquin swept into the room, his chief of security gave a quick bow.

"What have you learned?" Colliquin demanded.

"Not much yet. I was just preparing my report—"

"I don't want a report," Colliquin said with an icy stare. "I want to know what happened up in that lab room and where Ethan March is."

"Sir, we've finally solved a computer glitch and have now down-loaded a photo of Ethan March from the drone-bot database. We've shown the photo to your security detail. Two security guards thought they recognized him having entered the same elevator with them while using a lab technician's ID tag."

On hearing that, Colliquin clenched his jaw and glanced away for a nanosecond. He seemed to be lost in some embarrassing thought. Then he collected himself and shot back, "But that information doesn't answer any of my questions, does it?"

Martisse shook his head.

"And you are in charge of security, are you not?"

Martisse nodded again.

"And this incident constituted a security breach, did it not?"

"Yes," Martisse replied, swallowing hard. "Regrettably, it does."

Inexplicably, Colliquin reached out toward Martisse, holding a hand on each side of Martisse's head, though not touching him. Startled, Martisse began to take a step backward.

"Don't be frightened," Colliquin said in a cool, quiet voice. "I sense that you are anxious."

"Your Excellency," Martisse said in a plaintive voice, "I was going to warn you about something. The retina scan noted some 'anomalies' in your eyes. Perhaps you should have that checked out by an ophthalmologist."

"No, there is no need for that," Colliquin said. "But I can understand your concern." His hands were still poised on either side of Martisse's head, and now he brought his face close to the other man's. "You see, I had a remarkable experience recently. In my private chapel. The question now is an important one: To what degree have my otherwise extraordinary natural powers been supernaturally enhanced? Until I know that, how can I accurately determine the full limits of my power? You do see my dilemma, don't you?"

Martisse gave a confused nod of his head.

Colliquin closed his eyes, still holding his hands poised on either side of Martisse's skull. After a moment, he opened them again. But when he did, he seemed to be looking right through Martisse and all the way to the concrete wall behind him.

Martisse, frozen in place, began to whimper and moan. "What is happening to me?" he cried out, but his arms were fixed at his side as if restrained by some magnetic force.

A cracking sound became audible. Martisse screamed as his skull, right along the top of the neurocranium, began to fracture.

And then his eyes rolled back.

□□□

Colliquin released his hands from his invisible hold and Martisse's body dropped like a sack of meat to the floor.

As Colliquin studied the corpse, he addressed himself, as if he were delivering a college lecture. "The bony structure of the skull is quite thick. One of the thickest layers of protection for any organism known to nature. So, by my estimate, it appears that I have just exerted more than a ton of pressure in order to cause the fracture of that bony structure. And all of that by my mere act of mental will and concentration. Splendid. Absolutely splendid."

He stepped back and took a last look at the dead man on the floor. "Good practice for the moment when I meet up with Ethan March."

ㅁㅁㅁ

SATHER AIR BASE, IRAQ

As Rivka peeked out of the canopy of the military fighter jet, she spotted the military air base down below that was just outside of Baghdad. Ten hours earlier she had made a vow: with God's help she was not going to let the obstacles of time or distance keep her from reaching Ethan. She was getting closer to making good on that promise.

She had flown the first leg of her trip out of Hong Kong in Zhang Lee's private jet until they reached Bangkok, Thailand, where they landed. In the interim she had called on Gavi Davidson, a former spy partner from her Israeli Mossad days, and asked him for some urgent help. Gavi told her that a brand-new F-140 fighter jet from the IAF was fueling there in Bangkok, on a routine, long-distance test run. Gavi had to laugh when he told her that one of the few advantages of the "lousy" deal that Prime Minister Bensky had cut with Alexander Colliquin was that, at least for the time being, Israel's forces had more mobility traveling around the world, and refueling on the way—as long as the mission was peaceful, of course.

After landing at the Bangkok commercial airport, Rivka had grabbed a cab to the military air base and met up with a young Israeli pilot who had been flying solo in the new two-seater fighter jet. When IAF headquarters in Tel Aviv found out that one of their best former Mossad agents would be sitting in the second seat, they gave their lightning-fast approval. The pilot warned her about the Mach-two-and-a-half takeoff power of the new F-140.

When the fighter jet launched off from the Singapore runway like a missile, Rivka realized the pilot wasn't kidding—she felt as if her stomach had been relocated. But in the grand scheme of things, it didn't matter. She was winging her way to Iraq. Ethan was there somewhere, and she had the invincible feeling that she was getting closer and that God would bring them together again, even though she had no idea how that was going to happen.

But now, as Rivka studied the Iraqi air base far beneath them, and as the fighter plane began its descent, Rivka's brain went into hyperdrive. Her buddy Gavi had said he would try to rustle up a contact for her in the Baghdad area so she could catch up to Pack McHenry's team. But Gavi gave no details and made no promises. Even though her ride in the F-140 had cut her travel time down considerably, she knew Pack and his crew were still well ahead of her. The agreed plan was that Pack and company would begin advancing toward New Babylon the minute that they were in-country. Rivka and Pack had linked their encrypted GPS devices in the event they both were in the same part of Iraq around the same time. Pack said if it worked out, he would locate her geoposition and pick her up himself. If not, Pack said he had an idea about having some friends of his track her position and give her a lift.

As soon as Rivka's jet finished taxiing to a stop, and the landing gear was secured and the canopy popped, she stripped off her helmet and mask and began to scamper out of the jet. She yanked her Allfone out of her flight suit and hit speed dial for Gavi. It rang . . . and kept ringing. "Come on, Gavi, pick up," she muttered. But it didn't happen. She left a hurried message. "Gavi, it's me, Rivka. I'm at Sather Air Base. Where is your pickup guy for me? Do you have one? Call me, please."

She clicked off her cell and looked around. Huge concrete bunkers, a lot of large corrugated metal hangars and sheds, and several runways. Pretty much the same as when it had been turned over to the Iraqis from the U.S. military, and then later to the Global Alliance. Beyond the base she saw the flat, brown desert, with just a few palm trees and an occasional green tuft of shrubbery, and swirls of dust that drifted aimlessly.

Rivka hit another number on her Allfone, trying to get in touch with Pack and his team. But no luck there either, and she was forced to leave a message advising him of her location, asking for his, and wanting any update on the status of Ethan.

She glanced over at her F-140 pilot, who was now coming out of the air base security building accompanied by two Global Alliance security guards who looked to be Iraqi nationals. The three of them halted, and one of the Alliance guards passed some paperwork back to the pilot, who motioned toward Rivka. The Alliance guard shielded his eyes for a moment as he spotted Rivka, who was still in her flight suit. Then he nodded to the pilot, and he and his Alliance partner walked back into the building.

Rivka prayed silently. *Lord, I feel like I am stuck here now on a bad sightseeing tour. I want to be part of the rescue. Please keep Ethan safe. And bring us together, Father.* She paused. Then she muttered, "And forgive my impertinence. You're God, and I'm not. You're in control. I do believe that, Lord. Down to the marrow of my bones."

She trotted toward the pilot, who was walking her way. She had come from the other side of the globe to help in the daring rescue of the man she loved. But she was now getting a bad feeling about things.

Her Allfone rang. It was Victoria McHenry. "Hello, Rivka, dear. We're on the main artery coming out of Karbala and heading toward New Babylon. But we're sandbagged right now. About a mile and a half from our position is a massive military roadblock. The Alliance seems to have sealed off the Global Alliance complex. We're a small team, and we simply can't take on an entire company of Alliance special forces in a ground battle. Rivka, where are you now?"

"Just landed at Sather Air Base. I'm still trying to get a ride to where you are. I'm stuck here for now. It's maddening."

On the other end, Victoria sounded distracted, like someone was trying to get her attention. "Rivka," she announced, "Pack needs to tell me something. I've got to cut out—" The call dropped.

By then, Rivka stood eye to eye with the Israeli pilot. He was checking the time on his wrist Allfone watch and throwing her a look she didn't miss. He expected her to be ready to climb back into the F-140. And that was something she couldn't do.

"I told security here we had to make a fueling stop," the pilot explained. "They're giving us twenty minutes. Then I've got to get airborne. And if you aren't strapped into that second seat of the F-140 when I lift off, there's going to be some serious trouble."

FIFTY-TWO

SECRET SERVICE HOLDING ROOM W16 AT THE WHITE HOUSE

Washington, D.C.

Secret Service Agent Decker had to let Ben Bolling's telephone call go to voice mail because he was about to address a dozen White House agents and pass out assignments. But hearing Bolling's voice triggered some memories. Some good. Some bad.

Decker had known Bolling when Bolling was an FBI agent. They had once worked together on the presidential campaign trail guarding Hank Hewbright during the last election. Back then, Decker did the Secret Service perimeter work for Hewbright's activities. Meanwhile Secret Service Agent Owens was the guy physically closest to Senator Hewbright. Which is why Agent Owens was now buried in a cemetery in his hometown of Birmingham, Alabama, and why Decker was still alive.

During the assassination attempt against Hewbright, FBI Special Agent Bolling heroically broke into the middle of the attempted assassination scene in the political convention hotel room and put an end to it—unfortunately not until after Agent Owens had been killed. As Decker reviewed his e-clipboard, ready to address his cadre of agents, he wondered why Bolling was reaching out to him now. The two hadn't spoken for years.

When the agents were all seated in the holding room of the basement of the White House, Decker started giving them the POTUS briefer for the day. POTUS—the president of the United States—would be in meetings all morning, starting with his national security briefing and ending with a discussion with his economic advisors regarding the Alliance trade-sanctions issue. Then he would be leaving, via the south lawn, under constant Secret Service protection and would be boarding *Marine One*, the presidential helicopter, which would ferry him to Andrews Air Force Base. There, with the same team of agents in tow, he would be flown on *Air Force One* to New London, Connecticut, to deliver the commencement address to the graduates of the Coast Guard. Following that, POTUS would return under night skies to Washington and the White House, where he would retire for the night.

After the briefing, Agent Decker returned Ben Bolling's call. Bolling picked up after a few rings. At first, Bolling made small talk and painted an overly rosy picture of his life as a retiree. Finally, he got down to brass tacks. "I've got this friend . . . Well, a fellow FBI agent, actually. John Galligher. He used to do counterterrorism before he retired. A jokester and sort of a pain in the butt. But he definitely knows terrorism and threat assessment. So he contacted me recently and said he thought there was a threat against the president. A contact of his who used to work in clandestine services with the Company has traced this possible threat to an incident in Russia, and to a former KGB and FSB agent named Vlad Malatov."

Decker was silent, thinking through what he was hearing. "Okay. We'll run it through our system."

"No, that won't do you any good. This Malatov guy supposedly had a KGB-style extreme makeover. Face reconstruction. New fingerprints. Voice alteration. The works. He's even on an AllTube fight video, but he's wearing a mask. Anyway, he won't be in your system."

"Thanks," Decker said with hesitation. "I guess." He chewed on it for a second. "How about the staleness of this report? How current is it?"

"I couldn't tell you. I know this doesn't help you much, and I know you get a lot of vague threat data all the time—most of it pure malarkey—but I promised Galligher I'd pass it on to you."

"So that's it?"

"Yep."

"Well, Ben, considering that you're a grade-A hero in my book, I'll take your warning into consideration."

"Thanks."

"Anything else you can tell me?"

"No," Bolling said, "that's it."

"Any other names, places, leads?"

"No. I wish I had more."

"Well, thanks for letting me know," Decker said. "That doesn't give me much to go on." He paused and looked around to make sure he didn't have company. Then he added, "Things are weird around here, Ben. I don't know who I'm working for half the time. Hard to explain. Strange politics going on. Maybe we can arrange a time for you to stop by. Give me your take on things. Maybe I'm just getting tired of this line of work. I'm sure you know what I mean."

Ben said he understood and that he would be glad to visit the White House anytime.

Decker clicked off. He looked around the room and then went out in the hall where he found new transfer Agent Booth still hanging around, waiting for another round of follow-the-senior-agent-around-on-daily-assignments.

"Agent Booth," Decker said to him. "I just received a tip. Alerting me to a general risk, but nothing specific. Possibly directed at the president. I would like you to do something for me."

"Certainly," Booth replied with a grin, his teeth bright white against his Miami tan.

"Stay vigilant. Anything that looks out of the ordinary, please report it to me. I know you're new on the White House detail, but give me your eyes and ears. Okay?"

Booth nodded. "That's why I'm here."

"Oh, and something else," Decker said. "Your wish is about to come true."

"What's that, sir?"

"I heard about your being a fan of the president and wanting his autograph. Tomorrow you'll get your chance to meet him. You can get his autograph then."

The smile of Agent Booth broadened.

ㅁㅁㅁ

DESERT OUTSIDE NEW BABYLON, IRAQ

Ethan was constantly moving from one space to another within the labyrinth of crumbling stone walls that made up the interior of the ancient ruins. At first he'd been alone there and felt safe. But then the Global Alliance security forces started arriving. They were slowly beginning to flood the area less than a half mile from the ruins. As he peeked around the edge of the ancient walls, he could see the Alliance police with tracking dogs, sniffing the ground. He was glad that he had donned the clothes of the Alliance lab tech. Maybe that would throw them off. But he could also hear Global Alliance armed drone-bots flying in the distance, though they hadn't conducted a flyover on his position in the ruins. Not yet.

Most of the spaces between the high walls where Ethan was hiding were wide open to the sky, but a few had stone floors from the upper level that provided some cover. Ethan didn't want to stay in any one spot for too long. So he kept going along the walls, memorizing the exact pathways from his ever-moving positions back through the labyrinth to the safety of those few areas that had the big stone slabs overhead. The Alliance drone-bots and helicopters had heat-seeking sensors on board that could identify humans on the ground, but Ethan was betting that they wouldn't be able to detect him through twelve inches of stonework over his head.

His brain was still reeling, though, and the vertigo was still there. At times it seemed almost impossibly difficult to remember his way back to the areas with coverage from above. He wondered whether that experiment in the lab had permanently fried his brain.

□□□

SATHER AIR BASE, IRAQ

The pilot of the F-140 climbed back up into the cockpit, but he hesitated and looked down at Rivka. She stood in her flight suit, her feet glued to the tarmac. "Are you coming, Rivka?" he shouted down. "This bird is about to take off."

She hesitated. As long as Ethan might be somewhere in Iraq, there was no way she could leave. She felt as if she had jumped out of a plane without a parachute and she was free-falling. Unless something happened soon, she was going to hit the ground. But she still had no intel on where Pack's team was and certainly no idea where Ethan might be now.

"It's zero hour," the pilot called down. "Let's go."

Rivka's Allfone buzzed. She clicked it open. A message read: *Eyes only. Classified.*

She clicked the Options icon on the little screen of her Allfone. *Finger ID required.*

She pressed her thumb and index finger on the screen and hit *Send.*

After the confirmation was received, her screen read: *Eye scan required.*

She placed her wide-open right eye to the screen of her Allfone and hit *Send* again.

Ten seconds elapsed. Then the word *Confirmed* appeared. Another ten seconds went by, and then she received the message.

Meet us 300 yards south of the air base. Come alone. Look up.

She clicked off. In the cockpit, the pilot was looking down at her. Rivka took a deep breath and then called up to him, "Can't come with you. Thanks for everything. Godspeed."

The pilot gave a weary look, nodded, and closed the canopy, and a few moments later he was taxiing down the runway. A few seconds after that the tail of the jet lit up like a flame thrower and the fighter plane blasted up into the sky.

On the ground, Rivka pulled out a little compass from her flight suit to figure out which way was south. When she found it, she started sprinting full speed in that direction, out into the empty desert.

FIFTY-THREE

DESERT OUTSIDE NEW BABYLON, IRAQ

Pack McHenry sat behind the wheel of a vehicle that was dressed up like an Iraqi bakery truck, complete with a logo with a picture of pita bread and falafel on the side. But beneath the clever veneer the truck was armor plated, with heavy-duty suspension and a super-high-performance engine. His old days with the CIA and the contacts that he'd made there in the field always proved useful in providing him with some classy equipment.

Victoria sat in the back of the truck, along with Andre Chifflet and Vincent Romano. They were surrounded by a small depot of high-powered grenade launchers, ground-to-air shoulder-mounted missile launchers, and an assortment of automatic weapons. The bread truck had been parked there only a few minutes when Pack spotted a Range

Rover off in the distance coming their way. He'd hustled them all into the back of the truck, then got out and cranked open the hood as if it were having engine troubles.

Now the Ranger Rover pulled off the road and slowly crunched over the gravel and hard-packed sand until it was about twenty feet away. Pack noticed there was a Red Cross insignia on the side of the vehicle. The driver was either a plant from the Global Alliance or he was for real and had just passed successfully through the military roadblock a few miles down the highway.

Pack strode up to the driver, an Englishman in a sweat-soaked white shirt with the sleeves rolled up. The two of them sized each other up and engaged in some cautious conversation as Pack studied the Brit, who kept looking over at the pictures of pita bread on the side of the truck. Pack wondered if this guy was trying to piece the scene together, what with the fact that the bread truck was being driven by an American in the middle of the desert, just outside New Babylon, with a military roadblock not far away. It was clear the man had something on his mind; he kept meandering in his conversation, talking about an alert that had been sounded back at the New Babylon administrative sector and about the roadblock behind him, but he avoided specifics. Then he asked Pack what he was doing on the side of the road. He didn't ask an obvious question like, "Engine problems?"

Either the man was a professional actor along the lines of the Royal Shakespearean Theatre, or he was what he appeared to be—a nervous civilian sitting on some information. Pack knew when he needed to call in his wife to apply her talents. He asked the Brit if he could have a seat in his vehicle because Pack had someone who wanted to talk to him.

Pack went to the rear of the truck and knocked three times on the back of the truck, then twice slowly, then twice quickly. He then swung open the truck door—to be greeted with the barrel of Victoria's Glock semi-automatic with the pretty pink-colored grip. "Hello, dear," Victoria said cheerfully.

He explained what he needed. She quickly disappeared into the Red Cross vehicle.

Thirteen minutes later she came sashaying out of the Range Rover and back over to the bread truck. She sat down next to Pack in the front seat and told him everything the Brit had said—about the circumstances of his meeting Ethan March, about Ethan's apparent injuries, and how he had dropped him off at the ruins of the Hanging Gardens of Babylon. And that Ethan told the Englishman to be on the lookout for a rescue mission that he hoped was coming for him.

"Is he lying?" Pack asked.

Victoria gave it only a moment's thought. "Well, there was consistent musculature of the face during my questions. No inappropriate micro-expressive bursts. And no hint of deception in the dilation of the pupils. So, remembering that you are putting me under the gun here in terms of time, I would have to say no, he is not being evasive or deceptive."

Pack ginned. "You're the best."

Victoria smiled back. "Isn't that why you married me?"

"No," Pack said with a smirk. "It was a purely physical attraction."

With a grin of her own she slapped his shoulder.

Pack jumped out of the truck and trotted over to the Englishman, who had an anxious look on his face. The British man started first. "You know, I felt a little guilty leaving him back there. Is there anything I can do now?"

"Yes," Pack said. "You can drive toward Karbala and keep going. You don't want to be here when things start getting hairy."

ㅁㅁㅁ

SATHER AIR BASE, IRAQ

Rivka was about two hundred yards away from the air base, still at a full run across the desert, when she glanced back and saw the cloud of dust way back by the airfield. She slowed down just slightly so she could pull out her military spyglass and check it out. It looked like a jeep with two men in it, heading her way at a fast clip. It had to be Global Alliance air base security. Rivka had been an accomplished long-distance runner when she lived back in Israel. But all of that seemed like a long time ago. She was surprised that she was already getting slightly winded, so she slowed her pace a bit so she could fall into her stride and control her breathing.

There was a slight drop-off ahead to a lower plateau. Perhaps there would be somewhere for her to hide. She searched the skies but saw nothing. Who had sent the cryptic text to her Allfone? Was she following a wild-goose chase that would lead her nowhere—except into a Global Alliance jail cell? She was unarmed and had no survival provisions and was trying to outrun a vehicle in the Iraq desert.

This is not going to end well.

She reached the four-foot drop-off and jumped down, then picked up her pace again. Glancing to her left, she noticed a smooth transition area about a hundred feet away that could provide an easy ramp for the jeep to use in pursuing her down to the lower plateau. She abandoned the idea of pacing herself and pushed hard, sprinting full out with her legs wheeling like an engine. It was do-or-die time.

The jeep was getting close enough where she could hear its engine roaring up behind her. As she sprinted across the open desert with nowhere to hide, she heard gunfire and saw a puff of dust to her right and some to her left as the bullets from the Alliance airport security started zinging past her and hitting the ground.

The text message on her Allfone from the classified source had read *Look up*. She knew that she must be very close to three hundred yards by now. She tried to dismiss the echo in her head that kept saying this was crazy. She was now running pell-mell through the scrubby little bushes across the hard-packed sand. This had to be the spot, whatever it was, and so she looked up. But she saw nothing.

A desperate sinking feeling lodged in the pit of her stomach as she heard the vehicle of the Alliance security guards closing in. But she kept looking up . . . and finally she saw something. There was a black dot way up in the sky, and as she watched it she could see that it was hurtling down fast, like a huge anvil, making almost no sound as it descended.

Then the object in the sky fired on the Alliance jeep. Bullets ripped through the front tires and shredded the hood. The two Alliance airport security guards scrambled out of their vehicle and ran off in the opposite direction.

The object in the sky was still dropping fast and getting closer. Now she could make out what it was. She would have called it a helicopter except that it was clearly an advanced experimental model. It was black and strangely angular from the front tip to the rear tail that housed a fan-like propeller. The angular configuration was clearly designed to confuse radar detection. There was a large circular blade on the underside and larger chopper blades on the top and in between a large cockpit where she could see two men. Behind the cockpit that had two spare seats, there appeared to be a small booster rocket. The whole thing looked like a jazzed-up version of the older Comanche recon and attack helicopter developed by DARPA—the U.S. Defense Advanced Research Projects Agency—for use by the CIA.

When the superchopper reached a hover about fifteen feet off the ground, an alloy ladder dropped down to Rivka. She scampered up until she made it to a small opening where a bearded American in military fatigue pants and a black T-shirt pulled her in. Another man wearing blue jeans and a short-sleeved Hawaiian shirt was piloting the chopper. "Strap in," he told her.

She belted herself into her seat and started asking questions. "Do you know who I am?"

"Sure," the bearded man said. "You're Rivka. Actually, we're looking for your boyfriend. We figured the best way to find March was to connect with his girlfriend. We were given your GPS coordinates from the DOD. They got them today from a friend of yours. A Mr. Pack McHenry."

She beamed. "You have no idea how glad I am to see you!"

"You're one tough gal," the pilot yelled back as he put the chopper into a fast climb, "trying to out-run an armed jeep on the open desert."

"I didn't have much choice," she said. "Do you have any fix on Ethan?"

"No, ma'am. We were hoping you did."

She snatched her Allfone out of her flight suit and hit Pack's number. This time he picked up on one ring. "I was going to call you, Rivka," he said. "Did the U.S. military guys pick you up yet?"

"I'm flying with them right now."

"Good. Okay, we just received a credible report on Ethan's position," Pack said. "Hang on, we're pulling up the coordinates right now. He's hiding in some ruins south, southeast of New Babylon. The Hanging Gardens."

"What's his condition?"

"He's conscious and mobile. Some injuries. If we do this quickly we can get to him before the Alliance does."

Pack read off the coordinates for the ruins to Rivka, who yelled them over to the pilot. His copilot fed them into their onboard navigational computer.

"I assume you're American agents?" Rivka asked after finishing up with Pack.

"Red, white, and blue all over," the copilot yelled back.

"Time to ride the comet," the pilot called. "Hold on."

He pushed the turbine button and the small jet engine fired up. The chopper started streaking across the Iraqi flatlands toward Al Hillah and the ancient ruins of Nebuchadnezzar.

FIFTY-FOUR

DESERT OUTSIDE NEW BABYLON, IRAQ

Ethan could hear the drone-bot approaching overhead. He scampered underneath the shade of a big slab of stone. Off in the distance, and getting louder, were the sounds of the Alliance ground troops with their tracking dogs. They were close now, maybe a hundred yards, not more than that.

He stared at the weeds hanging down from cracks in the stonework that had been fashioned by Nebuchadnezzar's stonecutters twenty-six hundred years ago. In his gut, he felt that his own extinction might be rapidly approaching.

Then he heard the voice of Joshua Jordan in his head. It was something he'd said once about Moses being pursued by the army of Pharaoh. About Moses finding himself in a tight spot, with his face to the Red Sea and the Egyptian soldiers bearing down at his back with their chariots and their spears. What was it, exactly, that Josh had told him about that?

But then, Ethan really didn't feel like Moses. Not by a long stretch.

He remembered something else, and his mind shot back to the bedroom in Zhang Lee's penthouse, early in the morning of the day he'd met with Jo Li in Hadley Brooking's Hong Kong office. He had gone out to the porch of Zhang's beautiful high-rise residence and spent some time reading his Bible. It was a fine day, and the sky was clear blue and the sun was bright. Then Ethan had clicked on Josh Jordan's video log to catch a few more minutes of it before he left for the meeting.

Ethan had noticed a calm certainty about Josh in that video message. He spoke about Jesus and His excruciating moments in the Garden of Gethsemane. How Jesus knew exactly how bad things would get—that He would soon be led to the place of crucifixion. And that once there, even though He was the holy and perfect Son of God, He would be drenched with the putrid sins of the human race—not unwillingly, but intentionally taking them on Himself. He headed willingly to that place of torture and pain—that abysmal, blood-soaked hill—to be made a sacrifice, once and for all, for all sin. For all time.

At the time, there on Zhang's porch, Ethan couldn't shake a strange feeling about that, because it had been the same part of the gospel of Luke Ethan had been reading that day. When he turned on the video log, the image of Josh had been there, peering out from the screen as if he were in the room and talking about Jesus' obedience to the will of God: "Father, if You are willing, remove this cup from Me; yet not My will, but Yours be done."

Ethan was snapped back into his own drastic situation. He could hear the scuffling of Alliance soldiers on the sandy ground on the other side of the stone wall where he was hiding. He held his breath as he heard them making their way toward him through the labyrinth of the ruins, and he knew he was surrounded. They were only minutes away from capturing him. So, he thought to himself, maybe this was how it was all supposed to end. He whispered a prayer.

"God, not my will, but Your will be done."

□□□

The special-ops pilot in the helicopter had spotted it on his satellite surveillance screen: the small army of Global Alliance troops amassed at the roadblock that was situated some two miles away from the ruins of the Hanging Gardens. And they were armed with some heavy-duty weaponry.

Rivka saw it too. "Now what?" she called out.

"They've got a battery of ground-to-air missiles. Among other things . . ."

The copilot sized it up. "Time for some diversion," he said. The pilot nodded. He used his satphone to call Pack.

"Mr. McHenry, if we try to get in close to those ruins at the gardens at this point, we're going to face some serious salvos from the ground. I was wondering if you fellas—"

The pilot didn't have to finish his sentence. He was listening now and nodding, and gave a little sardonic chuckle at the end. "Okay, Mr. McHenry. Much obliged. Just keep your head down and don't get greased when they open up on you big-time, for they most surely will."

□□□

Pack rapidly explained the problem to his team: without a diversion, the helicopter was guaranteed to meet deadly resistance before even reaching Ethan's position. So Pack's group would have to race toward the troops at the roadblock, put some serious fire into the Alliance soldiers, and then speed away in the opposite direction, hopefully drawing fire on themselves and causing some of the troops to give chase in their armored vehicles. Once that happened, the rescue chopper would only need a few minutes to get to Ethan's position. If they weren't shot down first, of course.

"Wonderful," Vincent Romano groaned with an undertone of doubt. "I just love suicide missions."

Andre lifted both hands. "Buck up, Vince," he said. "It's just life or death. That's all."

Victoria, Vincent, and Andre strapped themselves into the special chairs that had been bolted to the metal floor of the truck. Each one was armed with a shoulder-mounted rocket launcher. Andre sat next to the lever that he would pull at the perfect time in order to spring open the double doors of the truck, giving all three of them a clear view of the enemy troops down the road.

The chopper pilot had described the location and where the amassed Alliance force had their most dangerous weaponry—the two ground-to-air missile batteries. The job of Pack's team was to hit those first. And then Pack would swing the truck around and jam the accelerator to the floor, luring the troops to give chase. Hopefully the Alliance pursuers would be looking everywhere except up into the sky where the helicopter would descend to the area where the Brit said he'd dropped off Ethan. Pack realized that ground radar would eventually pick up the chopper, but with its stealth-designed shape it should be cloaked until the last minute, when it was just passing over the area near the troops.

In the back of the super-charged bakery truck the three team members could feel Pack bumping the vehicle off of the sandy desert floor and onto the highway and then slowly picking up speed. Victoria was keeping time on her Allfone watch. Pack would have seven minutes to reach their firing point. The truck traveled around fifty miles per hour or so for the first five minutes, all according to plan. Pack didn't want to risk alerting the troops at the roadblock too early in the game.

Suddenly the trio could feel Pack put the truck into racing mode, and the supercharged engine roared as the truck began picking up speed. Victoria looked down at her watch. Sixty seconds to go. Pack had the truck really flying now. She looked down again. Thirty seconds. Twenty. Then ten. And five . . .

"Now!" Victoria yelled.

Andre jammed the lever back and the double doors flew open with a disturbing clang. At that same instant Pack put the speeding truck into a one-eighty spin. As he did, the three warriors in the back of the truck poised their shoulder-mounted launchers. They had a perfect shot.

Victoria, the eagle eye, had the antiaircraft battery to the left in her sights and would take that one by herself. Vincent and Andre aimed at the artillery unit on the right. The truck was fully turned around with the doors wide open, at a dead stop in the middle of the road. That would last for only ten seconds. Enough time for Victoria to let loose with her missile, which streaked out of the back of the truck with a thin vapor trail behind it.

In the distance they could see a red flash followed by a booming percussion and a cloud of black fiery smoke rising up from her target. "Direct hit," Victoria shouted to her partners. A half second later in perfect tandem Andre and Vincent both fired their rockets at the second target. Andre overshot slightly but Vincent's struck dead on into the antiaircraft battery. There was a second ground-rumbling explosion of fire and a plume of smoke.

Now Pack jammed the truck into gear as its six-hundred-horsepower hemi engine with the supercharger blower began to scream. The racing slicks on the back that had replaced the stock tires were spinning and burning rubber on the road as the truck lurched forward like a space program rocket sled and the front end lifted off the ground in a partial wheelie. Seconds later the truck was doing fifty and quickly seventy and then ninety-five and finally settling into a cruising speed down the highway at one hundred and thirty-five.

In the back of the truck Andre was furiously yanking at the lever to close the heavy hydraulic double doors that had been fitted with armor plating. But something was wrong.

"The doors won't close!" he yelled. "The hydraulics must have jammed when we took that one-eighty so fast." He used both hands to tug at it, but nothing happened. The back of the truck was wide-open. The Alliance troops would be shooting back any second. Vincent unbuckled himself and stood behind Andre, and together the two of them yanked at the lever as hard as they could. "I think I feel something . . ." Vincent grunted.

Victoria was peering through her military binoculars to the Alliance formation behind them. She saw something. "Incoming!"

An instant later rockets started raining down on the highway behind them blowing up the pavement and sending debris into the back of the truck. Vincent was knocked off his feet. Victoria wiped the dust from her face and asked if everyone was all right.

Before anyone could answer, a single Alliance rocket came flashing into sight and struck the highway at a point forty feet behind the team, exploding and sending shrapnel into the back of the open truck.

Andre, still buckled into his seat, screamed and grabbed his chest, which quickly began to surge blood. Vincent grabbed his own bloody leg and moaned. Victoria thrust her hand into her platinum-blond hair to try and stop the red trickle that flowed down her face.

In the driver's compartment Pack slid the window open to the back of the truck and yelled to them, "Are you hit?"

Victoria cried back in a desperate voice, "Drive faster! Drive faster!" Then she unbuckled herself and stumbled over to Andre. His face was already beginning to turn a grayish white and his torso was a sea of crimson. She ripped open his shirt and then his shredded

Kevlar vest and saw the irreversible devastation within. He tried to talk but nothing came out but a gurgle.

As Pack brought the truck up to one hundred and fifty miles per hour, racing toward Karbala, Victoria cradled Andre carefully in her arms and soothed him and prayed. A minute later he stopped moving. She knew he was gone.

FIFTY-FIVE

Ethan leaned against the stone wall, listening to the sounds of the drone overhead and the scuffling of the Alliance troops who were closing in around him on the other side of the wall. There was a certain dismal finality about it all. But then he remembered exactly what Josh had said about Moses in that video log. Yes, that was it. *"When you're surrounded on all sides, just like Moses, that's when you need to look up."*

With no other options left, Ethan started slinking along the wall that was at his back until he was no longer under the protection of the stone slab above him. He was now exposed to the open air and the blue sky above. Way up there in the sky was a black dot that seemed to be hovering. Ethan held up his hands to the sky. *Not my will, but Your will, Lord.*

The black dot grew bigger. It descended, coming straight down, dropping like a big black box. But it wasn't a box, and as it came into view he could see it was a strangely angular kind of helicopter with a fan blade on the underside and one in the tail.

Ethan saw the Alliance drone above him as it passed over and then disappeared. As the helicopter dropped quickly down toward earth it fired on the drone-bot, and Ethan heard the blast as it exploded. Then shots starting coming from the chopper, laying a suppressing fire down on the other side of the wall from Ethan, where he had heard the Alliance troops moving in.

Now the helicopter was about thirty feet above him, hovering, and a small door in its side dropped open. A collapsible metal ladder fell out. Then a head poked out of the door and a trim woman with short, dark hair in a flight suit scampered down the ladder and waved to him. Ethan yelled out loud and gleefully as he saw her.

Oh, I can see your beautiful eyes from here, Rivka, you amazing woman. But you've gotta hurry; they're getting close.

The ladder lowered closer to Ethan, with Rivka still hanging on, stretching out her hand to him. It was almost within reach when Ethan became suddenly aware of the sound of gunfire. He looked around to see where it was coming from, then looked up again. Rivka was clinging desperately to the ladder, trying to avoid the bullets being fired from the ground.

A defensive round of fifty-caliber gunfire burst from the helicopter toward the position on the ground where the Alliance forces were firing. Then it was quiet. Ethan leaped up and grabbed hold of the bottom rung of the ladder and began to pull himself up. Rivka was bending down, one hand on the ladder in back of her, the other reaching down.

"Ethan," she yelled. "Just one more rung up the ladder, darling. Then I can grab your wrist—"

More shots rang out from the ground. Ethan watched in horror as bullets ripped into Rivka's flight suit. She gave a dazed look at him. Her flight suit ran with red. And then she twisted slightly as if desperately trying to get a more secure grip on the ladder. But she missed and toppled backward off the ladder with a yelp, free-falling toward the ground . . .

Clinging to the ladder with his right hand, Ethan reached out with his left and caught her by the ankle as she fell. He panicked as he felt his right hand beginning to slip.

Oh my God, give me strength.

Rivka hung upside down, held only by Ethan's iron grip. He grunted loudly as he used his right hand to pull himself to a higher rung on the ladder, then locked his chin on the rung to steady himself as he snatched the next rung with his right hand.

Shots rang up from the ground and pinged off the metal ladder. Then the copilot appeared in the doorway with his large-caliber machine gun slung over his arm and blasted his weapon down toward the shooters until there was no more return fire. The copilot dropped his weapon and slid down the ladder like a circus performer. He landed right above Ethan and grabbed his right arm and pulled him up. And kept pulling until he was able to grab one of Rivka's ankles while Ethan held the other. Together the two men clumsily made their way up the ladder, each of them yanking Rivka upward until they were able to hoist her into the helicopter while she groaned.

The pilot yelled to them, "We've got to pull out quick. I've picked up six Alliance drone-bots on my screen flying this way and they're armed with missiles."

Ethan ripped Rivka's flight suit open to see the blood-soaked area at her shoulder and arm where she had been hit. "We need to stop the bleeding!" he screamed. Rivka looked like she was losing consciousness.

As the chopper gained altitude and then began to wing its way toward Karbala, the copilot jumped down next to Ethan with a first-aid kit in his hands. "Okay, partner," he shouted to Ethan. "You won 'Hero of the day.' Now strap yourself in, sit back, and leave the medic stuff to me."

FIFTY-SIX

OLD TOWN ALEXANDRIA, VIRGINIA

Sitting on an embroidered chair in Jessica Tulrude's study in her brownstone mini mansion, Vice President Darrell Zandibar downed his second glass of straight Johnny Walker. Tulrude was still confident about the plan. Yes, England and Canada had bolted from the Alliance. But otherwise, the Alliance was holding. And once the United States turned, those two traitor nations would come back begging. But she did worry a bit about Zandibar. As he drank, he wore an anxious expression that looked as if it had been drawn onto him, like a kid who had been face painted at a carnival.

"So, Darrell," Tulrude said in a deliberately soothing voice, "like I have been telling you all along, your job is simple. All you have to do is wait. And be ready."

"I'm unclear . . . on the plan," he said, sounding unsteady. He craned his neck back and forth.

"You don't need to know the plan," she said in a liquid tone. "Just that you will be the president of the United States. You want that, don't you? I know you do."

"The question is how? Hewbright has already beaten the impeachment trial in the Senate. He's not the type for a sex scandal. And besides, he's a widower. What could you possibly have on him?"

"Washington is always full of surprises," she said with a little smile. Zandibar still looked unsettled. Tulrude put her glass down on the coffee table. "Look, Darrell, I am going to ask you a very important question. And you need to answer it like a man. Do you really want to know all the details of Hank Hewbright's future? Because once you become privy to that there's no unhearing it. Wouldn't you rather retain a blissful state of deliberate avoidance? A plausible state of denial—even passing a polygraph test if necessary. Wouldn't that be better?"

Darrell Zandibar tipped his glass up and sipped the last drop. Then he threw Jessica Tulrude the kind of look that said he really needed a third drink but thought it would reflect poorly if he had to ask. "I suppose you're right," he said.

"Of course I am," she said, smiling. "Now let me freshen up your glass." She stood, grabbed the crystal whiskey glass out of his hand, and sauntered over to the bar to fill it up once more.

□□□

THE WHITE HOUSE

Washington, D.C.

Secret Service Agent Decker had made it clear he wanted to be with Agent Ted Booth when the man met with President Hewbright. It was something Booth had said in passing—something casual, seemingly irrelevant. But Decker had a paranoid side, and he'd decided to follow the new guy closely for a while, just to be sure. He'd even made arrangements to have someone else join them with the president, as an added precaution.

However, something had gone wrong. His third party was a no-show.

And then Decker had been unexpectedly called out to the outside portico on the report of a disturbance. As he stood there and surveyed the area, he saw nothing unusual. Confused, he asked the guards at the security booth if they had reported anything. They said no.

"Then why'd I get a code to come out here?"

"We just got a message from Ops Center that their system went down for a sec. Then booted back up. Must have been a computer glitch. You probably just got a random message code when it happened."

A bad feeling began to sweep over Decker and he tapped his earpiece. He wanted to alert the Emergency Operations Center to prepare for a possible move of the president to the secure bunker of rooms below the basement of the White House. Just in case.

But . . . nothing. His wireless earpiece wasn't working.

Sure, it could have been a malfunction. The encrypted radio channels for their earpieces were connected to the same system that had just gone down. But the paranoid part of his brain remembered something else—something that made him go cold. A security study done last month had indicated that, theoretically at least, someone inside the White House with his own password and enough cyber knowledge might be able hack into the communications system. They'd planned on doing something about it. But the Service had priorities that were higher on the "fix it" list. So it was never investigated further.

After all, it was just theoretical.

Decker spat out a few angry epithets, then turned and sprinted back toward the West Wing. *This better just be a systems glitch . . .*

A White House security guard strolling nearby called to him. "Hey, it took awhile, but that FBI friend of yours finally got cleared through security—"

But Decker wasn't stopping to chat.

ㅁㅁㅁ

Inside the White House, Agent Ted Booth, aka Vlad Malatov, and Agent Kevin Arnold waited side by side at the entrance to the Oval Office. As an added touch of authenticity, Malatov even had an old-fashioned ink pen in his top suit coat pocket. After all, he was supposed to be asking the president for his autograph today.

The agent on duty checked his e-pad for the orders. For that precise time of day, it read, *POTUS meets new SSA Ted Booth in OO.* President Hewbright insisted on conducting a short meet-and-greet with every new Secret Service agent. Today would be no exception.

The agent on duty reread the electronic orders again and then looked up at Agent Arnold. "Agent Decker is supposed to be here."

Agent Arnold explained, "He was called out to the portico. A report of a disturbance."

The door agent thought about it for half a second before he waved the two of them in and shut the door behind them.

Inside the Oval Office, the president was not in sight. But they could hear the water running in the sink in the private bathroom off the main room.

Malatov whispered, "You place the body behind the desk when I'm done. Then we both walk out."

Agent Arnold appeared stunned.

"Don't worry about the cameras in the room," Malatov continued. "I've put them on a timed failure. Part of my hack into the Comm system. They'll be out for the next seven minutes."

Arnold flashed an expression of distress. "I was told that this was only going to be an *intel* mission into POTUS operations," he replied in a hoarse whisper.

"Negative. This is a hit. You have a problem with that?"

Agent Arnold didn't respond. Not verbally. But a second later he gave his reply—he grabbed for the handgun under his coat. Malatov was faster and struck Arnold in the throat. As the agent gasped, Malatov grabbed him with his left hand, felt his chest where Arnold wasn't wearing his Kevlar vest, and raised his right hand into the air. Knifing his fingers together, he swung them down like a mechanical pitching arm into the man's stomach, piercing through his flesh and rupturing his stomach. Agent Arnold collapsed on the floor, bleeding profusely.

Malatov pulled out the SIG Sauer P229 pistol he had modified with a silencer just as President Hewbright strode into the room. Malatov dropped the gun to his side and out of sight.

Hewbright started to smile, but then noticed the fallen agent on the floor. "He's hurt—"

"No, Mr. President. I believe he may already be dead. And you will be too unless you do what I tell you." Malatov, who was standing over Agent Arnold, brandished the pistol and waved for Hewbright to step over in front of the famous Resolute Desk. Agent Arnold had changed the game plan, and now the kill shot would have to look like it had been fired from Arnold's position in the room.

Malatov thought he knew everything about White House security precautions. But as President Hewbright nodded in compliance with the order and shuffled slowly sideways toward the desk, his hand brushed across the top of a library table where there sat a paperweight with the presidential seal on it. The paperweight fell to the floor.

Malatov instantly realized the fall was no accident. It might have sent an emergency signal down to the Secret Service headquarters, and farther below that down to the Emergency Operations Center. He had to act fast.

Malatov raised his pistol at Hewbright's forehead, and before the president of the United States had a chance to react, he pulled the trigger. There was a muffled *zing* and Hewbright fell to the floor, bleeding from the fatal wound in his head.

Quickly Malatov tucked his gun away, then reached down and twice fired the weapon that was still clutched in Agent Arnold's hand, making it look like a firing by Arnold. The shots hit the Resolute Desk.

Turning toward the door, Malatov burst out of the Oval Office and shouted to the agent on duty outside, "Agent Arnold shot the president! I disabled him. But there's a coconspirator somewhere on this floor! I'm going to find him . . ."

As the other agent raced into the Oval Office, Malatov tore down the hall. But he was soon forced to an abrupt halt. Fifty feet in front of him Agent Decker stood in a firing position, with his pistol aimed at Malatov. He got off two shots, one of which zipped into Malatov's left leg, before the Russian got his gun out and returned fire. He hit Agent Decker in the hip and the man went down.

□□□

But Malatov didn't see what was approaching him from behind. Former FBI agent Ben Bolling, there for the meeting with the president at Agent Decker's request, charged down the hall like a fullback. He tackled the brute from behind and took him to the floor, knocking the handgun out of his hand. It clattered to the ground.

Enraged, Malatov tossed Bolling off of him, grabbed his pistol, and fired at him point blank. There was only an empty click. He had already fired the only two bullets in the clip that had been issued to him.

Bolling didn't have time to be thankful. Like a crazed bull, Malatov pinned him against the wall with his powerful left forearm and swung his right hand up in the air. Bolling knew what was coming; he grabbed frantically at the top pocket of Malatov's suit coat as Malatov swung his deadly hand toward Bolling's chest. But when it connected, it hit with a sickening metallic clang. Malatov recoiled in pain.

Taking advantage of the assassin's confusion, Bolling angled the sharp end of the ink pen he had snatched from the man's suit pocket and thrust it into Malatov's jugular vein. He watched as the Russian killer stumbled forward for a few feet, grabbing at the pen in his neck and at the jugular that was now surging blood. After a few more unsteady steps the assassin collapsed to the ground.

Bolling pounced on him and searched his limp body for other weapons but found none. By then the agent on duty was standing over them with his own gun drawn.

Vlad Malatov, with his last moments of consciousness, looked at the broken fingers of his right hand with a confused look of bewilderment. Bolling leaned into the assassin's face. "I know your moves, creep. I thought it was you on that UEFM fight video." Then he unbuttoned his shirt, revealing his homemade defense system—the uncomfortable seventeenth-century metal breastplate from his private armory collection that he had worn that day. It had caused him to be delayed in getting clearance through White House security.

He slipped off the breastplate and scampered over to Agent Decker. The hall was now crawling with Secret Service agents and special-ops men in black attack fatigues. But they were all too late. That was when the scope of the somber tragedy really started sinking in.

"Did he get to the president?" Decker asked, choking on his words as another agent applied pressure to stop his bleeding.

"I'm afraid so," Bolling said, trying to fight back tears. But he couldn't stop them, and they started to stream down his face.

Bolling stayed with Decker, even after they loaded him in the EMS vehicle and it raced toward Georgetown Medical Center. "I had a kinda weird feeling about that guy," Decker explained, trying to raise his voice above the siren as Bolling squatted next to him in the ambulance. "Couldn't put my finger on it."

The medics told Decker not to talk, but Decker ignored them. "I had this hunch, but nothing concrete, except our first conversation. Kept thinking back to it. That's why I asked you to come today, to check out the new guy, just on a lark . . ."

"What about that first conversation?"

Decker was trying to manage a smile. "His papers said he was transferred from the Miami office. He told me he was a Marlins fan. He said that only *after* they fired Ozzie Guillen as manager way back in 2012 did the team start to take a nosedive. But any Marlins fan would know that wasn't true. The season before that, they were in last place in the National League East."

FIFTY-SEVEN

NORTHERN IRAQ

Rivka had been flown to a hospital where the Kurds were still friendly to the Americans. Ethan didn't want to leave her alone, but the two helicopter pilots from the CIA promised they would arrange trusted guards to keep her safe for the next few days while she recovered. That had to be good enough for Ethan.

He bent down at Rivka's hospital bed and gave her a long kiss. "There's more where that came from," he said, smiling. "When I get back."

But she didn't smile in return. Ethan figured she had a pretty good idea where he was going next, and she knew that for him the danger was only just beginning.

"You have to promise me you'll be safe," she said with a gentle quality to her voice. "You're going into the belly of the beast."

He nodded and took her pretty face in his hands. She was shockingly pale from blood loss, and they had her hooked up to a transfusion line. Although he was preparing to leave her, he was drenched in lingering regrets. *Man alive, I wish I could stay here with her.* He bent down next to her ear and whispered, "When I get back, I have a question to ask you. I'll even get down on my knee to ask it. And the answer has got to be a yes."

In her bleary state, Rivka just stared back at first, but then a light bloomed in her eyes. "Oh, Ethan . . . I love you so . . ."

With a final kiss, he let her go and stepped out into the hall where the two CIA helicopter pilots were waiting for him.

Ethan had already heard the shocking news that Hank Hewbright had been assassinated. The mainstream press was spinning the story that it had been a hit orchestrated by Moscow as revenge for Hewbright's support for Israel, the nation that thoroughly embarrassed Russia by miraculously withstanding Russia's terrifying coalition attack a few years before. But Ethan knew better than that. Bart Kingston and his staff at AmeriNews would now have to tell the real story: that Alexander Colliquin wanted a new president in the White House for his own purposes, someone who would do his bidding and bring the U.S. into the Global Alliance. And so he'd made it happen.

Ethan was one of the few people who saw the really big picture. He had experienced it firsthand as a guinea pig in one of Colliquin's cruel labs. Colliquin's plan was to track and then control the human race through his 3-D digital holography system. But he still needed a computer data center that had adequate computing power to accomplish that. But which one, and where? Dr. Iban Adis was the one who had been tasked to nail that down for him. Ethan needed that intel immediately. It had been nearly two weeks since he had heard from him.

The pilots told Ethan that the Agency had received orders to transport Ethan back to the White House for a debriefing regarding the Global Alliance. The chief pilot added, "Even with President Hewbright gone now, and with President Zandibar sworn in, we still have to follow a standing order, unless someone—the director or DOD or the White House—reverses it."

They looked as if they were waiting for Ethan to fill in the blanks. So he did. "That's fine with me," he said. "I just need to ask a favor: you may need to take me on a little side trip first. I just have to figure out *where*."

The two CIA guys nodded. "Just name the place."

Rivka had given her Allfone to Ethan before he left the hospital. He needed it to call into his encrypted Remnant site to pick up messages that may have collected for him after his capture in Hong Kong. As he was being driven to a secret CIA air base in the north outside of Kirkuk to be flown back to the U.S., he logged in. On his digital message bank there were calls from Rivka and Pack. There were also several from Remnant supporters in Iraq, mentioning the torture and killing of an unnamed lab scientist in New Babylon. Following those, he saw a text from someone he didn't recognize at first—Farrah Adis.

Then it struck him. She was Dr. Iban Adis' wife. And judging from the other messages that he had received, he realized she must now be a widow. It was clear that Alexander Colliquin's people must have found out Dr. Adis was undercover for the Remnant. But apparently not before he sent an encrypted e-mail to his wife containing three vital pieces of information she was now sharing with Ethan.

The first thing she shared was the location of the computing center that Colliquin was after: the National Data Center at Bluffdale, Utah. Ethan nodded at that. *Of course, it all makes sense—why Colliquin needed access to the United States. To take over its massive intelligence computer center.*

Second, Farrah recited a Bible verse that her husband had messaged to her. Revelation 13:15. Ethan knew that one by heart: *"And it was given to him to give breath to the image of the beast, so that the image of the beast would even speak and cause as many as do not worship the image of the beast to be killed."*

But the third piece of information in Farrah's message was perplexing. It read, *Binary aka base 2* and was followed by a string of ten binary characters in *0*s and *1*s.

Ethan immediately forwarded the text to Chiro Hashimoto up in the Yukon Territory with an urgent plea for him to call back. He then leaned forward in the sedan and addressed the pilot and copilot in the front seat. "I've got the location I would like to visit first."

"Shoot," the pilot said as he drove.

"Bluffdale, Utah. Or as close as you can get."

The two CIA operatives shared a quick side glance. Ethan wondered if the U.S. government wasn't already aware of the importance of that location to Alexander Colliquin.

"There's a military airport right next to the National Data Center," the pilot shot back. "We'll give you door-to-door service."

As they drove through Kirkuk, heading to the air base miles outside of the city, Ethan leaned his head against the window. He was exhausted, and his head was still dizzy and swimming in pain, but there was no time for that. He watched the scenes of life in Kurdish Iraq flash by the window—the modern office buildings, the neighborhoods that had been bombed into rubble interspersed with palm trees and a few gardens.

The car pulled to a stop at an intersection. Ethan spotted a group of old men in turbans sitting in a courtyard, smoking and talking. They seemed oblivious to the cataclysm that would soon be visited on the earth. They had to be warned. They had to be told about Jesus Christ. Everyone needed to hear that. Back in the lab, God had given Ethan a glimpse of the heavenly kingdom to come. Ethan wanted everyone to have a chance to be transformed by the love of Jesus. Before it was too late.

But there was still much work to do before that. Suddenly, Ethan felt the urge to catch up with world events. He waved his finger over the AmeriNews icon on his Allfone. The headlines of the day popped up. He felt relief that at least for today the Roundtable's news feed was still being distributed on the Allfone communications system. But now that Darrell Zandibar was president and the White House controlled all Internet information sites, that could end at any time.

The major story was the assassination of Hewbright. AmeriNews questioned the official story that blamed it on a Russian plot—as all the other media outlets had been claiming—and suggested that the Global Alliance actually had a hand in it. But the second story was all about President Darrell Zandibar's agenda and his first comments as chief executive. His "highest priority," he announced to the American people, would be "to unite America with the Global Alliance, to forge a new and prosperous tomorrow."

There it was. Ethan had to get to Bluffdale. And more important, he needed Chiro to transport his quantum computer down there immediately. He was about to call Chiro when his Allfone buzzed. Chiro was beating him to the punch. He had already read the forwarded message from Farrah Adis. Chiro's voice cranked up a notch as he exclaimed, "Ethan, this is it."

"Break it down for me. Not the Bluffdale, Utah, part. I understand that. But that long binary code, the series of *0*s and *1*s."

"Binary code—with the 1 representing *on* and the 0 representing *off*—is the basis of all digital communications and computer language," Chiro said. "Basic on/off, true/false, open/shut kind of commands. Based on the fundamentals of logic."

"But what does Dr. Adis' string of binary characters mean?"

"Those ten binary characters Dr. Adis discovered in the program at the New Babylon lab are the new internal code for everyone's BIDTag."

"Speak English," Ethan pleaded.

"Alexander Colliquin is going to link his 3-D holographic image to the global BIDTag grid, which is already synced to the Internet. That way he'll be able to appear at will before every man, woman, and child with a BIDTag. But first his technicians will have to reprogram the entire QR code system in the grid so that everybody's BIDTag is imbedded with the same universal binary code."

"Accomplishing what?"

"I think it's going to do two things. First, it will give Babylon the ability to use a person's skin implant as a direct access to their neural pathways."

"Make it simple, please."

"Influence their brain functions. Control them."

Ethan nodded. "Yeah, I know something about that one. Been there, done that. And the second?"

"It is going to prove how true the Bible is."

"How?"

"This binary string of ten characters in base 2 that will be fed into everyone's BIDTag, the code that will control them, actually represents a whole number."

"And the number is . . ."

"Six hundred and sixty-six."

Ethan could feel the little hairs on the back of his neck standing on end. He had thought that if he ever arrived at this point in history, he wouldn't be shocked, that he would be mentally prepared. But now he was here, and he felt himself trembling. He had to silently tell himself to get a grip.

Remembering that he was not alone in the sedan, Ethan said to Chiro, "I'm about to send you an encrypted text. Read it. Then you must follow it immediately."

A few minutes later Ethan messaged Chiro: *Pack up your C-Note quantum computer, and you and John Galligher need to get it down to the National Data Center in Utah. I'm activating the plan. I'll take care of the other arrangements. Further instructions to follow.*

Then Ethan called Bart Kingston in New York. He was in the newsroom, and Ethan was put on hold for a few minutes before Bart picked up.

"Good story on Hewbright," Ethan said. "He was a brave American and a Christian statesman. The forces of darkness are closing in. Do you have our special project ready to roll?"

"Oh yeah. We'll blow the lid off the lie about the supposed mass suicides of Christians as the reason for their disappearances. We'll include the video statement from our image forensics expert. And a side feature exposing how the Alliance and Alexander Colliquin were behind the attempt to cover up the truth about the Rapture."

"Good to hear it."

"We can feed our video feature to any site you want."

"I am counting on that fact," Ethan said. "We'll be in touch."

FIFTY-EIGHT

JERUSALEM, ISRAEL

The Two Witnesses stood in the middle of a huge crowd on the plaza below the temple. Their codes names of Mashah and Tishbite had given way to their true names—those that were inscribed in the pages of God's dealings in human history. Moses and Elijah. At the top of the Temple Mount next to the temple, Bishop Dibold Kora stood on his private stage with its grand view of the Old City. As he stood over the crowds below, Kora wore a wireless microphone connected by satellite to every household in Israel. His spiteful message against Moses and Elijah could be heard by every family in the tiny nation.

"The two of you," Kora cried out, with his finger pointing down to Moses and Elijah, "are false prophets of catastrophe. True religion should bring peacefulness, comfort, and abundance. But you bring only death and destruction. You have blood on your hands, having massacred our Alliance soldiers. Soon enough we will be rid of you, and then the whole world will see the divine light that rises in the east and the world will embrace the image of the all-powerful one who comes out of New Babylon like a bright and shining star."

Moses raised his right hand and the chatter in the crowd around him stopped abruptly. He cried out in a loud voice, "You speak of blood? Then blood you shall have! That all of Israel may know I have been sent from the God of Abraham, Isaac, and Jacob, and that the earth may know that the Lord God is the Father of Jesus the Christ, His Son. I now declare by the power of God that all the waters of Israel shall become blood. And the stench of it shall rise up in the nostrils of this people so that the whole world might repent and might believe on the Lord Jesus Christ and receive Him by faith and be saved."

Bishop Kora tried to respond, but his voice was drowned out by the screams from the crowd. People were pointing to the large fountain in the plaza with the plaque at its base that commemorated "the great covenant of peace" reached between the Global Alliance and Israel. Something bizarre was happening. The crystal-clear waters that cascaded down the statue of the Greek goddess Aphrodite in the fountain had now turned to a thick, red flow staining the white marble statue and streaming down the sides of the fountain and onto the stones of the plaza.

Then Elijah cried out with a loud voice, "This is only the beginning of the wonders of the Lord. So that you may truly know that the Lord is God."

Along the banks of the Jordan River, a disgusting current of blood had replaced its muddy waters. Bathers floating in the Dead Sea started running back to the shore when they realized that they were surrounded by a lake of blood. Faucets in the homes of Israel were choked with the thick red fluid and wells pumped it. Irrigation systems for the lush agricultural fields north of Jerusalem sprayed crimson rather than water. And the waves on the Sea of Galilee lapped red, to the horror of the commercial fishermen and the hotel owners in Tiberias.

Soon the decaying, sickly stench of blood would begin to fill the air in Israel, from Elat at the southern border with Egypt all the way up to Golan Heights in the north. And after that the flies would begin to flock by the billions to the coagulating pools of blood.

ooo

On the following day, on the other side of town, in the affluent Rehavia district of Jerusalem, Sol Bensky sat in his prime minister's mansion. He had been brooding all day over the ghastly news that his nation was drenched in scarlet. He had heard it first from the deputy assistant to the chief scientist in the Ministry of Health, who told him about it but then exclaimed that "it couldn't be blood—that would be an event of Old Testament proportions. No, it must be some substance having the same appearance and some of the same chemical properties." That was immediately followed by a call from the minister of environmental protection, who was having a meltdown over the disastrous impact the bizarre phenomenon would have on Israel's ecology.

It then became very personal for the prime minister. He and his wife, Esther, were unable to bathe or drink water or make their morning tea or coffee, as all of the water in Israel had mysteriously disappeared and been replaced by a repulsive flow of coagulating blood.

Later that day Bensky was given a security briefing in his home about the entire incident on the plaza with the Two Witnesses and how it seemed to have precipitated the grotesque turn of events. That evening when Bensky and Esther were in bed together and the lights were out, he turned to her with anguish. "I wonder," he said in a pained voice, "whether it is too late for God to hear my pleas. To hear my regret and failures, and my repentance, and yes, my sins also. Is it too late?" And then he asked, "Is there still hope for Israel?"

Esther was silent for a long time. And then she said quietly, "God answers those who seek Him with an open, honest heart. Doesn't He?"

□□□

NEW BABYLON, IRAQ

As the citizens of Israel labored with fits of restless sleep, the lights remained on in the news division of the Global Alliance Information Network in New Babylon. Alexander Colliquin had tasked the staff there to create a cover story—anything—that would explain the miraculous event in Israel as a mere environmental accident.

At dawn a press statement was released by the Alliance. It explained that a catastrophic oil spill within Israel had tainted its water supply and that the reddish-black color of the oil "was being used by Jesus Remnant rebels to subvert public opinion to their cause, spreading lies that Israel's water had been supernaturally turned into blood." The news release suggested that "Jesus Remnant rebels orchestrated the oil spill, and a criminal investigation has been launched by the Global Alliance International Security Department to bring the responsible parties to justice."

FIFTY-NINE

IN THE SKY OVER UTAH

The small CIA transport plane was now over Utah. The navigator had his classified e-pad in his lap and was checking the latest national security risk assessment dispatch from the Central Intelligence Agency. The Red Memo that had just been issued from the agency's Incident Management Center contained a similar enigma—breaking news about an America that was on the verge of disappearing from the map, soon to reappear as a territory belonging to Region One of the Global Alliance of Nations. It also contained a message for the two pilots, advising them to treat Ethan as a person authorized to receive classified information regarding the data center takeover by the Global Alliance and explaining what the CIA knew thus far about Ethan's plan.

The navigator turned to face Ethan, who was sitting behind him. "Mr. March, I just received an interesting update from Langley. We have a bead on your mission, Mr. March, and I say, *hooah*, sir. But here's the sticky part. The Incident Management eggheads at Langley are telling us that the minute POTUS took the oath he authorized a takeover of the U.S. by the Global Alliance. Alliance forces are already moving into place in Bluffdale. They are ringing the outer perimeter of that facility with a fleet of five hundred well-armed, high-caliber shooting droid-bots that will patrol on foot—or whatever you call those things they walk on. So the outside turf at Bluffdale will belong to those robo-cops. Any unauthorized person entering the grounds will be shot on sight."

Ethan was nonplussed. "Sounds pretty extreme."

"Yeah. Extreme to the extreme." Then he studied Ethan. "You don't look worried."

"Not about that," Ethan said with an attempt at a smile. "It's the rest of the mission I'm concerned about. *My mission.* If everything doesn't work perfectly—and perfectly on time—there's going to be an unparalleled disaster."

The CIA agent nodded and grinned. "Mr. March, welcome to the club."

□□□

NEW BABYLON, IRAQ

In his own suite of offices, Ho Zhu, Alexander Colliquin's deputy, had just finished up a private phone call with Beijing, and specifically with the associate to the general secretary of the central committee of China. Those phone calls had become routine for months, though he had never discussed it with Colliquin, or anyone else in the Global Alliance leadership, for that matter. And he intended to keep it that way.

The call was ending when his contact in Beijing closed by quoting an old Chinese proverb: "'Water can both float a ship as well as sink it.'" Then he added, "The difference, Mr. Ho, comes in the size of the waves. You would be well advised to prevent Mr. Colliquin from making waves. His ambitions must be delayed."

An hour later Ho Zhu was summoned to the master control studio of the Alliance Communications Center building. Alexander Colliquin was already there, sitting in the large swivel chair belonging to the chief of communications, which was positioned in front of a recording-and-transmission consol. Colliquin had shooed all of the digital engineering staff out of the room. Now it was just the two of them.

"Ho," Colliquin said, "this is the final hour. Now that the Americans are coming around, we will be in complete command of their computer center in Utah, the new hub of our worldwide digital matrix. Shortly we will launch our first worldwide holographic transmission. My digital image will reach every human being on this planet. The little setback in the experiment with Ethan March has been rectified. We're operational."

Colliquin rocked a little in the chair. There was an air of satisfaction on his face. "We also must launch an attack on England. And without mercy. Their rebellion must be punished. Once we incinerate Great Britain, Canada will surely do an about-face. Mr. Ho, you will release a statement that England attempted to sabotage global peace through their act of treason, thus leaving us with no other alternative but to launch our military assault. That will also serve as a warning to any other nation members that might be thinking about leaving."

"I am wondering," Ho replied, "whether we shouldn't carefully consider our next move. Buy a little more time. For instance, Mr. Chancellor, rather than an expensive, time-consuming invasion, we could seek to remove the English prime minister, as we did with the head of state in the United States. That proved effective and—"

"Excuse me," Colliquin snapped, interrupting him. "But this is not a *dialog*. I talk and you listen. I give the orders and you follow them. Is that confusing?"

"No, Your Excellency."

"Good. Now do as you're told."

As Ho turned to leave, something came to mind and he turned back to mention it to Colliquin before he left. "One other matter, Chancellor. Jo Li is here in New Babylon. He turned Ethan March over to us as promised and then traveled all the way from Hong Kong to speak with you. As you recall, he has benefited from the *temporary* loophole in the Alliance law that we gave him, the one that has allowed him to operate his underground economy if, in exchange, he gives us unlimited access to his confidential list of customers and clients and as long as he cooperates with us whenever we want to snatch someone on his list. Like Ethan March, for instance. But now he is driving a harder bargain, asking for his exemption—set to expire in two months—to be made permanent."

Colliquin opened his eyes wide. "Oh?" After only a few seconds of consideration, he delivered his verdict. "I need to keep Jo Li on a short leash. Tell him I said no. And if he doesn't like it, then I have an alternative. I can grant him that permanent loophole—*posthumously*—after I have him crucified in the desert outside New Babylon with the other traitors."

Colliquin's face exhibited a new, even more brutal kind of resolve, one that even Ho Zhu did not recognize. He bowed and fast-stepped out of the room.

□□□

ENGLISH CHANNEL OFF THE COAST OF NORMANDY

The CB90 high-speed assault boat manned by the Royal Marines hit seventy knots as it raced toward the Isle of Guernsey, a protectorate of

England. Night was falling as British prime minister Derek Harrington was transported to his new command post in the Guernsey Government House as a precaution against an impending Alliance attack against London. Intelligence gathered by MI6 dictated that travel by sea would be the safest route, even if slower.

The prime minister stared at the screen of his Allfone, watching the telecast of the long procession of mourners passing by the coffin of Hank Hewbright, whose body was lying in state in the Capitol rotunda. "They finally got to him," Harrington murmured out loud.

"Hewbright once told me that this would all come to pass," Harrington added, addressing his chief of staff next to him. "Detailed in the Bible. The prophecy about a union of ten kings from ten kingdoms and how three kings would revolt from the power of a future, global Babylon. And how the Bible says that those three leaders would be struck down."

"Sir, with all due respect—" his COS began.

But he was cut off by the prime minister, who plowed ahead. "America, England, and Canada. Three nations have now revolted from the Alliance of New Babylon. The president of the United States has been hit." The military boat took a momentary bump over some choppy waters and it jolted the prime minister, who then added, "One down. Two more to go . . ."

SIXTY

IN THE AIR—DESTINATION BLUFFDALE, UTAH

Chiro had conveyed Ethan's order to Galligher: they were to immediately transport the C-Note quantum computer from the Yukon to a huge government compound in the desert of Utah. Galligher put in a call to Alvin Leander at the Roundtable in Colorado and lined up transportation, hiring the same private pilot Joshua Jordan had used for his charter flights. Manfred would stay behind to run things back at the computer headquarters in their Yukon Territory hotel in White Horse, with Bobby Robert in charge of security.

Now Galligher leaned back in the cushy seat of the jet with his eyes closed. He listened to the hum of the dual engines as the Citation X jet streaked through the night sky. But his mind clicked, mentally adding up all the things he didn't know about this mission that was the brainchild of Ethan March. Like why he was going to Utah. And exactly what he would do when he got to his destination. And why Chiro's computer was so critical. Which led him back to the issue of leadership.

Ethan March had better be right. About all of this.

He told himself he needed to close down his brain and get some sleep. Chiro, in the seat next to him, was already snoring. But a few minutes later Galligher opened his eyes, like he'd been slapped in the face.

This mission is going to be dangerous. Real rock 'em sock 'em. The president has been assassinated. America's being sucked into the evil empire. And I'm supposed to bring a homemade computer created by my genius buddy Chiro down to a secret government installation, sneak it in, and hope that nobody minds.

It hit him once again that he needed to connect with Helen, his ex-wife, before it was too late. Things had been bad between them for a long time, but he needed to tell her something. Forget the fact that she basically hated him and had told him never to call again. This was too important to let that stop him. Considering what was up ahead, he just hoped he lived long enough to make that call.

He closed his eyes again. Maybe if he was lucky, he could get a three-hour nap.

□□□

IN THE SKY OVER UTAH

The sun was just breaking over the horizon. Ethan March had spent the flight praying and trying to figure out the details of his game plan. He figured the CIA transport plane could land him at the military airstrip right next to the National Data Center.

But then the CIA copilot received another classified bulletin and relayed the bad news. "Ethan, we already knew that our newly installed president has ordered a complete turnover of our National Data Center facility to the Global Alliance. But now he has forbidden any unauthorized personnel to set foot down there. That makes you persona non grata. So, barring new orders, we'll have to take you directly to Washington. We're going to turn this bird around and head east. Sorry about that."

"Negative," Ethan bulleted back. "I need to be down there on the ground in Utah."

"We're stuck with this directive from the White House. The CIA is not a domestic intelligence agency, so we're already sticking our neck out by even transporting you over U.S. airspace. But now, with this new twist, completing the turnover of the Bluffdale computer headquarters to the Alliance, you're shafted."

"Hang on," Ethan said. Then he hit the speed-dial number for Judge "Fort" Rice at the Roundtable headquarters at Hawk's Nest, Joshua Jordan's former Rocky Mountain lodge. A sleepy Rice answered and asked what time it was. "About five in the morning," Ethan replied. He immediately briefed Rice on the current legal quagmire—that the new president had ordered the U.S. to join the Global Alliance and had turned over America's computer headquarters to the Alliance, thus preventing any federal agency from interfering with that order.

"Give me a couple minutes to wake up, throw some water on my face, and figure this out," Rice said. "I'll call you back in fifteen."

Ethan talked the agents into circling above Bluffdale while they waited for the return call from Rice. One thing Ethan knew about Rice from what Joshua Jordan had told him: even though the former Idaho Supreme Court justice was slow to make decisions, he was never late. Fourteen minutes later Rice called back. He told Ethan to put him on speaker phone. Now Ethan, the pilot, and the copilot were all listening.

"This is Fortis Rice speaking. Here's what I've turned up. Back when Barack Obama was president, in his second term he tried to get Congress to give him sweeping powers to control the Internet in the event of a cyber attack. But the folks on Capitol Hill wouldn't go for it. So politically he was forced to sign a much less drastic executive directive, giving the Department of Defense, rather than him, the power to oversee America's Internet infrastructure in the event of a perceived cyber attack. To my knowledge, that directive was never rescinded by any of his successors. So that gives the DOD the trump card."

No one in the airplane spoke for several seconds. Fort Rice asked, "Are you all there, or did we lose the call?"

"No, still here," Ethan called out. "Thanks a million, Judge Rice."

After Ethan clicked off his Allfone, he suggested that the two CIA operatives contact the DOD. If the Defense Department thought a cyber attack on America's Internet infrastructure was imminent— in this case by Alexander Colliquin and the Global Alliance—then wasn't the Department of Defense, rather than the president, authorized to thwart it by any means necessary, including using Ethan March and his compatriots?

The pilot and copilot conferred together. Then the copilot sent a rapid-fire series of text memos. As the plane continued to circle above Bluffdale, the copilot asked Ethan only one question: "Are you willing to swear that an attack on America's Internet capabilities will be imminent unless you are allowed to intervene?"

"Absolutely," Ethan said. "Without hesitation."

A few minutes later the pilot spoke up. "Ethan, I'm afraid if we don't get the okay from DOD to land you at Bluffdale in the next fifteen or so, we're going to have to start heading east, and stat. Otherwise we may not have enough fuel to make the trip to Washington. And our agency has ordered us not to stop for refueling at any commercial airports along the way. Too many questions."

□□□

MASTER CONTROL STUDIO—ALLIANCE COMMUNICATIONS CENTER

New Babylon, Iraq

Alexander Colliquin was holding his final meeting with his digital communications staff. The newly appointed chief of digital imagery gave the briefing. "Mr. Chancellor, we will be ready to go live in the next two hours. I can assure you that no failures will occur, like that embarrassing incident with Ethan March in lab number six."

"Which is why you are now in charge," Colliquin replied. "Continue."

As the new lab chief launched into his explanation, his voice bordered on the ecstatic. "In the next two hours we will simultaneously override all of the major root server addresses for the Internet around the world. A few in South America, Australia, and Africa, a number in the United States, and the remaining ones in Europe and Asia. That will effectively shut down the Internet and the World Wide Web across the globe. The shutdown will last approximately forty minutes. During that time we will program all of those servers to allow overrides from this office in New Babylon and to receive the reprogramming of the BIDTag grid so everyone with a laser imprint will be subject to your holographic 3-D image messages. The digital hub for this is, of course, the National Data Center in Utah. We have all seven of the ICANN Internet start-up codes, and we will use them to restart the Internet. Then you will commence your first global transmission. Your holographic image will appear to every person on the planet, wherever they happen to be situated—in deserts, cities, jungles, or on a mountain top. Our global GPS locator will target each of them via their BIDTag laser implants."

"And those without the laser tag?"

"Well, those without—like the many Jesus Remnant rebels—will be located by blanket thermal imaging, which of course will immediately determine that they lack the necessary QR code data that is part of the BIDTag. Once identified, our computers will classify them as subversive nontaggers and present them with your holographic 3-D image, and then proceed to use the laser impulse from your image to directly control the neuromuscular response center of the brain. I am happy to announce that after the Ethan March debacle, I used this technique successfully on three human nontagger subjects."

"Jesus nontaggers?" Colliquin asked hopefully.

"I'm afraid not, Your Excellency. Merely political dissidents."

Colliquin sighed. "Let's proceed as quickly as possible. Tell me when I can come into the holographic studio to deliver my first message. I don't want to be late."

ㅁㅁㅁ

LAS VEGAS, NEVADA

In their little efficiency apartment off the Sunset Strip, Dillon Ritzian's girlfriend, Darlene, was throwing everything at him she could lay her hands on—lamps, dishes, books.

"And to think I was planning on marrying you, you sick, pathetic scum of the earth!" she shouted as she tossed Dillon's empty bowling bag at him.

"Come on, Darlene, give me a chance to explain," he pleaded.

"Explain what?" she screamed. "That you sold out the United States of America for twenty thousand bucks?"

"Well, I was supposed to get another eighty grand if these guys ended up using my schematics to hack their way into the computer system, but with the new president bringing us into the Global Alliance, this mob enforcer guy, Henry Bender, said his people didn't really need my information after all."

"You're not getting it!" Darlene shouted as she shoved him back with both hands. "My dad died a Marine, a hero for this country serving in Iraq when an IED exploded under his truck. I was just a kid when it happened, Dillon. And now I find out that my boyfriend's a traitor to his country."

"I needed the money for some gambling debts—"

"I don't care if you needed it for a heart transplant! What kind of person are you? I'm seriously thinking about moving out. Going back to work at the nail salon."

"Hey, Darlene, please let me make this up. I'm not a bad guy. How can I prove myself to you? Make this right?"

She grabbed her car keys and headed to the front door. "How about being a man? Use your brain to figure that out, and whatever guts you still have left, unless you've pawned those off too." Then she was gone.

Dillon dejectedly dumped himself down onto the couch, clicked the web TV on, and perused the channels. He stopped on the AmeriNews network. A man in his late sixties was talking about the Global Alliance takeover of the United States and calling it "a crime against humanity." Underneath his image the network flashed his name: *Former Senator Alvin Leander.*

As Leander lambasted the Alliance, Dillon Ritzian's eyes widened and he leaned closer to the TV set.

SIXTY-ONE

LANGLEY, VIRGINIA

The message from the plane carrying Ethan March streaked through the CIA and ended up on the desk of the director. The agency chief, William Tatter, had his own opinions about the killing of Hank Hewbright, even if he couldn't prove it yet. But there was no way he was about to ignore a possible coup within the White House, especially now that the United States was on the verge of being absorbed into the Global Alliance empire.

He called Secretary of Defense Rollie Allenworth and laid out the three points: President Zandibar's executive order turning America's top secret national defense computer system at Bluffdale over to the Global Alliance; Ethan March's plan to sabotage that Alliance takeover; and the rather dated but never rescinded presidential directive that gave the Department of Defense, rather than the White House, special powers to block any Internet cyber attack that threatened American national security.

"And this Ethan March fellow, he's ready to enter the Bluffdale area?" Allenworth asked.

"He is. At this very moment. I have some people ready to drop him there, but not without your authorization."

Allenworth mulled it over out loud. "It looks like we're caught between a rock and a hard place. Our new president has explicitly turned over our entire Bluffdale computer complex to the Alliance. But there's also a prior executive directive that President Zandibar may not know about yet, but soon will, that gives me the authority, not him, to stop a hostile attack on America's access to the Internet. And in the middle of all that, we have the murder of a sitting president that raises some very ugly questions. So how do we reconcile all of that?"

After a few moments the secretary of defense answered his own question. "Bill, remember your military history? During the eighteenth century, England would deputize privateers—private ships' captains who were empowered to attack and plunder enemy ships on the high seas with only two stipulations: the attack had to be consistent with English interests, and the privateers had to split the loot with the English Crown."

"Sounds intriguing," William Tatter replied. "Ethan March as a privateer? The difference here is that there's no loot to split."

"I beg to differ," the secretary of defense said. "Some things are more valuable than gold or silver."

□□□

IN THE SKY OVER UTAH

The CIA plane had already turned eastward and was almost out of Utah airspace when a supervisor in clandestine services at Langley contacted the two agents and gave them the plan. The DOD was authorizing them, as "loaned agents" of DOD, to drop Ethan March as close to the National Data Center facility as possible, but under no circumstances to land at the military airstrip that was part of the National Guard facility located adjacent to the computer complex.

"So what, exactly, do they want us to do?" the copilot said.

"Seems clear to me. They want us to help Ethan March. But we're supposed to stay invisible while we do it," the pilot shot back. "In other words, we can get him to the target site, but we can't land the plane."

The copilot rolled his eyes as the plane slowly banked and then headed back toward Bluffdale. No one spoke until Ethan broke the silence.

"What's in this box back here?" he asked, pointing to a large cargo case a few feet from him.

"Parachutes," the copilot said.

Ethan smiled. "When I was training in the air force, I took a lot of jumps out of planes."

"You don't say," the copilot said. Now he had a grin of his own.

ooo

BOUNTIFUL, UTAH

The charter jet carrying John Galligher, Chiro, and the quantum computer landed about thirty minutes outside of Bluffdale at the nearest civilian airport—Salt Lake Skypark Airport in a town called Bountiful. Galligher and Chiro carefully wheeled the C-Note computer down a little chute from the jet to the tarmac. It was big and bulky, but light enough for the two of them to manage.

Ethan had arranged for the Roundtable in Colorado to provide a truck for the mission; it was already on the tarmac waiting for them. Ethan had had his people print the words *Triple T Construction* on the side—the name of the primary contractor involved in the construction of the National Data Center. That, plus a file containing phony authorization papers lying on the front seat, would hopefully get them at least through the first security gate on the property. It was risky, but what option did they have?

Galligher and Chiro rolled the big black computer up the ramp and into the back of the truck, where they used four-inch straps to cinch it against one of the inside panels. Galligher had also put in a special request of his own to Alvin Leander and his Roundtable partners—he wanted a Croatian RT20 20mm elephant gun loaded into the rental truck. Galligher knew a former FBI buddy of his who had one at his retirement cabin in the Utah mountains. So when Galligher opened the double doors in the back of the truck, he smiled when he saw the big gun case waiting for him.

After the two men transferred a few toolboxes full of gadgets and equipment into the truck and laid a tarp over the gun case, Chiro insisted that he ride next to his computer in the back. Galligher pointed to the tall machine that was bigger than a refrigerator. "Make sure your child stays in his car seat," he cracked before telling his partner he would see him in about half an hour. He shut the double doors in the back and slid the locking lever into place and then trotted to the driver's side.

The rendezvous point with Ethan was supposed to be three miles outside of the National Data Center, but two miles past the first guardhouse. Galligher made it to that first security checkpoint in good time. The gated guard booth on Redwood Road was surrounded by a high razor-wire fence stretching into the Utah desert. The National Guard had previously manned that post, as Camp Williams was adjacent to the computer complex, but now they had been replaced by Global Alliance security guards. Galligher handed over the phony paperwork. It contained a persuasive-looking order for him to repair a damaged fiber-optic line.

The two guards whispered something to each other. Then the one with the electronic clipboard said to Galligher in an Eastern Bloc accent, "But you are not on list."

"Fine," Galligher said. "When your computer system doesn't work today, and New Babylon strings you up by your fingernails, don't complain to me."

More hushed whispers between the men. Finally the guy with the e-pad said, "When you report to operations department, have them call me. If you don't do that, there will be big-time trouble." Then he touched something in the booth and the gate over the road opened wide.

Galligher nodded, but added, "Okay. But it may be awhile. First, we've got to run some field tests on the outside connections."

Galligher geared up the truck and took off down the paved stretch of Redwood Road that meandered through the desert until his odometer read two miles from the guardhouse. He climbed out and opened up the back door and told Chiro to sit tight while he checked things out.

Galligher could see, off in the distance, the mammoth computer complex on the rise of the plateau, with the mountains in the background. He used his high-powered binoculars to get a closer look at the computer headquarters that was several times larger than the Houston Space Center. There were ten huge buildings grouped together, and off to the side about a hundred yards sat two square, windowless structures that he figured might be power substations to run the digital intelligence center.

But he wasn't much interested in the architecture now. He was concerned about the fact that the place was swarming with security. He could see hundreds of blue, well-armed droid-bots marching around the place. And Global Alliance armored jeeps patrolling with big-caliber guns. And more Alliance guys with automatic weapons at various sectors just inside the inner razor-wire perimeter. But not a sign of American military presence. President Zandibar had obviously put a massive rush on the transfer of power here at Bluffdale.

Galligher kept searching the area, but Ethan March was nowhere to be found. Galligher was about to blow a gasket. He had his own doubts about Ethan anyway, but now he had traveled across the country and was parked outside the target site right on time, yet the Remnant's fearless leader was AWOL. He took his binoculars again and scanned the sandy flats around him.

Then he spotted something moving. It was a man crossing the desert toward him, about a mile away, and he was walking fast. Galligher kept peering through his binoculars until he could make out the man. Then he smiled. "Okay," he muttered to himself. "Nicely done."

Ethan March was walking alone through scrub brush heading toward the truck. The whole thing reminded Galligher of the old John Wayne movie *Hondo*, with the Duke shuffling out of the badlands on foot—his horse having given out—carrying only his saddle. But Ethan wasn't the Duke, and anyway, that was just a movie. What was happening around him today was real, and so were the bullets in the weapons that studded the framework of those droids and in the clips of the machine guns carried by the Global Alliance security forces down there in the complex.

Ethan was dirty and tired looking by the time he reached the truck. He was wearing a sand-colored jumpsuit that blended with the landscape and the hills. He quickly unzipped it and pulled it off. "Had to parachute down," he said. "They gave me one of those nifty triangle canopy stealth chutes—super-fast descent and almost invisible to detection." Galligher gave him a confused look and Ethan added, "It's a long story. Anyway, I buried my chute in the sand. Any sign of drone-bots flying overhead yet?"

Galligher shook his head no and trotted over to the back of the truck to tell Chiro to climb out and join them. As soon as the three of them stood next to the truck, Galligher jumped right into it. "What's the plan?"

Ethan raised an eyebrow. "That's what I'm trying to figure out."

Galligher started to boil. "You're kidding, right?" When Ethan said that he wasn't, Galligher mumbled loud enough for everyone to hear, "God, give me patience with this guy."

But Ethan shrugged it off. "We're going to have to improvise, John. That's the fact. Time to put our game faces on."

Chiro joined in. "Up at our hotel in White Horse, I tried to figure a way to hack into the system from the outside, using an Internet virus, like a bot-net," he said. "But it's impervious to initial entry that way. Maybe if I had more time . . . This transfer of American facilities over to the Alliance came way too fast. I owe everyone an apology for my failure—"

Ethan cut him short. "Listen to me, Chiro. You're a godsend. The Lord is going to use your computer brilliance today, I'm sure of it."

As Ethan turned to give Chiro a pat on the shoulder, Galligher noticed something. There was dried blood in the inside of Ethan's ear. Galligher moved around to the other side of Ethan's head and saw more blood, and some of it caked in his hair. Galligher looked intently at Ethan's face. The man had dark circles under his eyes and looked like he hadn't slept for a few days. And something else—his left eye was vibrating like a little NFL figurine on a car dashboard.

Back when Galligher worked in the Bureau, a few of his fellow agents had sustained serious head injuries in the line of duty, and he'd learned to recognize some of the signs. "What did they do to you in that lab anyway?" he asked Ethan.

"Messed with my head," Ethan replied quietly.

Galligher nodded, struggling with how to respond to this younger man he had resented for way too long and for all the wrong reasons. Finally he said to Ethan, "Okay, chief, you're the boss. What do you want us to do? The security guard told me if I didn't check into the computer complex we'd be up a creek without a paddle."

Ethan lowered his head as he thought it through. "We know that the Global Alliance will be shutting down the Internet world-wide—that's why they needed all seven of those ICANN code cards to restart it again after they've finished reprogramming it for their own purposes. Knowing that, Chiro, what are our options?"

"Just two. One is that we go down there"—and he pointed down to the uber-guarded National Data Center—"and we get *inside* the building so I can reprogram directly into the guts of their computer hardware."

"My guess is that's a long shot," Galligher grunted. "I got past the first guard with my doctored papers, but down there in Tron Central, how long do you think it'll take them to find out that we're part of a Trojan horse?"

"You're right," Ethan said. "So option two?"

"We do it old school," Chiro said. "We cut into the fiber-optic lines running into the data center. But we'd need to locate a junction box somewhere around here. My research leads me to believe that they've located the core switches underground out here in the desert somewhere, possibly as a backup system in case the data center itself suffered an attack. But I don't know where they buried it."

"Great," Galligher grunted with desperation. "I noticed your toolboxes in the truck, Chiro, but I didn't happen to see a tractor or maybe a well-digging rig or even a team of geologists who could locate it under the ground. Anyway, I thought there was sonar for this kind of stuff."

"There is," Chiro snapped back. "But I didn't have access to military-grade ground sonar equipment on such short notice. It's not easy to come by."

Ethan was trying to keep the group focused. "Let's deal with what we know. We need to break into their system during the short window of time when the whole Internet is down, right?"

Chiro nodded.

"How short a window?" Galligher asked.

"Maybe an hour," Chiro replied. "Maybe longer. I just can't be sure how long it will take Colliquin's people to shut down the web and load their program into the data center's computer system. But we'll know when it happens, because our Allfones will all go down at the same time."

Ethan held his hands up to the sky. Galligher studied him closer and then noticed that Ethan's eyes were closed and that he was praying out loud.

Oh, Lord, as You took pity on Hagar and Ishmael and found them water in the secret place in the wilderness, and as You led Abraham to dig a well and find water at Beersheba, so now, Lord God, help us find the entrance to the core switches to this computer center. The evil one has captured this place for evil, but You, Lord, still have plans for good.

When Ethan was finished he looked around the flat wilderness area. "I say the three of us start walking in three different directions and look for signs of a ground entrance or disruption of the soil—power lines, cables . . . anything."

Galligher suggested that Ethan was looking pretty lousy and that he ought to scout out the area while driving the truck. Meanwhile he and Chiro would go it on foot. But Ethan shook his head. "Can't do that. The terrain's too rough. It could shake up Chiro's computer."

Chiro reluctantly nodded in agreement.

As the three men started to stride out into the brush, it became obvious to all of them: they were looking for a needle in a haystack, and the haystack had a ticking time bomb inside. Not the explosive kind, perhaps, but something even more insidious—a sick, warped plan to capture and control the human race from the inside of everyone's cerebral cortex.

Ethan's Allfone went off. He checked it. "It's the Roundtable," he shouted out to the other two men. "Probably wants to make sure we arrived safely. I'll call them back later."

Galligher was scanning the ground, but he stopped every few seconds to search the sky. It was just a matter of time before they caught on to the fact that Ethan's team had not officially checked in with the data center as required, and then the drone-bots would spot them from the air, or maybe the droid-bots would start running at them from the ground. Galligher had heard those Alliance robo-cops had a top speed of forty-five miles per hour, and once the droids started chugging their way, it wouldn't take them very long to reach the truck, find the computer, and then scuttle the entire mission.

SIXTY-TWO

JERUSALEM, ISRAEL

Jimmy Louder and Rabbi ZG sat in the back of a little shop where the Remnant's secret communications office was located. The place was just off of Batei Mahseh Square in the old Jewish Quarter section of the city with a storefront made to look like a fish market, complete with a Jesus Remnant person dressed in a fishmonger's apron ready to wait on customers. But now that the waters of Israel were flowing with blood rather than water, killing the fish trade, shoppers wouldn't be bothering them today.

Their job now was to wait with their Allfones on. They were hoping to get an encrypted message from Bart Kingston in New York; in turn, they knew he would be waiting for a secure message from Ethan March.

"Come on, Bart," Jimmy Louder whispered. "Let's hear from you."

□□□

AMERINEWS HEADQUARTERS

New York City, New York

Bart Kingston and Terri Schultz had cued up the video feed, checked their connection to the Yukon computer station where Manfred was running things, and tested their link to Jerusalem. But they hadn't received the go-ahead from Ethan. The small staff had brought sleeping bags to the office and were prepared to stay through the night until they did.

The buzzer sounded on the outside of the double entrance doors to the AmeriNews lobby. Kingston checked the video surveillance monitor. It was the guy from the office next door. Terri had checked them out and said they had a sparse but active website and their corporation was registered in Delaware, but there were no other public filings.

The buzzer kept sounding. Kingston clicked on the intercom. "Sorry, but we're unable to come to the door."

"Mr. Kingston," the voice came back, "this is Kasmir Dellatar. I am with the ISA—the Global Alliance Information Security Agency. The ISA has authorized me to search your premises."

"On what grounds?" Kingston replied curtly.

"Illegal possession of news footage obtained in Amman, Jordan."

"Have you ever heard of freedom of the press or the First Amendment?" Kingston threw back.

But Dellatar had an answer. "Have you ever heard of the Global Alliance, which is now in control of your country?"

□□□

BLUFFDALE, UTAH

Ethan was fifty yards into the desert, looking for something, anything, but not knowing exactly what. Suddenly he had the nagging feeling that he was forgetting something. The call from the Roundtable—was it Judge Rice again? More information on the authority of the DOD? He decided he ought to return the call after all, before things got really crazy. He dialed the number on his Allfone. But instead of Fort Rice, Alvin Leander picked up. Leander immediately launched into details regarding a call he had just received from a guy named Dillon Ritzian. The man had called from Las Vegas. At first Ethan only half listened as he scoured the ground and kept an eye out for Alliance security forces. Leander said the man had complained about a girlfriend named Darlene and said he had a defense security clearance with the United States government. But when Leander said the caller had worked with Triple T Construction Company in Utah, Ethan heard Fourth of July fireworks going off in his brain.

"He was contacted by some shadowy characters months ago," Leander said. "They wanted his schematics and codes for the National Data Center. He said it has something to do with the Global Alliance takeover."

Filled with excitement, Ethan told the retired senator that he needed to get back to Ritzian. "You need to get the GPS coordinates from him for the underground entrance to the fiber-optic core switches just outside the data center complex. This is urgent."

After that, Ethan messaged Galligher and Chiro and told them both to head back to the truck immediately. As he sprinted toward the truck with the Triple T logo painted on it, his head reeled. He hadn't told anyone what the world looked like from inside his skull. He had been wracked with relentless pain and nonstop vertigo, and out of his left eye he saw things in a constant state of vibration. But this was the bottom of the ninth inning. He had to just push through it.

When the three men rejoined, Ethan gave a rapid-fire account of his conversation with Leander. Now they could only wait.

Ten minutes later Leander called back with the coordinates. Two minutes after that, the three of them were in the truck, with Galligher driving slowly so as not to rock the computer in the back. Chiro had his eyes glued to the GPS location-finder as they eased their way over the terrain, until he finally shouted, "Stop here! This is it."

The trio piled out and began to survey the area dotted with scrub brush and cactus. Then Ethan pointed to something about fifty feet away—a five-foot-square metal hatch set into the hard desert floor.

"Wow, that was too easy," Galligher called out with a smile.

"You're right, *too* easy," Chiro said. He was nodding to the ring of little red lights creating a perimeter of about twenty feet around the hatch. "Infrared security."

"Right," Galligher grunted. "We trip those, and the electric goon squad shows up."

Chiro scurried around to the back of the truck and snatched one of his big toolboxes and lugged it outside. He opened it up and pulled out a plastic container with a hook on the top. The device was the size of a Kleenex box, and it looked like a homemade science experiment, with a battery pack connected to the bottom and large orbs on each of the four corners that looked like hemispherical lenses. He began to narrate his plan as he pulled out the segments of two portable aluminum fishing rod lengths and started to assemble them together in one long pole. "I figured that the government had an advanced infrared system for this site," he said. "Which means the type that uses the newest PWM system—pulse-width modulation—that keeps the LED lights cool and avoids overheating with a rapid on/off pulse. Which means there's a digital code for those pulses. Which also means I had to build a decoding device that tells the LED lights to stay on the *off* pulse until we are safely out of here."

Galligher cocked an eyebrow and gave Chiro a confused look. "I'm glad you know what you're talking about . . ."

After switching his box on, Chiro hocked it to the end of the fishing rod and clumsily lifted it into the air. Galligher studied him for a moment and then reached out toward the extended rod with the strange bait on the end and gently lifted it out of Chiro's hands. "I've done more fishing than you," he said. "Let me give that a try."

Chiro told him the plan: the goal was to drop the box down as close as he could to the center of the metal hatch. He had a pair of night-vision goggles and he handed them over to Ethan, telling him to make sure the infrared beams were off. But Ethan shook his head. He was still seeing the left side of the world from a carnival tilt-a-whirl ride. "You'd better do that part, Chiro."

As Chiro coached him, Galligher dropped the box right down over the center of the metal hatch until it was about two feet off the surface. Finally Chiro announced that the LED security lights had been deactivated; he snapped the night-vision goggles off while Ethan grabbed a wrench from the toolbox and carefully crawled through the dirt and over to the metal hatch, where he unscrewed each of the lug nuts. Ethan slid the hatch off to the side of the opening. He could see a metal ladder that extended thirty feet down to the underground computer vault where green safety lights illuminated a corridor at the bottom.

While Galligher held the pole and decoding box steady over the hole, Chiro and Ethan scrambled back to the truck. They released the straps from the C-Note computer and wheeled it down the ramp and then began to roll it through the sand and dirt until they could cautiously lift it up and over the infrared light perimeter and set it down next to the square opening in the ground, close enough so they could run cables from it to the core switches underground.

Chiro snatched a few more devices from his toolbox and filled his pockets until they bulged. Ethan fetched a large roll of fiber-optic cable from the truck and Chiro hooked up one end of it to the computer while Ethan plugged the power cord of the computer to a cable that fed into the power outlet in the truck's dashboard. Chiro thumbed the On switch, and the big black computer started to scream in a perfect-pitch high-C note. Ethan and Galligher both smiled. Chiro's name for the quantum computer now made sense.

Ethan ducked under the box dangling from the end of Galligher's fishing pole and started down the ladder first, lugging the big roll of fiber-optic cable that was connected to the computer. Chiro was beginning to climb after him when Galligher called out to him with a cocky grin, "Hey, Chiro, I thought you said this wouldn't be that easy."

Chiro nodded as Galligher announced that the box at the end of the line felt like it weighed about ten pounds and his arms were getting tired. He asked exactly when he could put the fishing rod down. "You can't," Chiro called back to him with a smile and then he disappeared down the ladder.

□□□

Two miles away, in the security control room in the National Data Center, the Alliance staff was receiving an operational crash-course from a National Security Agency advisor from Washington. The NSA official had to respond to all of their questions, even if it meant answering through gritted teeth.

"What about the signal here," one of the Alliance technicians asked. "It says that the infrared LED system out there in the desert is showing an anomaly: the system protecting the outside bypass hatch is reading *Low Power* on the PWM pulse. Maybe there was an intrusion into the exterior data vault out there. Someone could be accessing the fiber-optic core switches. Perhaps we should send out a squad of droid-bots to check it out?"

The NSA man gave a nonplussed shrug. He had read the most recent top secret memo—the one that was now circulating through the FBI, Homeland Security, the NSA, and the CIA. It described the status of the formal investigation into the assassination of President Hewbright and the nefarious ties between the now president Darrell Zandibar and Jessica Tulrude, the regent for Global Alliance Region One. And the obvious partnership between Tulrude and Alexander Colliquin. With no vice president yet named, the next in line of succession—the Speaker of the House, a former head of the CIA himself—was demanding that President Zandibar surrender his executive powers until the investigation was completed. The memo also described the link between Alexander Colliquin and the assassin Vlad Malatov, aka agent Ted Booth. The death of President Hewbright had all the makings of an insidious White House coup, and the Pentagon and the intelligence agencies were siding with the Speaker.

The last thing the top secret memo had mentioned was "a heroic attempt to countermand the handover from the U.S.A. to the Global Alliance of the Bluffdale computer data center, spearheaded by a former air force special-ops pilot who is a loaned asset of the CIA."

The NSA man, just like his superiors in the intelligence agencies and like the Pentagon brass, had no intention of giving in to the Alliance until every last question about Hewbright's murder had been answered to their satisfaction. Until then, the orders of the late president Hewbright to treat the data center and every other inch of American soil as free of Alliance control were considered reinstated.

As the NSA official looked at the blinking signal light on the computer console, he remarked casually, "Nothing to worry about."

The Global Alliance technician kept insisting that something was wrong. But the NSA man simply replied, "That PWM system in those infrared LEDs is the newest design model." He grinned. "I never trust the newest model off the assembly line—whether it's a car from Detroit or an infrared security system. Don't worry about it."

The Global Alliance tech guy still looked unconvinced. After glancing down at his Allfone watch, he said, "An Internet shutdown is scheduled to occur soon. But we'll be down only for a short time. Then I'll launch our droid-bots to check out the perimeter. Just in case you're wrong."

SIXTY-THREE

As Ethan walked through the long, cement-floored computer vault, he carefully unrolled the fiber-optic cable that was connected at the other end, above ground, to Chiro's C-Note quantum computer. The underground hall was lined on both sides with data racks; each rack was nineteen inches wide and just under two inches tall, and rows and rows of them were stacked one on top of each other from floor to ceiling. Together, they created a tunnel of blinking lights that looked like a Future World ride at Disney World.

At the end of the vault were two big machines on the left. "Routers," Chiro announced in the green illumination of the safety lights as he pointed to them. There was a smaller data machine on the right with yellow, black, and purple cables running out of it. Chiro pointed to it and, in a whisper of hushed awe, said, "This is it. The core switches. If we can access this, we can override everything."

But Ethan wasn't next to him; he stood a distance away, down the corridor from Chiro, and he had a distressed look on his face as he held the end of the fiber-optic cable. It was clear now that the length of cable was too short to reach the core switches. "It won't reach," Ethan said.

Chiro pulled out his digital measuring tape, held it at the face of the box containing the core switches, then focused it at Ethan's feet. "Maybe I can fix this," he said. But after reading the little meter he said with a groan, "We still need twenty-three feet."

"Is there any more cable?"

Chiro shook his head. Ethan bit his lip. "I thought you just said you could fix this?"

Chiro pulled a small red box from his pocket. "I could," he said, "with this signal extender. Only . . ."

"What?"

"It only works up to *twenty* feet."

"Lord," Ethan prayed, "You extended the length of a day during the life of Joshua. We need You to extend the capacity of this device by three more feet."

When Ethan was done praying, he noticed Chiro's anxious face in the ghostly illumination of the green lights. The young Japanese man was a genius, and Ethan was tempted to believe that his word on matters of digital technology was always final. Except for one thing: God was God. Ethan was now banking everything on that single fact.

Chiro connected a fiber-optic signal receptacle to the core switching box and then attached his red signal extender to the end of the cable, which lay twenty-three agonizing feet from the core switches, nothing but empty air between the two. He reached his hands out toward the core switching box as if he were trying to somehow make the distance disappear between it and the end of the fiber-optic cable connected to his C-Note computer above ground.

Ethan touched Chiro on the shoulder. "Faith is the evidence of things not seen," he said, paraphrasing from the book of Hebrews, "the substance of things hoped for." He pulled the reluctant Chiro away from the dead end of the corridor and urged him toward the other end of the hallway and the ladder leading up to the ground level. "So we walk by faith. But *quickly*."

ㅁㅁㅁ

MASTER CONTROL STUDIO–ALLIANCE COMMUNICATIONS CENTER

New Babylon, Iraq

Alexander Colliquin stood alone in his New Babylon penthouse, studying himself in a full-length mirror. In the Internet headquarters of the Alliance, Colliquin's digital engineers had sent their state-of-the-art denial-of-service signal through the Internet, aimed at every root server address across the planet. It was now just a matter of time. As soon as the Internet went down, the new 3-D holograph program would be imbedded and then the global system would reboot. That's when they would call Colliquin and invite him over to the studio to begin his first 3-D global image transmission to the human race.

Thirty minutes later it started.

ㅁㅁㅁ

NEW YORK, NEW YORK

In New York, the software-controlled lights of the huge Jumbotrons that filled the sides of buildings along Time Square started to blink off, along with the digital stoplights in the intersections. On Wall Street, inside the New York Stock Exchange, the electronic trading boards went dark. Subway trains running on Internet-driven schedules and directional systems ground to a halt. The radar screens in airport control towers shut down as jets circled, waiting for clearance to land.

□□□

LAS VEGAS, NEVADA

In Las Vegas, Dillon Ritzian was sitting next to Darlene, who had reluctantly returned to the apartment when the nail salon didn't pan out. The two of them were watching Internet television together as he tried to explain the whole back story to her—about how Henry Bender had pressured him for information about America's central web hub in the data center at Bluffdale, Utah, and how sorry he was he'd gotten involved. Especially when he finally figured out somebody was trying to take over the entire Internet, or shut it down, and maybe use all of that against America. And how he'd decided to put a stop to it and had placed a call to a television studio and tracked down an ex-senator he'd seen on TV. That is how he—Dillon Ritzian—had blown the lid on the whole conspiracy.

Darlene flashed a skeptical expression, the kind usually reserved for stories about alien abductions.

"I'm just sayin'," Ritzian said, "I was actually trying to save America. I think something heavy is goin' down on the Internet."

She shook her head. But just then the image on the TV in front of them disappeared. They both noticed that the electricity in the apartment was still on. Simultaneously they pulled out their Allfones. Both devices showed no signal. Darlene looked at her boyfriend. "Okay, so, tell me this again . . ."

□□□

BLUFFDALE, UTAH

Up on ground level, John Galligher was grinding his teeth and grunting loudly as he struggled to keep Chiro's decoding box two feet above the entrance to the underground computer vault so the red laser security lights would not be tripped. When Ethan's head popped up, Galligher yelled out, "Thank You, Lord!"

After Ethan and Chiro were both out of the hole and back on ground level, Galligher used the fishing rod to swing the digital box out of the way and then let go of it with a grunt. All of them simultaneously checked their Allfone watches. No one had a signal.

"The Internet is down," Chiro shouted. Then he scampered over to his C-Note quantum computer. The On power switch was already engaged, but one additional switch with a little light panel next to it had yet to be flipped. Directly beneath it, Chiro had typed the words on a label: *The Great Commission.* If the light illuminated, that meant that connectivity had been achieved and his computer was connected to the underground core switches. Which meant that somehow the signal had managed to jump twenty-three feet from the end of the fiber-optic cable to the master switch—three feet more than his signal extender was ever designed to achieve.

Chiro whispered a prayer and toggled that switch. A little white light lit up on the panel. When it did, he leaped into the air with a cheer. Then he snatched his Allfone and stared at the screen, waiting for the first evidence that the Internet was back up. A minute later Chiro's Allfone digital display illuminated. He immediately called Manfred, who was waiting in the computer lab on the second floor of their Yukon hotel. "I've got the C-Note connected!" Chiro yelled. "Are you seeing the de-encryption working?"

Ethan and Galligher watched as for several minutes Chiro stood motionless, waiting for the answer. Then Manfred told him something on the other end, and Chiro threw his head back with his eyes closed. "It's working! My C-Note has deciphered the data center passwords, and now our Remnant program is being uploaded globally."

Ethan balled up his fists and swung them in the air with a whoop of laughter. He then hit speed dial on his own Allfone. At the other end, Bart Kingston picked up in New York.

"Bart, this is Ethan. It's a go. We're in the system and we've overridden the Alliance program. We got there first. I want you to start the transmissions from Rabbi ZG in Jerusalem first and follow up with the video testimony from Dr. Radameyer. Do you have the AllLanguageTranslator program synced?"

Kingston had to yell over some noise at his end. "Yes. The rabbi is ready in Jerusalem. We're set to link his message to our facility here. We'll sync him with the taped statement of Dr. Radameyer momentarily. Then we'll shoot it to your routing station in White Horse."

"Great," Ethan said. He could hardly hear Bart over the sound of loud banging in the background, so he raised his voice to a shout. "Then Manfred up in the Yukon will transmit to Chiro's quantum computer here in Utah. And if all goes well, we'll go global in a matter of minutes." The banging at the other end continued. "What's going on out there?" Ethan asked.

"Alliance forces," Kingston explained. "Three of them. They're breaking down the AmeriNews entrance as we speak. I'm hoping we can get this transmission out before they make it through the security door."

"Can you get out of there?"

"We'll climb out the balcony to a construction chute that's still up against the building. I think we can slide down the chute to the floor below us. Pray for us."

Galligher suddenly strode up next to Ethan. "Visitors!" he shouted and pointed down to the data center complex where a squad of blue titanium droid-bots were running in their direction. Galligher turned and took off running back toward the truck.

Ethan called out, "Where are you going?"

"Getting backup!"

Chiro was wide-eyed. "This is when we find out if my computer friend at IntraTonics really did program that *Disable* code into the droids."

In two minutes Ethan and Chiro were surrounded by a squad of seven-foot droid-bots with the barrels of automatic weapons sprouting from their chests. The robot leader, who had a dark, bulletproof Plexiglas shield for a face, was bellowing for them to lie down on the ground or be shot. Chiro strode up to within inches of the leader, who was now giving his final warning. He gave a quick glance up to the sky, then began to recite the *Disable* code in a slow, methodical voice. "For God so loved the world, that He gave His only begotten Son, that whoever believes in Him shall not perish, but have eternal life."

There was a pause and a little red flash behind the black face screen of the robot. A few seconds elapsed. Then the droid announced, "You are free to go. Have a good day." The squad of droid-bots turned and began to march back toward the data center.

Ethan grabbed Chiro by the shoulders. "You did it, Chiro! I told you God would use you mightily today!"

Chiro was beaming. Ethan looked around for Galligher, figuring he was still in the truck. But something else caught his attention. Even with the wavering vision in his left eye he could see trouble off in the distance, kicking up dust and approaching them with the speed of an accelerating sports car. He closed his left eye so he could limit his vision to his right eye and study it closer.

What came into view was a huge black droid, considerably bigger than the rest, churning his legs like an industrial forge and sprinting toward them. The squad of other droids who were retreating back to the data center dutifully stepped out of its way as it blew past them.

"Must be the new generation droid!" Chiro said with mild hysteria. "And it won't have the old *Disable* code programmed into it."

Ethan ordered Chiro to run back to the truck.

"What about you?" Chiro yelled as he started sprinting.

"Don't wait for me." As Ethan studied the droid, he could now see it held something in his hand.

Chiro was just a few feet from the truck when the droid started firing at them. As the bullets started zinging up to his position, Ethan leaped to his right and barely missed being hit. Facedown in the dirt, he looked back toward the truck. Chiro was down on the ground.

"Chiro, are you hit?"

But Chiro didn't answer. He was trying to lift his head off the ground and flailing one of his arms in the air in a pitiful movement.

The huge black droid was now about seventy feet from Ethan and lifting an arm over its head. Ethan could see it had in its grip one of the new variable-impact grenades he had read about, the kind designed to explode instantly on impact with rigid, impervious surfaces like the side of a vehicle. But on impact with any elastic surfaces like human flesh or clothing, they were timed to detonate only after three seconds—a safety feature to mitigate possible "droid error" in pitching the explosive at friendly troops.

As the droid reached sixty feet, Ethan realized it was aiming at the side of the truck. The explosion and resulting shrapnel would kill them all.

"Throw it, you monster. No mistakes this time." As Ethan shouted that, like a flash of lightning he remembered it all—his failed last catch in the last inning in the losing baseball game against the Yankee farm team from Scranton/Wilkes Barre.

The droid let loose in Ethan's direction at ninety miles per hour, the white impact grenade spinning in a perfect fastball. It headed straight toward the truck. Ethan squinted, closing his left eye and using only his right side vision. At the last millisecond he leaped to his right almost parallel to the ground and with his bare hand extended caught the high-velocity pitch in the fleshy palm of his hand. Howling in pain, he hit the ground while holding the grenade aloft so it wouldn't strike the hard ground. He quickly rotated the grenade, frantically searching for the detonator-off thumb switch. *Found it!* It was recessed within the skin of the explosive. He flicked it off with the thumb of his other hand, just shy of three seconds.

The droid was now thirty feet away and closing. It reached down to the button that would have let loose another volley of bullets. But Galligher appeared from the truck and raised his Croatian RT 20mm armor-piercing gun. He let go with a single blast. The bullet hit the mark. It blew the head of the droid completely off of its shoulders. The torso of the giant robot came to a slow stop and then collapsed to the ground. Galligher leapt over to Ethan and reached down with delicate care to lift the grenade out of Ethan's broken hand. "Sorry, Ethan. I guess I was wrong about you. Wrong about everything."

As Galligher cradled the grenade, Ethan stumbled over to Chiro, who had been shot several times in the chest and was bleeding out profusely. With tears welling up in his eyes, Ethan bent down over Chiro and searched for words to comfort his faithful friend. But Chiro spoke first. His face was ashen gray and his voice was barely audible.

"Blow up the C-Note computer. Don't let the bad people get it . . ."

In a choking voice, Ethan said that they would.

Chiro looked up, as if he had seen something in the sky, a vision that only few could ever see this side of the grave. "Oh," he said with a faint tone of wonder to his voice, like a child. "I see Jesus . . . heaven open . . . on a white horse . . . the Faithful and True . . ." With that, he stopped talking and his head fell against Ethan's chest.

Ethan choked back tears. He reached down and touched the face of his dead friend and gently closed his eyes, and as he did, he remembered his own vision. Ethan March had been there. In the heavenly realm. For only a short time, but he was there, and he knew that even though Chiro was now gone, he had found his way home to a land of light and peace. No more chaos, fear, or death. A region where everything would finally make sense, because Jesus was in that place.

Next to Ethan, Galligher struggled against a sob.

In the silence of that moment they both heard an unsettling sound. Jumping to their feet, they swiped the tears from their faces to take a look. About two miles away, a pack of armed drone-bots winged their way skyward toward their position.

Without a word Galligher took the impact grenade and set it carefully inside the C-Note quantum computer. He then gathered Chiro in his arms and shouted for Ethan to grab the gun and run after him back to the truck. Galligher tenderly laid Chiro in the back of the truck and then jumped behind the steering wheel with Ethan next to him. He gunned the truck until he was a safe distance away and slammed it to a halt. Then he took the rifle from Ethan and aimed it one more time. Squeezing the trigger, he detonated Chiro's quantum computer, which exploded in a fiery blast. Then he jammed the truck into gear, spitting stones and dust, and floored it toward the gatehouse.

Ethan turned around to see that the drone-bots in the air above them were gaining fast. As he turned back he noticed several helicopters in the air ahead of them, beyond the perimeter of the razor-wire fence that marked the edge of the Alliance's geographical control of the data center. They were heading straight for the truck. "We're pinned!" he shouted.

The drone-bots in the sky behind them started firing, but the truck was just out of range. The guard gate was up ahead and by now Galligher's foot was to the floor and they were doing eighty. They could see the two Alliance security officers running out of the guardhouse and looking for cover.

Confused, Ethan looked closer at the choppers and recognized them. "U.S. Army Blackhawk helos," he yelled. "They're ours!" They were cutting the air and maintaining their position just above the wire fence. Ethan saw the situation instantly: maybe there was a question about who controlled the data center grounds, given the political mess in Washington. But the Pentagon had apparently decided that everything beyond the wire still belonged to the U.S.A.

Galligher gunned the truck and crashed it through the security gate. The instant that happened, the Blackhawk choppers took aim at the squad cf drone-bots flying toward them and blasted them out of the air.

As he gripped the steering wheel and straightened the swerving truck, Galligher shouted over to Ethan, "Well, well. It looks like the DOD doesn't want America in a shotgun wedding with the Alliance after all."

SIXTY-FOUR

In the shadow of triple-roofed Buddhist temples and the ancient royal palace built to honor pagan goddesses and forgotten kings in Durbar Square, hundreds of local residents of Kathmandu, Nepal, flocked together in the open courtyard. They were stunned at the sight before them. Multiple 3-D images of Rabbi ZG floated in the air, appearing before them, addressing them in their own language. He was explaining the state of the world. "The evil one has planned this technology for evil, but God has permitted it for good, at least for this short period of time."

"In a few minutes," he said, "you will hear from one of the world's great experts in video forensics. He will tell you how the story told by the Global Alliance and the pictures they showed you in an effort to explain away the disappearance of millions and millions of Christians was a lie. In truth, Christians disappeared because they were taken into the presence of Jesus Christ in the Rapture, the gathering of all

Jesus followers who were then on the earth. But do not despair, for I will share with you now the great love of God. You too can have peace with God through His Son, Jesus Christ. For sin has kept all of us at a distance from God. But God sent His only Son, Jesus, to bridge that gap by being the sacrifice for our sins—shedding His own holy and righteous blood on a cross—so that our sins can be forgiven. Yours and mine. Casting your sins away forever, as far as the east is from the west. Farther than the deepest ocean and farther away than the top of the highest mountain."

Some in the crowd looked up at the towering, snow-capped mountain ranges that rimmed their city and nodded.

"You need only believe in Jesus, and believe in what He did on the cross," he continued, "and believe that after being killed for your sins and mine, then, just as He predicted, Jesus rose from the grave. This very same Jesus is coming back to earth again. Will you be part of His family? Or will you be counted among the followers of the evil one? Today is the day of decision. Won't you invite Jesus, the Christ, who is the King of the universe, to come into your heart and to dwell there forever?"

At that same moment across the border in neighboring India, hundreds of thousands of forgotten and malnourished souls in the slums of Dharavi and Calcutta, having witnessed and heard the same message in their Marathi and Hindi languages, knelt down in piles of garbage and prayed for Jesus Christ, the Savior, to redeem their souls and to enter their hearts and to grant them eternal life. In upscale Bangalore, the city of seven million, with its international hub of IT companies, Indian technicians and professionals halted their work to consider what they had just seen and heard.

Identical scenes were taking place throughout the world: in the Balkans and in Red Square in Moscow, and on the stark plains of Mongolia among the tent dwellers, and across all of Europe and down through all of the Arab nations of the Middle East, and over the entire continent of Africa in all of its cities and towns and among the far-flung tribes living on the veldt, and in the deep rainforests of Brazil and the remote mountain villages of Peru, and up through Central America and Mexico, and across the U.S.A. from New Orleans to Duluth and Bangor to San Francisco and all points in between, and across Canada, and on every Pacific island with human inhabitants, and in every city in Australia and among the ranchers and the Aborigines in the remote regions of the Outback.

The four and a half billion people living in China and in the rest of Asia all witnessed the message from Rabbi ZG that day. In Beijing alone, it was estimated that some six million Chinese citizens bowed their knee to Jesus of Nazareth.

In the ravaged city of Athens, Gikas, the local go-between for Jo Li, stood with his bodyguard when he was confronted with the stunning 3-D message that spoke about salvation by God's grace and through faith in His Son Jesus Christ. Gikas quietly dismissed his bodyguard and walked up to the Areopagus hill alone, to the place where Ethan March had told him the story about the apostle Paul and his preaching about knowing the "unknown God." As he sat up on the stone outcropping, he knew that this was the time for knowing. And for the first time in his adult life he talked directly to God and said that he wanted to trust in Jesus and be saved.

□□□

HONG KONG

In the city of Hong Kong, with a view of Victoria Harbor, Hadley Brooking was a man with a lot on his mind. He sat in the penthouse of Zhang Lee, jiggling the ice in the glass of tea that Zhang had served him. He didn't know exactly how much the easygoing Christian real-estate mogul really knew about him. But regardless, even if Zhang had an inkling about the truth—that Brooking had been working as a double informant for the governments of both England and the United States for years and that even his superficial collaboration with Jo Li was just one more part of that mission—still, the former English solicitor-turned-spy hadn't called on Zhang because of that.

He had come because of something else. For personal reasons. It started when he was confronted, like billions of others, with the 3-D video statement from Dr. Terrance Radameyer, the imagery forensics expert who explained how the hoax perpetrated by Colliquin and the Alliance had camouflaged the disappearance of millions of Jesus followers in the Rapture. But even more than that, it was the message from Rabbi ZG that had jabbed at something deep inside of Brooking, as if he had been poked with an ice pick.

"You see," Brooking said, "I was raised in the Church of England. Baptized and as a boy learned the catechism and all of that, and I became rather knowledgeable about all of the Christian doctrines of the faith, you know. But never felt, well, transformed by any of it, you might say. It stayed in my head. But never went any further."

"It's good to have it in your head," Zhang said with a smile. "But it's very, very necessary to have it in your heart too. That's where the transformation comes."

"And the sin business . . ."

"Sin resides in the human heart," Zhang said. "When you willingly invite Jesus to reside in your heart, sin is forgiven. A new life begins."

"New life, yes. That's what I'm thinking about. I've lived a life that's been rather full of secrets."

"Yet there are no secrets from God."

Brooking nodded. He knew that, but had avoided it all of those years.

Zhang studied the Englishman closely. "Jesus is knocking on the door of your heart. You must decide today. Will you open the door?

Will you tell Him what you believe about yourself, and about Him, and about what Jesus did on the cross and how He rose from the dead? And then will you allow Him to enter? Will you?"

Such a decision seemed to Brooking, for the very first time in his life, to be so effortless, so self-evident. Those doctrines he had once learned in his head but that felt as cold and dead as the stone walls of the little country church in Staffordshire he had attended in his youth—those truths now seemed to have been birthed into new life.

"I shall," Brooking said, nodding as he said it. "Yes. The time has come."

Zhang invited his guest to pray. Both men knelt down on the floor, and Brooking began a halting prayer, acknowledging that God had sent His Son, Jesus, to save sinners like himself by dying on the cross as the perfect sacrifice—and yes, he was such a sinner, Brooking added. He spoke to God about how he did believe the Bible's account of Jesus, and about His life, and about His death. And yes, that he believed in Jesus' actual resurrection too. And that he knew Jesus could redeem him from judgment and rescue his soul in every way that such a rescue could be accomplished. And that he now wanted that, more than any other thing in the world.

But when Brooking was about to finish, his throat tightened and his voice wavered. "Oh, God, I have wandered so far from You," he said with a frankness that held nothing back and with tears that began to fill his eyes and would soon stream down his cheeks. "I have ignored the knocking on the door of my heart. I always knew some-how that the Savior was out there, on the other side, waiting for me. But I ignored Him. Dear God, please, if You would, permit Your Son, Jesus, to enter. I've bolted the door for too long. I open it now. My heart is ready. I do not want to waste another minute living apart from You. I have known the face of evil. Its shadow is spreading over the entire world. But You are mighty, Lord. I put my trust in You and in Jesus, my Savior . . ."

□□□

UTAH

Somewhere in the desert in Utah, John Galligher pulled the truck over to the side of the road so they could await a U.S. Army transport helicopter. They had been told that it would soon pick up Galligher and Ethan and, of course, the body of Chiro Hashimoto. While they waited, Galligher told Ethan he needed to make a call, so he climbed out of the truck and strolled out a few yards onto the sandy ground by a big yucca bush and he dialed Helen, his ex-wife. When it rang eight times and she hadn't answered, he figured she'd seen the incoming number flash on her Allfone and that she wouldn't pick up. But on the ninth ring, she did.

Galligher stumbled over himself a little at first as he spoke. Helen didn't say a thing. He apologized for his failings as a husband and as a man. And then he told her that something pretty amazing had happened to him over the last two years and how he had become a follower of Jesus. And that for the first time in his life he had peace inside—and it reminded him of that lake in New Hampshire where they had taken their honeymoon, the one with the long, funny Indian name. The place where the surface of the water in the early morning was as smooth and peaceful as glass and everything about life seemed right at the time. But this peace that he had now was even better than that, he said, because he knew that it was real and it was forever.

Galligher ended by saying that he had to tell her about his new life with Jesus, because if he didn't, it would be the biggest mistake of his life.

Finally Helen spoke up. She said simply, "You sound different."

"I am," he replied.

After a moment of silence she added, "Okay. So, John, go back to that part about you and Jesus. Tell me that again . . ."

SIXTY-FIVE

Ethan March had heard rumors about Colliquin's reaction to the Remnant victory at Bluffdale. An inside source in New Babylon had told him that when the Remnant's, rather than Colliquin's, message went global, the Alliance chancellor happened to be standing before a wall of a hundred monitors keyed to different parts of the globe. The video feed had been designed to verify the successful launch of Colliquin's digital control over the planet. But instead, Colliquin caught the horrifying sight of millions of humans receiving a message about Jesus and then bowing their knees to Him.

As the story went, Colliquin then turned from the wall of monitors, stunned, almost robot-like in his movements, tripping a bit and then striding out of the room with a face scarlet with rage, saying nothing. It was shortly after that when Colliquin began making his terrifying threats to retaliate against Jesus followers everywhere. His rage would now build to epic proportions. Ethan was sure of that.

And then there were some things that Ethan was less certain about. Like providing an economic system for his Remnant followers while Colliquin tightened his net. Interestingly, a courier of Jo Li had contacted Ethan and said his boss now wanted to meet again and to offer his apologies. That he was done with Colliquin and he wanted to talk terms with Ethan. The messenger shared a quip that he said was straight from Jo Li himself. "'Better to do business with a Jesus-cross than with a double-cross.'"

On any other day, all of that would have occupied Ethan's mind. But not today. Not on this occasion.

In a small fishing village on the island of Great Cumbrae off the coast of Scotland, Ethan gathered with his closest friends. Jimmy Louder was there, and John Galligher, and so were Pack and Victoria McHenry, Zhang Lee, and Nick Akonos. Bobby Robert had come all the way from White Horse, the heart of the Yukon. Alvin Leander showed up, although Judge Rice was unable to attend—he had recently suffered a mild heart attack and couldn't travel.

Bart Kingston and Terri Schultz, however, had disappeared from the AmeriNews headquarters. Neither Ethan nor his leadership had heard directly from them, but a Remnant contact in North America reported that they had made it to a safe house in Nova Scotia. Everyone was anxious to verify that.

Ethan also thought of some others. Those who couldn't join in the festivities. The ones who had died valiantly while resisting the evil empire. Brave ones like Chiro and Dr. Adis. And Andre Chifflet, who gave his life in the rescue mission to save Ethan's.

But those who had come were now gathered together in a little church perched on a hill that overlooked the waters of the Firth of Clyde. The usually somber Rabbi Zechariah Gamaliel stood before them with a grin that spread over his bearded face. Ethan was wearing his best suit, the only one he owned. And next to him, in a white dress full of delicate lace, Rivka held tightly to his hand with one of her own, as if she would not let him go. A lesser bride would have been exasperated at having to wear her other arm in a sling, but not Rivka. Nothing was going to dim this day for her.

Ethan had just slipped a plain gold ring onto her finger, and the joy on her face was incandescent. Marriage, Rabbi ZG had just told them, was a reflection, a portrait, of the relationship between Christ and His church. He was the Bridegroom and the church His bride. Rabbi ZG spoke of the love and honor and respect that was to be exchanged between a husband and a wife.

Ethan cracked a little smile when his strong-willed bride unhesitatingly declared her pledge to obey her new husband, because at that exact moment Rivka's bridesmaid, young Meifeng, the Hong Kong teenager, had started to giggle.

When Ethan finally wrapped his arms around his new bride and kissed her passionately, a cheer rose up from the small crowd. As Ethan studied the pretty, smiling face of his bride, he saw the glint of tears starting to show. He only hoped he could live up to the standard set before him—to love her as Christ loved the church and gave Himself for it. The Bible commanded that of him, of course. But Ethan also believed Rivka deserved it, more than any woman he'd ever known.

After the ceremony there was a modest supper in the basement of the church and lots of laughter and a few tears—and many stories. Jimmy Louder went on and on about Ethan's courageous leadership while Ethan's face blushed and he tried in vain to get his friend to stop. Victoria McHenry had everyone laughing when she poked fun at Ethan about his being married to a woman like Rivka, as she wondered out loud what would happen the first time Ethan refused to take out the garbage or forgot to bring home milk from the office. "Rivka is a martial arts expert, after all," she cracked.

John Galligher talked about some of the crazy, laughable experiences he'd had with Chiro in the Yukon Territory. Halfway through he had to stop and turn away in order to compose himself so he could continue. He told the group that he couldn't help thinking about Chiro when he finally made good on his promise to reconnect with his ex-wife, Helen. They were on talking terms now, he said, and the whole thing was a miracle.

Later that night Ethan and Rivka slipped outside together, hand in hand, into the moonlight. They looked at the little harbor filled with fishing boats that rolled and bobbed gently in the water. Standing there under a sky studded with stars, Ethan knew he couldn't keep the world or the devil at bay indefinitely. But he could today, and perhaps for a little while, at least.

Rivka broke the silence, and when she did, standing there in her wedding dress, she surprised Ethan with her comment. But then, she always had been an interesting combination of true romantic and stone-cold realist.

"By my count," Rivka announced, "we are still somewhere within the first half of the Tribulation, not even at the midpoint yet. Colliquin will only grow stronger, and his atrocities will increase." Then she turned to Ethan and kissed him hard. "Which is why I'm glad we will go through this together, my darling."

Ethan held her face in his big hands. "I thank God for you, Rivka, more than you will ever know." Yet as he said that, Ethan knew they would soon be plunged into a life-and-death struggle with demonic forces—waging a spiritual battle against a cruel and soulless enemy. He wanted to protect Rivka, keep her safe, and he knew that he would lay down his life if necessary to do that. But he also knew that ultimately he would have to entrust her to the safekeeping of God. After all, she had belonged to God long before she had ever belonged to him.

Rivka shivered a little in the evening air, and Ethan covered her shoulders with his jacket and pulled her close. He felt the weight of the future bearing down on him. *How long, O Lord?* Ethan wondered to himself silently. But before he could take his next breath, the answer to his question seemed to envelop him from some unseen place; the message was as real and as certain as the breeze that now swept to shore from across the moonlit bay, brushing over Ethan's face and rustling Rivka's wedding dress.

    Yes, I am coming quickly.

EPILOGUE

The apostle John, known as "the disciple who Jesus loved," served as bishop of Ephesus for over twenty-five years. He was the last living eyewitness to Jesus' life, miracles, death, and resurrection. John wrote in AD 90 this challenge to all Christians everywhere:

> The Revelation of Jesus Christ, which God gave Him to show to His bond-servants, the things which must soon take place; and He sent and communicated it by His angel to His bond-servant John, who testified to the word of God and to the testimony of Jesus Christ, even to all that he saw. Blessed is he who reads and those who hear the words of the prophecy, and heed the things which are written in it; for the time is near. (Revelation 1:1–3)